Media and the City

Global Media and Communication

Media and the City
Cosmopolitanism and Difference

MYRIA GEORGIOU

polity

To Elektra and Leon, explorers of the urban world

Contents

Acknowledgements

The journey that led to the realization of this book has been long, challenging but also enjoyable. The latter would not have been possible without the intellectual and emotional support of a number of people. First and foremost, I would like to thank Lilie Chouliaraki for her insightful comments, tireless support and constructive criticism during the last phase of this book's completion. Also, for valuable feedback on different versions and presentations of the chapters of this book, I want to thank Valentina Cardo, Nick Couldry, Gareth Dale and Nikos Papastergiadis.

Kindred spirits, Sandra Ball-Rokeach, Susan Drucker and Gary Gumpert inspired me in many ways and at different times of my engagement with media and the city. Thank you. I am grateful to my colleagues at the London School of Economics and the University of Leeds who offered their time generously and helped me see what this project was all about when I was struggling in seminar rooms and pubs. Special thanks to Sonia Livingstone, Robin Mansell, Alison Powell, Polyanna Ruiz, Nancy Thumim and Katharine Sarikakis for inspiring exchanges and to Max Ahy-Hanska and Jean Morris for their help during the production phase.

My PhD students Heba Elsayed and Rahoul Masrani have been great companions in many exploratory intellectual journeys about the city and the media. And throughout this project, Roger Silverstone, as always, was somewhere there in spirit to inspire and guide me.

But this book would have not been possible without the enormous and unconditional support of the people closest to me. I want to thank my parents, Clara and Aris, for always having faith in me. Kevin James, who had no free weekend for two years, and Elektra and Leon, who kept holding my hand, and all this with a smile – thank you. My biggest gratitude goes to them: they knew this book would come to life even when I didn't. Leon and Elektra, you are the inspiration behind this book. I hope it will some day speak to you.

1 Introduction: The Mediated Cosmopolis

Fear and anarchy spread across the city. The citizens are hostages of the mysterious, violent and nasty *others*.[1] The camera frantically moves from an aerial overview of the city to the globally familiar urban skyline defined by skyscrapers and landmark buildings. The camera continues moving fast, now down at street level, taking the audience on speedy travels along the metropolitan avenues so often seen on the screen, so often used as symbolic and physical attributes of the big city. This is Gotham, one of the fictional incarnations of the city. In the latest Batman movie, *The Dark Knight Rises*, this is the city whose citizens single-handedly try to save the world; this is the city that attracts envy and which is always on screen. As dramatic events take place in the film, the rest of the world is irrelevant but at the same time ever present: television cameras and surveillance cameras provide instant and constant access to all that takes place in this important location: the city that really matters. The big and unpredictable city is integral to the film's plot, aesthetics and appeal. At the same time the urban locale cannot be separated from its mediated representations. The inevitable question that this example raises, among so many others in the media, is whether we can imagine less fictional cities, such as London, New York, Paris, but also Rio de Janeiro, Cairo and Shanghai, outside their representations, their representations' making and their consumption. After all, the ubiquitous presence of the city in the media is familiar, a tested and repeatedly affirmed choice in so many films, television series, fashion magazines, music lyrics and news stories. How possible is it to separate New York from cinematic imagination, Cairo from news headlines, or Shanghai from media visuals of its futuristic globality? And if what we know about cities is increasingly mediated, where are the meanings of these mediations and why does it matter?

While more than half of the world's population now lives in cities (UN 2010 [2009]), most of what we know about the city – the one we live in and the one we consume, desire to visit, migrate to, or avoid – is mediated. Films, television series, music lyrics, news headlines, but also social and personal media shape urban cultures both through representations and through communication practices. Utopian and dystopian representations of the city and responses to the challenges that the urban world presents to humanity are as much negotiated in the media as they are in the street. The city needs Batman as much as Batman needs the city. Depending where one sits, Batman saves the city from troubles associated with diversity or the city with its diversity provides the necessary platform for Batman to even exist. The role of media and communications in making the city is multifaceted and, importantly, dialogical. Media support the symbolic power of the city by exposing its many layers, its differences and its rich trajectories that can be commodified, as the case of the Batman films demonstrates. But media also need the city as a global node in communication flows that support exchanges of information, images, commodities and narratives of 'the urban'. In both cases, urban dwellers, global consumers and prospective visitors are constantly reminded that the city is unpredictable, exciting and fearsome but also possibly welcoming, potentially a place of opportunities and potentially a space to see the *self* and *others* as part of the urban story.

Among all cities, a small but growing number, the so-called global cities, most forcefully invite us to consider the expressions and consequences of these possibilities. The global city is probably the most mediated city but also the most diverse and open urban centre in the world: it is welcoming to the cultural industries but it is also globally recognized for the long and intense flows of people, ideas and media that link it to the rest of the world and bring the world to it. Powerful imagery and histories of domination symbolically mark the territory of global cities and shape its cultures of creativity, experimentation and diversity. A global city is a city that, day in, day out, requires us to think of how we live in close proximity to each other and how we communicate across difference. With long histories of political and cultural domination, London, New York, Paris, Berlin, and Los Angeles are quite distinct. In their global appeal as destinations for people and money and in their reputation as centres of concentrated difference, they are very particular. But they are not isolated cases. These are the cities that help us understand the uneven, hierarchical global order of the urban world; these are the cities that capture most intensely urban trajectories in global times. These are also the cities that most vividly reveal the politics of a changing mediated world.

In a world where the Empire and western capitalism are not in full command, the symbolic power concentrated in cities of the global North relies on transnational networks of people, cultures and information for its reproduction. The media constantly remind urban dwellers, global consumers and prospective visitors that the city is open, potentially welcoming, potentially a place of opportunities. Paradoxically, the same symbolic forms that enhance and secure the hegemony of top-tier cities in a global urban order are the ones that destabilize their exclusive access to symbolic power. A number of cities of the global South, ranging from Shanghai to São

Paulo, are currently gaining ground as attractive destinations for prospective tourists, migrants, consumers and cultural industries. Emerging global cities provide a glimpse into the diffusion and intensification of some of the key challenges of the urban world, which we now associate with cities of the global North. While this book sustains a focus on the established global city of the global North, the issues it addresses are far from contained in it. Given how much is at stake, especially with the vast and fast growth of urbanization, the ways in which the city is shared, communicated and symbolically constructed can have enormous consequences for cultural and social life: most importantly, in the ways in which we are exposed to each other, and understand or misunderstand each other, in an increasingly mediated urban world.

The book explores these issues through a particular relationship of growing significance: that of the media and the city. The media need the city to feed their industry with talent, powerful representations and consumers for their media products and technologies. The city needs the media to help brand its global appeal but also to manage its diversity and communication landscape. From the mobile phone that helps tourists navigate the city to social media that help protesters organize trans-urban action, this relationship is becoming more and more one of interdependence. As discussed in the next chapter, this interdependence starts with the over-concentration of media industries in certain cities and the domination of those same cities in media representations. But, importantly, it expands to and depends upon the urban street: where appropriations and uses of media and communications invent, become evidence and reaffirm the uniqueness of the city as a creative hub, as a consumer paradise, as a space of identity, community and even possibly political recognition.

The conceptual and methodological proposition of this book is for the study of the media and the city from street level. The book approaches their relation through an analytical matrix that includes the four main interfaces where this relation unfolds: consumption, identity, community and action. These interfaces allow us to record and problematize the different layers of a complex and contradictory relation. The discussions of these interfaces develop in chapters 3, 4, 5 and 6 respectively and present evidence of the intensification of the media and city synergies and their consequences, especially as expressed in cosmopolitanization. Cosmopolitanization is discussed as the process through which urban subjects are constantly exposed to difference through mediated and interpersonal communication. As music produced in the margins of the city, for example, reaches global audiences, both those on the margins and those in the centre of the urban world are forced to think of the *self* in relation to the *other* (as discussed in chapter 4).

Or, when media and city authorities brand the city as a cosmopolitan shopping destination, many urban dwellers adopt a celebratory cosmopolitanism discourse and adapt their own cultural practices to the branded city (as discussed in chapter 3).

The argument of this book is twofold. On the one hand, the intensification of mediation and urbanization advances proximity to one another. Close encounters with difference, when rubbing shoulders with others in the street or when being reminded of their proximity through the media, forces urban subjects to become more aware of the challenges and opportunities difference presents. On the other hand, those close encounters with difference become necessary ingredients for the media and the city to sustain their symbolic power, precisely because they feed back into invaluable creativity, branded cosmopolitanism and a city which represents marketable material for film-makers and advertisers. Chapter 2 starts from that top level of the media and city synergies, precisely in indicating the uneven concentration of symbolic power in corporate headquarters and their support through neoliberal policies. It shows how cosmopolitan narratives and practices are selectively incorporated into hegemonic discourses of the city but also how elites both desire to control the city's diversity and get access to it. A starting argument here is that we need to understand hegemonic ideologies while expanding our study beyond the corporate media headquarters. Most studies on media and cities focus on the top level of their interdependence. For this book, the corporate vision and practice of the mediated city represents just the beginning of the story. While starting the next chapter by recognizing the over-concentration of power in media corporations, the book invites its readers to navigate the city as a mediated space and to think of power not statically but as subject to the dynamics of mediation beyond the glass buildings.

Adopting a street-level analysis, the book aims to surpass the bird's eye view of the city and show that the symbolic power of the media and of the city is reaffirmed in everyday life. The media and the city take their meanings through communication practices across the city: from upmarket shopping malls where the representations of the city are made and consumed (chapter 3), to backstreets of impoverished neighbourhoods where creativity becomes a symbolic bridge to the other side of the world (chapter 4), to mediated networks that invent and re-invent communities (chapter 5), all the way to claims for recognition through acts of revolt in the urban and virtual street (chapter 6). This approach emphasizes that social actors are makers of *meanings* of the city and of the media: the urban dwellers, the consumers, the visitors, those seeking refuge are part of the story of the city, even if always from unequal positions. But there is a consequent and important element of this argument: the city is a site of struggle. And the very many struggles for symbolic and material resources in the city increasingly unravel at the meeting of the media and the city: when protesters use social media to gain local and global presence or when music becomes a tool for representing marginalized urban identities.

The book's empirical focus is London. London is a very powerful but far from unique case: global connectivity, cultural diversity, representational appeal and histories of mobility, creativity and political action take their distinct forms in each location but they reflect conditions that are increasingly shared across cities, especially global cities. Thus London provides a comparative starting point for understanding a synergetic relation which is most powerful in the established global cities of the global North, but which is far from exclusively contained by those cities as argued throughout the book. London provides a platform for developing a thick analysis, avoiding indiscriminate generalizations. A starting point and an empirical basis, the discussion sets forward an agenda and an argument of wider relevance.

Grounded in the mediated city

The case of Batman, among so many cinematic representations, news agendas and consumption patterns shows that the relation of media and the city has become synergetic but ordinary, so much so that it is rarely spoken about, even in media and communications studies. In research agendas, this taken-for-grantedness is expressed as a paradox: the more mediation shapes and is shaped by growing urbanization, the further away we move from studying cities. The intense, and partly novel, centrifugal power of networks (Castells 2009) has become so overwhelming that the centripetal power of the city has ended by being almost ignored. Yet, the global city's power to attract people, ideas, money, technologies and media encapsulates in the most vivid and intense manner the empirical meeting point of Appadurai's 'scapes' (1996) and reveals the core nodes of Castells's network society (1996). No other city is more connected, more networked and diverse than the global city (Sassen 2001).

In this context and in the first instance, this book arises from a necessity to study what becomes obvious: those increasingly important synergies described above. Beyond the obvious lies the unexplored. This book represents an attempt to understand the ways in which media and the city co-constitute each other and the consequences of their synergies for cultural and social life. In the global city, these expressions and consequences are most striking, though not unique. If we start by looking from the top down, these synergies are expressed in the over-concentration of cultural industries in a small number of global cities – elsewhere called global metropoles, alpha cities or world cities – as will be discussed in the next chapter. Neoliberalism's advance, expressed in the domination and celebration of the market as the driving and organizing force of public and private life (Lemke 2001), has been aggressively promoted in the urban governance of many cities around the world (Sassen 2001; Harvey 2009) – global or other – with direct benefits for the cultural industries. If we then look at these synergies from the bottom up, they become messier. They reflect neoliberalism's domination, especially when it comes to the commodification of culture and the neoliberal celebration of difference reduced to 'ethnic cuisines' and urban fashion. But they also reflect moments of resistance to the political and economic order through practices of revolt and urban dwellers' daily attempts to manage difference and inequality in the ways in which they communicate with others and use the media as interpretative tools for understanding the world that surrounds them. Most importantly, if we look at the media and city synergies as a dialectic relationship which is both bottom-up and top-down, it becomes possible to observe a complex and contradictory relationship, one that intensifies the proximity between individuals and groups and their ability to communicate across difference, while at the same time enabling them to hide from each other in segregated, mediated spaces and in individualistic and competitive spheres of self-interest.

The ambivalent consequences of the relationship between media and the city reflect the tensions of cosmopolitanization. If we think of cosmopolitanization as a process (Beck 2006, 2009), associated with Sennett's definition of cosmopolitanism as grounded in social experience (2002) and Robbins's definition of cosmopolitanism as lived (1998), then the city is where we can observe this with all its intensity and contradictions. The intensification of mobility and mediation has advanced cosmopolitanization as a process of individuals' constant exposure to one other, of boundary erosion, and of challenge to the domination of the nation-state as the primary organizing system of cultural and political life (Beck 2006). While cosmopolitanization opens up spaces for communication, it does not predetermine the ways in which we communicate, construct our identities and our sense of citizenship. As will be argued, cosmopolitanization in the city is work in progress, an unresolved condition: an asset for the city and its brand, an inescapable and constant exposure to difference, yet a process with uncertain consequences for citizenship, equality and recognition.

In the absence of much academic research on the ways in which media and the city become shaped by and shape cosmopolitanization, this book begins an empirical exploration of a familiar but under-studied territory. I start by recording the evidence of powerful synergies – the over-concentration of cultural industries in global cities, the branding mergers of city and media as shown in numerous cinematic and televisual representations, and the collaborations between urban government and cultural industry, to name but a few. I then move outwards and downwards from these top-tier synergies in order to understand what happens beneath the surface and the glamorization of the media and the city synergies: when it comes to messy and uneven spaces of creativity, claims to urban territories or representation of urban difference in the media. Synergies at the top are the ones best recorded in media and communications research and in urban geography. Yet a singular focus on economics, even on the political economy of the media and city relation, is far from enough; most importantly it fails to understand the city as a multi-layered site of struggle. Corporate media and city government synergies play a strategic role in the reproduction of economic and symbolic power, precisely because neoliberalism depends on symbolic forms – information, communication systems and perceptions (Garnham 2011; Lemke 2001) – as commodities but also as regulators of the market. Importantly, these synergies represent the top tier of a complex and diffused cultural economy, which, however, expands across all layers of urban life in ways that both reproduce hegemony and occasionally challenge it.

Since every city is a place of inequality as well as a place of excitement, a place that is lived in and a place that is consumed, a symbolic space that is imagined on screens and on the street, a multi-focal and interdisciplinary approach is required. In both its spatial dimensions, the city reveals the ways in which place is currently configured through the media. The ways in which it shifts between the real and the virtual shape place as a commodity, as well as a space of expression and participation. The book engages with these conceptual and empirical incarnations of the city, as discussed in global city literature, but most importantly with the ways in which everyday life and the urban street become meaningful contexts for understanding complex and contradictory experiences and media appropriations in all cities. While strategic collaborations originating in corporate headquarters or urban government offices are driven by interests in profit, market growth and the expansion of networks and business capabilities, the story of the urban street is much more complex. Do we see only the reproduction of neoliberalism and its reinforcement through the enactment of prescribed roles among urban dwellers: as consumers, as labour, as audiences? Movements such as Occupy, urban riots, but also more nuanced forms of action such as graffiti and music production suggest otherwise, as will be argued. Communication practices, which involve a vast range of ordinary acts, including the languages we speak in and over or the music we play or unintentionally hear, also challenge a prescriptive and top-down understanding of the mediated street.

Thus, and if we accept that cosmopolitanization is currently taking place in the involuntary close encounters of difference, especially as a result of the intensified transnational flows of people, ideas and media, it presents us with a challenge: the need to understand the cultural and political consequences of close – and intensified – proximities. Cosmopolitanization as a process (Beck 2006, 2009) is not neutral; it is confronted by the dual meaning of cosmopolitanism: as operational concept grounded in social experience and as an ambivalent vision attached to contradictory ideologies of worldliness, responsibility and citizenship (Gilroy 2004; Harvey 2009). Cosmopolitanization as a messy, lived reality in the global city forces us to pay attention to encounters of difference and their consequences. Expanded and extended in all layers of city life through physical and mediated encounters with difference, cosmopolitanism demands a particular kind of visionary orientation that challenges the taken-for-grantedness of Eurocentrism, western liberal democracy and the advance of neoliberalism. The increasingly intense, multiple and complex encounters with difference resulting from the diversification of flows of people, ideas, media and technology cannot be taken for granted merely as reflections of cosmopolitanization. Instead, we need to ask whether they give rise to possibilities for cosmopolitan agency (Papastergiadis 2012) and for cosmopolitan democracy (Calhoun 2002; Gilroy 2004). Cosmopolitanization may be incomplete, unpredictable and unresolved, but it creates unique opportunities for cosmopolitan trajectories and for making claims to symbolic and material resources in the urban mediated world.

Chapters 4, 5, and 6 will show that any claim to the city as a space of identity and citizenship is constantly confronted by and negotiated through the claims of other groups who occupy the same physical and symbolic spaces. If the city is a space of alterity (Isin 2002), it is also a space of communication: close proximity to difference makes contact inevitable, with consequences for the ways in which the city is lived and symbolically constructed. The multitudes and multiplicities of identities, communities, consumer cultures and political action associated with the city are not a result of things happening elsewhere; they are not small-scale representations of what happens on the national level or in the global markets. They take their forms *in* the city, but only and increasingly through the inevitability of physical and mediated encounters with difference. Since urban subjects have no choice but to encounter difference, they also have no choice but to think of the self through the *others* (even if this means in opposition to them). How much this process becomes dialogical, and how much confrontational, depends on context and on a number of variants. Some of those most important variants will be discussed in the following chapters.

We can perhaps for a moment think of the mixed and contradictory meanings of cosmopolitanism through a historical and metaphorical reference to *flânerie*. *Flânerie*, i.e. the experience and method of wandering in the city, observing, reflecting on and possibly acting upon the opportunities and challenges presented by the concentration and the intense contact of differences, has historically captured the many different trajectories of cosmopolitanism. Representing one of the earliest forms of cosmopolitan exploration through wandering and a method for analysing the city, *flânerie* has also been associated with an elitist viewpoint for observing with fascination the city and its difference. If we think about cosmopolitanization we might consider whether this presents yet another way in which those subjects who are media savvy and well connected through networks can wander as contemporary *flâneurs* through the city in aesthetic explorations of difference. A possibility, and one of the many expressions of cosmopolitanization, this kind of aesthetic experimentation in the city can be observed in the middle classes' return to the inner city, in new forms of alternative tourism, in advertisers' appropriations of graffiti and urban music. At the same time, and if we go back to Benjamin's cosmopolitan *flânerie*, we can see that his cosmopolitan wanderings can be far from aesthetic explorations. For Benjamin, *flânerie* was a way of understanding the city as a site of struggle, as an unequal place, but also as an unpredictable place, precisely because it has always been a point of meetings of difference (1997, 2004). This possibility – both academic and urban – represents a very different expression of cosmopolitan practice from the one described above. This different kind of wandering in the city links to a possibility for cosmopolitan agency and cosmopolitan politics that are reflexive, critical and potentially more inclusive. As will be shown, different *flâneurs* – elite and working class; reflexive and aesthetic – exist next to each other in the city, in the same way that they exist next to each other in the academic community.

In this context, I am interested in exploring the contradictory expressions of cosmopolitanism in urban narratives and practice while reflecting on its diverse academic theorizations. More specifically, I am interested in the ways in which neoliberal cosmopolitanism can exist next to vernacular cosmopolitanism and in exploring different kinds of possibilities and limitations of cosmopolitan democracy (Calhoun 2002) and of a liberatory cosmopolitanism (Harvey 2009). Unlike Beck's analysis, which emphasizes reflexive individualism and the retreat of class antagonism, I want to explore the persistence of classed and antagonistic versions of cosmopolitan discourses in the city. Thinking of cosmopolitanism through cultural and social experience, especially as this has been changing through mediation, I discuss the ways in which cosmopolitanism involves diverging discourses and practices that are subject to class, gender, ethnicity and urban and national identities.

This discussion captures a particular spatial and historical moment in the city's construction through difference, which is explored through the contradictory experiences and effects of cosmopolitanism. This moment is about the present: a time of intense human mobility, but also of intense mediation. This moment is about certain places of significance in our times: the cities with an intense concentration of symbolic power and diversity. These are the cities that cannot be imagined, internally or externally, without the intense juxtapositions of difference between people or outside sophisticated mediated systems that construct both the city's cultural identity and its value as a commodity. These are the cities that have accumulated these characteristics through centuries of colonialism, postcolonialism and concentration of capital. These are the cities in the top tier of the global order which so many cities aspire to compete with. These are the cities we need to turn to in order to most vividly observe and understand the tensions, limitations and promises of cosmopolitanism.

Revisiting the global city

The urban imaginary that emerges out of these processes is divided and political. Familiar images associated with the urban age (Burdett and Sudjic 2007) start with grim and overcrowded shanty towns, the homeless and the unemployed and expand all the way to sleek skyscrapers, affluent urbanites and prestigious cultural buildings. Turn to the publications of policy and charitable organizations and images of the first kind appear in abundance. Open up a tourist brochure or a popular magazine and representations of the second kind are plentiful, colourful and reaffirmed as familiar. Try to find representations of these two sides of the urban story in the same media location and it becomes almost impossible.

There is something about the two sides of city life that are hard to reconcile in urban representations. Perhaps these are sides hardly reconciled in human experience of the city. Indeed, there are at least two sets of realities in the city that appear to be worlds apart. Do shanty towns have anything to do with rich, gated communities or global financial centres? Do illegal migrants living in grim, inner-city neighbourhoods have anything to do with urban socialites? The answer is again unsurprising, yet less obvious. When illegal migrants build the sleek skyscrapers and their music is overheard on their mobile phones on the urban street, when filmic representations of shanty towns premiere in cinemas full of urban socialites being served cocktails by shanty-town dwellers, and when global capitalism sustains the position of certain cities as desirable destinations for migrants, different stories become entangled in a single urban reality.

According to the United Nations (UN), not only does more than half of the world's population now live in cities, but by 2015 it is expected that twenty-two megacities will each host more than ten million people (UN 2010). These megacities include the likes of New York and Los Angeles, but also Calcutta, Cairo and São Paulo. The challenges that urbanization presents to the cities of the North and of the South vary enormously, but, even within this complexity, a universal challenge for all humanity lies in the mere domination of the urban. Globally intensified urbanization reflects to a great extent the city's qualities (real and imaginary) as a refuge, as a location of hospitality (Derrida 2001b) and as a location of concentrated financial power (Sassen 2001). These qualities inform and reflect urban diversity, which cannot but be recognized as central to any discussion of the city. While human mobility goes back to the beginning of human history, it has presently reached unprecedented volume, intensity and diversity (IOM 2010). Long-standing and sustained human mobility shapes the contemporary city and has a particular significance in the case of the global city. The global city has its distinct characteristics as a cultural, social and political formation: intense diversity; an over-concentration of economic and symbolic power; high-level communication infrastructure and a significant level of autonomy from the national government (Sassen 2001). In this book, the global city is discussed in its complexity and diversity as a concept and as a context, as a node in mediated networks and as a container of symbolic power.

Within the present discussion, the global city's role as a centre of cultural command is crucial. This role is sustained through the accumulation of power by cultural industries, but also through the sustained reputation of the city as a location where global culture *is produced*. The global city's cultural hegemony depends on its strategic position in different flows, most influentially defined by Appadurai (1996) as mediascapes, ideoscapes and ethnoscapes. Mediascapes provide 'large and complex repertoires of images, narratives, and ethnoscapes to viewers throughout the world, in which the world of commodities and the world of news and politics are profoundly mixed' (ibid.: 35). Ideoscapes represent contrasting ideologies – especially those associated with the hegemonic and Eurocentric interpretations of

Enlightenment, on the one hand, and its diversified interpretation, especially via the city's diasporas, on the other. Ideas, narratives and imageries are often initiated in the city and in its rich cultural production that spreads from the cultural industries all the way to the urban backstreets. Alongside these, the ethnoscapes emerging and shaping the city's openness have become diversified, with migrants originating in different places and moving for different reasons. Transnational human mobility has also turned ethnoscapes into (trans-)urban communities, increasingly linked (or opposed) to other local and transnational communities. Cultural forms and flows of people, media and ideas are fragile, their particularisms are contextual and their organization and paths non-isomorphic. Thus, different cultural forms overlap and clash, becoming shaped through meetings and disjunctures that are local in their expressions and global in their effect.

The global city represents a site where encounters with difference have always shaped urban life, yet at no other time in history has the mobility of ideas, images and people followed such diverse, rapid and rich paths. While these paths do not by definition go through the city, they often do. They come together, cross-fertilize one another and clash in their top-down representations by the media and the authorities in the global city, in its organic communication unfolding in urban neighbourhoods, in the claims that are made to a presence in public life and in the clashes arising out of the city's intense social and representational inequalities. The global city is an unsettled place. In its political autonomy from the nation and its immense concentration of power, it is simultaneously a location of liberty and of order (Isin 2002).

The media embrace and enact an ambivalent and powerful role as they give voice to people, creating spaces for representations of difference, while at the same time supporting systems that control and discipline any deviance through state and corporate surveillance. These struggles around the media as technologies of control or emancipation can be observed in most elements of city life: where popular culture, such as fashion and music, sometimes suppresses diversity and pushes it to the margin and at other times gives it space for expression; where meanings of urbanity and diversity become battlegrounds of ideas as politicians and advertisers place groups into bounded social categories or where they realize the impossibility of this boundedness. These power struggles are expressed in tense juxtapositions of competing forces: between cultural industries and creative labour; between projects of identity and commodification; between claims to presence and surveillance. What these power struggles also produce is the actual city. As Isin (2002) puts it, the city is a difference machine, a producer of identities in its dynamics. 'Neither groups nor their identities exist before the encounter with the city,' he argues (ibid.: 49). One of the key elements of Isin's analysis is the constant possibility – and often the realization – of conflict in the city through the awareness among urban dwellers of oppositions and differences rubbing against each other when they make shared or conflicting claims to the physical and symbolic spaces of the city. The possibility of conflict, and certainly of opposition, is inherent in the city – and in the identities formed in its territory – as much as it is in communication. Opposition is largely concerned with awareness of difference. And the city leaves little space for lack of this awareness.

Does the intensification of city and media synergies represent just another story of neoliberalism's advance? Or does this relationship reveal the ways in which our social and cultural life changes precisely as a result of the city becoming a mediated and complex meeting place? While the city – especially the capital city and recently the global city – has long been the most important site of struggles associated with the emergence and establishment of capitalism, these struggles have become increasingly complex. As neoliberal capitalism is flexible and global and as market values saturate all elements of social and cultural life, it also becomes diffused in everyday life and in the way family relations, leisure and work are organized. Media and communications play a contradictory role in the neoliberal project. On the one hand, the global city is the ultimate neoliberal city: it reinforces its global leadership through digital networks that bring back to the city investment, information and people attracted to opportunities for work and for wealth. In this process, communication technologies have become enablers of social and cultural change, especially in two ways: in making possible the constant exchange of money and information between the global city and other parts of the world and in circulating within and beyond its territory neoliberal values and practices. On the other hand, the advance of media and digital communications has diffused access to media production, consumption and circulation, providing opportunities for new forms and new platforms of production and possibilities for a diverse and rich consumption that surpasses the singularity and boundedness of national mediascapes.

Among the global cities where neoliberalism thrives and where struggles for access to symbolic and material resources are intense, London represents a powerful case. Not a unique but a representative case of a global city, London is a city of 'multiple actors, trajectories, stories with their own energies – which may mingle in harmony, collide, even annihilate each other' (Eade 2000; Massey 2007: 22). London, Massey continues, is 'not a kind of pyramid, with finance as its shining citadel and the rest of us in one way or another dependent upon it' (2007: 22); rather the city is a multi-layered organism with interaction, communication and interdependences flowing between its different layers, even if the result of these flows is often reinforced inequalities.

As all cities, London provides a framework that 'allows us to reflect on the cultural consequences of globalization from an other than national perspective . . . to open up some alternative cultural and political possibilities', as Robins writes (2001: 86). Indeed, each city as a living and lived space allows us to observe the emergence and circulation of meanings of the *self* and of the *other* through contact, through mobility and through urban transience and openness, as intensified by digital communication. London, like every city of course, is also a unique place. It is a city with a long history of exercising hegemony through the Empire and more recently through its neoliberal leadership in financial markets. London is also a city with established flows of migration, but also of cultural exchange, partly as a result of migration, partly of the incorporation of the local popular culture into national and global media representations. It has become known as the ultimate global city in a uniquely powerful way of celebrating its image as a global centre, a world city, a cosmopolitan hub.

Importantly, like most cities and certainly like other (established and emerging) global cities, London is not only loaded with mediated representations. It is also a place producing mediated representations and framing meanings of mediation on local, national and transnational levels. This becomes apparent in the ways in which music, art and fashion created on the urban streets spill across the city and beyond, in the ways in which political protests and conflicts in the city are linked to claims made across the city, the nation and the globe, and even in the ordinary ways in which residents and tourists navigate the city's territories: through tourist guides, 'apps' and media that inform them of desirable destinations and no-go areas. As media are shaped and made sense of in the city, they both function in enabling the diffusion of neoliberal values and in destabilizing their orthodoxy. Possibilities for the destabilization of the neoliberal project are presented when urban dwellers, especially those not traditionally linked to centres of power, acquire access to media forms and communication systems that are themselves involved in the production of symbolic power. Minority, diasporic and alternative media, digital activist networks, but also music, graffiti and certain cultures of consumption are some such cases discussed in this book.

Mediation and power

The chosen interfaces of consumption, identity, community and action and the corresponding cases discussed in the book reveal the deliberately inclusive definition of the media that I adopt. I do so for two reasons. Firstly, urban communication is fluid and may be face to face, communal, grounded in place or mediated over long distances. Secondly, the convergence of media industries, technologies and platforms, alongside the fluid circulation of symbolic forms of digital social media, challenges any neat separation of what can be called mediated and non-mediated systems of communication. For this reason, I turn to the concept of mediation as a more useful concept vis-à-vis *the media* as distinct and separate technologies. Drawing on Silverstone's definition of mediation (2007), I study the dialectical processes in which institutions and audiences are involved in the circulation of symbolic forms enabled through the media, but not exclusively located *within* the media. Mediation does not exclude interpersonal communication; rather, interpersonal communication is a requirement of mediation as it is precisely in the practice of everyday life that symbolic forms take their meanings. Behind Silverstone's (2007) definition of mediation lies the almost unspoken recognition of the central significance of symbolic power in contemporary societies. Producing, having access to and consuming the variety of symbolic forms that surround us means participating in, even occasionally controlling, the symbolic processes associated with the construction of identity, of the city, of the proximate and distant social world. It is these moments of production, access and consumption of symbolic forms at the meeting of the city as a lived space and the media as communication systems that intrigue me. This is where cosmopolitanism becomes associated with the social and communicative experience, where the increased exposure to one another becomes a way of making sense of the city, but also of making claims to symbolic power in the city.

The global city's symbolic power is reproduced in images of the city as a unique location of diversity and of a fascinating openness. Such images have come to frame its corporate representations as a market and as a product. Its qualities and representations as a site of difference, and thus of indifference, tolerance and hospitality, have made the city recognizable as a social form and as a cultural space that is attractive to media producers and consumers. The attractiveness of the city to the media has in many ways reinforced global hierarchies: day in, day out, the media represent the city as powerful, culturally diverse, but also an almost inevitably unequal place with over-concentration of symbolic and economic power at the top. At the same time, the wide circulation of such representations has reinforced the identity of the city as an attractive destination for its different consumers and (potential) dwellers. Importantly, it is these same processes of mediated disembodiment and un-placing of the city that make it marketable as a commodity and a potentially inclusive place open to different people

– those seeking refuge, a space of identity, community, expressivity and action.

At the same time, transnational flows of money, people, commodities, ideas and technologies show that 'the global' in the global city is multi-layered not only internally, but also in its external interconnections. It only takes a glance at the city centre constantly crowded with tourists to realize that one of the core elements of 'the global' is expressed in the cultural transience of the city. The activities of cultural industries include the circulation of media products such as television programmes, music and film that, arguably, contribute as much to a global city's importance as do its museums. Alongside these, diasporic and migrant networks, although less glamorous than the core of the metropolitan city, globalize the city in two ways: by circulating such media products as diasporic film, television and music, and by establishing transnational interpersonal communication as an ordinary, daily element of city life. It is such corporate, creative and interpersonal activity that turns 'the global' into organic, rooted and powerful urban realities. Airports and train stations link locations and people's lives and enable the interconnection, continuity and transience of place. Computers, digital networks, television screens, cables and satellites expand further connections of people's relations, their understanding of the world and human interaction. It is in this complex and constant production of globality through internal and external heterogeneity, and in internal and external networked connections, that cosmopolitanism becomes rooted, routed and challenged.

Ruptures, disjunctures and multiplicities emerging in social and cultural fields as a result of the constant mobility of people and the expansion of media flows are most visible in the growing interdependence of the city with other cities, especially through urban and trans-urban networks. These networks are corporate and associated with markets (as primarily recorded in the global cities literature) and they are cultural and social, especially when associated with exchanges of media products and interpersonal and communal long-distance communication, such as in the case of diasporas. Such trans-urban activity supports the symbolic power of global cities as it reproduces its centrality in global networks, but also makes it conditional and relational. Participants in these networks may be proactively looking outwards – e.g. the global capitalist class, diasporas – or they may unintentionally incorporate their city's globalness and relational symbolic power into their own everyday lives (e.g. when they use different media or when they come across people of different backgrounds). Urban dwellers are different from one another, of different origins, but share the same city, even when they do not always converge or converse. They live in the same city, next to one another, separated by thin walls, streets, gates and fences and they are seen on surveillance cameras, on social media and represented in the mass media. Living in difference, they often project their difference into the future, but through it they sometimes also project common trajectories arising precisely through their close encounters with others in the city.

The now and the here

The synergies between media and the city may indeed intensify proximity and awareness of difference. But the close interrelation of media and the city is not new, as classic cinema and photography demonstrate (Gordon 2010; McQuire 2008). McQuire (2008) argues that the role of the media in reconfiguring city space goes back to the early days of modernity, through photography and cinema. Gordon (2010) argues that it was not until the late nineteenth century, when the handheld camera and cinema were introduced, that the American city took on its contemporary meanings as an important place signifying more than mere urban concentration. Yet there is something particularly important in the historicity of this relationship and in the current moment as shaped within the context of globalization. This book pays more attention to the present than to the past precisely because of the distinct characteristics of this present relationship: most importantly, digitalization and the expansion of mediation in all elements of urban life; the intensification of urbanization and migration; and the neoliberal advance in the urban world. In this context, and now more than ever, the relationship between media and the city is one of interdependence. It is expressed in corporate synergies associated with cultural globalization and with the liberalization of global communication markets, but also in new forms of politics and projects of self-making currently emerging in movements outside formal politics and in forms of creativity beyond bounded communities. It is also a relationship that is chaotic and so dispersed across every element of city life that its recording and analysis present a real challenge. It is informed by the constant interplay between mediated recognizability and urban unpredictability.

In an attempt to unfold the complexities of this story, the book focuses on the four distinct, yet interrelated, interfaces where this relationship takes its forms. Within these, we can observe oppositional meanings in making the city a symbolic and a lived place. These emerge through competing ideologies, practices and uses of media and communications that often merge into contradictory narratives that make the city. The brand of the global city, for example, is celebrated and capitalized on by the city authorities and the cultural industries. What happens in the underbelly of the global city and on the margins of its socially and culturally diverse world is deliberately missing from the celebrated brand. Yet poverty, the social divides and tensions around inequality often creep back into the brand of the city in the form, for example, of celebrated subcultures. Media and communications outside the core of the major cultural industries remain unnamed, even named as *other* to the successful and global brand. Yet, creativity and communication practices associated with marginality, with conflict and with the politics of exclusion find their way back into the symbolic space of the city through music, graffiti and the politics of protest. Of course the challenge remains: do these voices end by being incorporated into the neoliberal brand of the city, or do they contribute to the recognition of alterity as part of the city's story?

This book hopes to contribute to an understanding of the complex and partly untold story of the city, as it is currently made through the intensification of mediation and urbanization, especially in the global city. While the role of the media in communicating, sharing and managing difference is not new, it has now become a constitutive role. This happens in three ways. First, the city becomes the place it is through its representations – it is not just a location with taken-for-granted characteristics. The media both construct and reproduce images of the city as a place of opportunities and of fear; they construct and reproduce images of specific cities as desirable or undesirable destinations. Most of the information we hold about individual cities comes through the media. Even when we visit these cities or live within them, our choices of where to go or not to go are largely dependent on the mediated representations of these locations. Even perceptions about where we live and who we live next to are filtered by the media. When coming across other people, other attitudes and behaviours, we already know from the media something about what they (are supposed to) mean to us. And at the same time, as part of the urban world, when living in cities or when visiting them, difference is never completely strange: it has long been on the screen, constructed, explained, demonized and celebrated. For prospective migrants and visitors, the mediated representations of the city play a role in their desire and effort to reach it. Secondly, the city is always connected. The global economy and transnational migrant networks, alongside the expansion of individual media worlds to include a range of media and technologies, keep the global city always online, always in open systems of communication. Castells (1989, 1996), perhaps before anyone else since the Chicago School, discussed the relation of media and the city in shaping urban and trans-urban networks within the space of flows. More recent works on media and the city have looked at the city's connectivity as an expansion of and a counterpoint to its internal socio-economic and cultural dynamics. Urban space is a relational space, McQuire argues, and 'the horizon of social relationships has become radically open' (McQuire 2008: 22). The global city is a node in global networks, but it is not a node like many others in the network. Thirdly, mediations of difference become mechanisms of separation and negotiation of co-presence, both within the city and beyond. Representations and communication of difference have become transnationalized, reaching urban dwellers and (prospective) migrants, visitors, investors, media professionals and consumers when they try to make sense of the city-destination and the city-commodity. Within urban and transnational flows, difference is not only a characteristic of others, but also of the self. Desired, undesired, physical and mediated, close encounters with difference define the character of the city and the scale of its attractiveness as a destination, its financial growth, its cultural identity and its viability as a representation and as a centre of power. In light of the complex conditions that characterize the mediated city, rather than approaching the city through the financial networks of global capitalism, I focus on cultural networks and mediated negotiations of spaces of *we*-ness, *other*-ness, inequalities and exclusions.

Outline

In the chapters that follow, I explore these issues, while aiming to understand the ways in which the symbolic power of the media and the city becomes reinforced, and sometimes redistributed, through processes of cosmopolitanization. Chapter 2 provides a contextual and conceptual starting point. Evidence from the cultural industries and branding initiatives reaffirms the unequal distribution of symbolic power in the global city, which reinforces its identity as a neoliberal city. The unevenness of symbolic power is strengthened in synergies among cultural industries and between cultural industries and government. Yet, it is argued, the neoliberal city represents only an element – even if the most prominent one – of the ways in which the city is constituted through its synergies with the media. In chapter 2, it is argued that, in order to understand the contradictory consequences of those synergies for cultural life and for cosmopolitan practice and vision, we need to study their expressions across different layers of social and cultural life. Initiated in chapter 2, this discussion becomes empirically grounded in chapters 3, 4, 5, and 6 and through detailed and grounded analyses of the interfaces of consumption, identity, community and action respectively. In interrogating the expressions and consequences of cosmopolitanization,

I explore a number of key issues: concerning the mediated city as a place where we might come together to clash but also to communicate; concerning our inevitable urban proximity, advancing reflexivity, but not necessarily equality; concerning the intriguing manifestations of media culture that link consumption and creativity to identity, community and politics.

In chapter 3, I examine the first interface where media and city synergies unfold: consumer cultures. More particularly, I study some of the ways in which the organization of consumer cultures vis-à-vis histories of diversity in the city promote contradictory ideological systems for understanding difference. I discuss these with reference to the tense coexistence of neoliberal and vernacular cosmopolitan discourses and practices. Counterposing two quite different urban spaces of consumption, I explore the construction of a clean, stratified and conditional neoliberal cosmopolitanism and a messy, experiential and historically framed vernacular cosmopolitanism.

The second interface explored in chapter 4 is that of urban creativity, especially as expressed in graffiti and music. I focus on the subcultures of marginalized youth associated with urban music and graffiti, examining some of the ways in which spaces of identity expand across the local and the global and in the dialogical relation between the mainstream and the marginal. While injustice, deprivation and marginality mark the city, its sociocultural spaces are never fully bounded. Popular culture as a form of (self-)representation and identity demonstrates that there are always communication flows connecting different parts of the city. These continuities have been strengthened through the media, which have brought certain forms of expression from the margins to the mainstream global stage. I argue that urban music and graffiti are some of the very few forms of self-representation originating on the margins that are heard and seen across the city and across the globe. Precisely because of their visibility across different communication flows, these cultural forms become central referentials to the project of identity.

Chapter 5 focuses on the city as an interface of community, constantly shaped and redefined through transnationalism and migration. At the meeting of the media and the city, solidarity within communities, as well as with urban and distant *others*, takes on new forms and new urgency. With reference to diasporic, urban and new trans-urban communities, I discuss the rise of a reflexive awareness of urban and trans-urban subjectivity among their members. In becoming more aware of the conditionality and fragility of their own identities, some of these subjects are exploring new and global forms of solidarity beyond the boundaries of existing and long-standing communities. At the same time, the discussion invites caution in celebrating hyper-mobility and mediation: the ability to move between different physical and symbolic spaces sometimes revives communitarianism and re-invents communities as self-referential domains. In some of these cases, however, cosmopolitanism becomes an individualistic tool for new forms of separation, not an expression of solidarity towards others.

The fourth interface, unfolding in chapter 6, is that of action in the city. The city, in its physicality and as expanded in media (self-)representations, presents renewed opportunities for the presence of marginal political and social groups. As marginal groups occasionally and momentarily achieve a central position in mediated systems of representation, they can develop a political presence and a voice that can challenge the current political order. In examining the challenges for politics presented by such empirical evidence, we need to renew our interest in thinking about the possibilities of representation, recognition and redistribution (Fraser 2003). Different forms of political action, alongside processes of identity and community construction, demonstrate the ways in which living and communicating in cities of difference shape spaces of cultural and political representation. The possibilities and limitations of solidarity and mutual understanding within such spaces presents us with significant points of reference, as well as real challenges, in addressing urgent questions about injustice, inequality and participation. These are precisely the questions addressed in the concluding chapter. This last chapter presents a point of reflection on the challenges emerging in the processes of cosmopolitanization for identity, community and citizenship in a mediated urban world as discussed throughout the book.

2   Media and the City: Synergies of Power

There is a paradoxical divide in social scientific research on the contemporary city. Research on the powerful cities – especially global cities – has focused on neoliberalism's advance and the domination of economic interests over the city's social and cultural landscape (Hackworth 2007; Harvey 2007; Sassen 2001). The city as a space of communication, of understanding and misunderstanding of difference, and potentially of cultural and political representation, is almost a different city, an *other* city. The city where migrants, the urban poor and social movements have agency and presence is part of a different scholarly agenda: that of the study of identity, community and communication (Binnie et al. 2006; Davis 2000; Eade 1997, 2000; McQuire and Papastergiadis 2005). While academic agendas might diverge, either looking at the top or the bottom layer of the urban cultural and social landscape, the city constantly reminds us that those layers are organically interconnected and that conflicting interests converge in urban space. This convergence is largely mediated – when media constantly reaffirm the city's reputation and importance and when they enable the incorporation of selective discourses of cosmopolitanism in the city's story. The outcome is indeed the neoliberal unequal city, as will be shown in this chapter. But, as will also be shown, this is a city which is also lived and made as much through corporate projects as in communication and cultural struggles between its social actors.

When looking at the city from the top down, reputation, histories and present realities of concentrated economic, political and symbolic power visibly merge. This is most powerfully the case in the global city. Largely sustained in media representations produced for itself and for consumers around the world, the city is reaffirmed as a rich, powerful and cosmopolitan place. Skyscrapers, monuments, concert halls and studios constitute familiar imagery through which we often recognize a particular city. Creative people and media celebrities, alongside urban fashion and music, are also significant and compelling urban identifiers. Such symbols and imagery increasingly depend upon powerful cultural industries, especially the media, for the reaffirmation of their importance. Cultural industries, alongside the financial sector, are now widely recognized as holding the sceptre of the global city's power. For critical political economy, this recognition presents evidence of the almighty role of the cultural industries in advancing the neoliberal project (Garnham 2011; Herman and McChesney 1997; Golding and Murdock 2005). For city authorities and cultural industries, such recognition offers evidence of invincible and celebrated synergies of mutual benefit and profit. In these powerful narratives, both sides underestimate what lies in between: the practices of social actors (Couldry 2012) within the city and the cultural industries. Such practices, across all levels of urban and cultural life, both reaffirm synergies and complicate their consequences. The complex system of power emerging out of such synergies is at the core of this chapter's discussion. The chapter provides an anchoring and contextual starting point for understanding the media and the city synergies in current times and vis-à-vis conceptualizations of symbolic power and of cosmopolitanization.

Depending as much on money as on the production, circulation and consumption of symbolic forms, this power is not only economic, but also symbolic. Symbolic power is crucial in understanding the ways in which media and city synergies become dispersed and effective, but also complex. A central argument that runs through this book is that, while unevenly distributed, symbolic power is made and concentrated not only on the top tier of a media and city pyramid. Neither the city nor the media are neatly organized systems, and their complexity makes them sites for tension, contestation and conflicting claims to presence and representation. Thus, and while their synergies may play a key role in the reproduction of hegemonic relations and ideology, they are also battlefields of ideas and practices, as discussed in the following chapters with reference to four interfaces. Possibilities for self-representation, dialogue and solidarity emerge from time to time through struggles and competing claims to the city and the media.

As these possibilities are always subject to hegemonic economic and cultural relations, to understand them we need first to recognize the top-tier synergies and their complex consequences for urban and global cultural economy. More often than not, these synergies organize culture and communication around market criteria and potential profitability. But if the top-level relationship of media and the city is examined from a less horizontal viewpoint, the complexities of symbolic power which challenge the rigidness of the neoliberal project become more visible. These provide a glimpse of the peculiar and intangible workings of symbolic power and the oppositions between a systemic reproduction of power and its cosmopolitan incarnations. In the first part of this chapter, I introduce the hegemonic expressions of media and city synergies. Here, already, a contradiction becomes evident: corporate and government interests and synergies involve little or no intentionality to advance the city as a space of understanding and participation. Yet both corporate and government sectors increasingly depend on the recognition of (a selective) cosmopolitanism. Building on this discussion, I then explore the ways in which the dependence of media and of the city on urban cosmopolitan realities problematizes relations of power in the city and almost inevitably opens up spaces for communication across difference. I do that by drawing the main conceptual parameters of the discussion, primarily on cosmopolitanization as a process and cosmopolitanism as vision and on mediation and symbolic power.

The cultural and economic hegemony of the global city

Pratt (2012) argues that cultural and economic leadership go hand in hand as far as powerful cities are concerned. Skórska and Kloosterman (2012), comparing financial activity and creative activity indicators, emphasize that this relationship is far from straightforward and these indicators are not always comparable. Yet, when it comes to the top tier of the urban and economic order – the global cities – the correlation of financial and cultural leadership is persistent and comparisons can be drawn. Krätke and Taylor's (2004) city benchmarking indices show that New York and London take the first two places among the twenty most important global business centres in the world (ibid.). The media activity of London and of New York is also ranked on the same level, demonstrating the merging of media power and economic power (ibid.). A liveability index developed by the *Financial Times* (Norwood 2013) positions New York at the top, followed by London and Hong Kong, with Singapore rating third, followed by Paris, Melbourne and Shanghai in joint fourth place.

Importantly, and as the *Financial Times* index indicates, the global order of cities is changing, though London remains in all different accounts on the top tier. Evidence supports its hegemonic position in global affairs. According to the City of London's *Key Facts* (2012), financial services generated a trade surplus of more than £40 billion and professional service firms a surplus of £6 billion in 2009, while London's share of the UK's gross value added was 21 per cent in the same year. While there is significant evidence of London's place as a global centre of financial command, its 'globalicitysation' (Gordon 2003) is more than financial. London is also a global centre of culture, with galleries, theatres, museums and concert halls. Authorities such as the City of London, the Greater London Authority and the London Mayor have an easier task than other cities in building their city's reputation and advancing its symbolic power. Firstly, there is the high concentration of cultural industries in this global city. MediaUK (mediauk.com) lists more than 600 media which have their headquarters in London. It is not only the mere number that is impressive, but also the range of media, which extends from local neighbourhood newspapers to transnational television corporations, and from local ethnic media all the way to highly profitable and globally recognizable digital media firms.

Urban and national government celebrates and advance the attractiveness of London, as a global city, to cultural industries by promoting established, experimental and diverse cultural production and consumption as sources of wealth and growth. London authorities, for example, put considerable effort into branding the city as a global cultural centre, a cosmopolitan location and a business magnet (Mayor of London 2012). In the self-representation of the City of London as a global brand, it is emphasized that the financial city's prosperity and influence rely on excellent communication infrastructure and technological innovation. Equally, it does not fail to emphasize the enormous concentration of cultural institutions and activities in its territory (City of London 2012) and their symbolic value. The reproduction of a powerful brand also benefits from the growing appeal of London to the global film industry. Alongside a handful of other cities that are used in films as simulacra of futuristic utopian or dystopian worlds, London is gaining ground as a setting for big Hollywood productions, like the 2013 *Star Trek: Into Darkness*. Government fosters many of those projects, extending invites and developing business plans for attracting cultural industries, which both bring in money and reproduce the 'London brand' as a key element of the industries themselves. For example, Film London represents a publicly funded organization promoting London among American and other non-British film studios as a desirable location for filming. It is also one of the many initiatives that aim to maximize the benefit that cultural industries bring to the city. Along the same lines, the mayor of London's recent cultural strategy, introduced under the compelling Cultural Metropolis brand, has recognized the significance of the cultural and creative sectors in making London a successful world city (Mayor of London 2012). In the mayor's own words: 'On any measure you choose, you will find that London is a cultural powerhouse justly renowned across the world' (ibid.: 5). In the report, the decline of the local workforce in the cultural industries is brushed off as a result of the recession. At the same time, the fact that consumption of cultural industry products – especially film, theatre and live music – has held up or increased during the same period is presented in an emphatic and celebratory tone. The city as a commodity and as a place of consumption is celebrated in this neoliberal discourse, which at the same time downplays the importance of the city as a place for secure living and employment.

Alongside established cultural industries, fashion is being globally promoted by cities as a key element of their appeal and symbolic power. Fashion Weeks, which now spread from the established fashion centres of Milan, Paris, London and New York to new destinations such as Singapore, Dubai and Toronto, are embraced and celebrated in media and government discourse. 'Fashion is a very serious business' and 'I am proud to be minister for fashion', Ed Vaizey, UK's Minister for Culture, Communications and Creative Industries, declared during the February 2012 London Fashion Week (*Time Out* 2012: 14). *Time Out*, the leading London magazine, adopted a similarly celebratory, but also uncharacteristically didactic, tone in its special story about London Fashion Week. That 'fashion matters' is a repeated message from political, urban and media leadership. For the Minister for Culture, Communications and Creative Industries, the reason we should care is clearly market-driven: 'Fashion contributes £20 billion a year to the economy. It's not just about catwalks, but the high street, photography, hairdressing, magazines and lots more. More and more manufacturing is returning here as well' (ibid.: 14). The very title of his ministry merges the different creative and media industries, as does the practice of these industries that bring attention and money to the city.

The cultural leadership of the global city is celebrated and cherished by urban and national government, but also used by cultural industries in their efforts to sustain environments of low taxation and deregulation. The fact that creative labour decreases while the industries' activities and income are actually on the rise presents some evidence of the increased insecurity of creative labour and the lack of political intentions to change this. This is no surprise, since the concentration of cultural industries and their products in global cities has developed in ways not dissimilar to other industries. The global city, Sassen (2001) argues, is a strategic epicentre, bound to other global cities by the dynamics of economic globalization. Certain cities sustain their centrality as systems of global command through the over-concentration of know-how, innovation and infrastructure in their territories. The symbolically significant cities represent a combined force, exerting power collectively and forming a transnational urban system; they are produced and enhanced through trans-urban networks that link these cities and their economic activity (ibid.) and host industries that sustain their power in the 'repetition of institutionalized practices' (Giddens 1987: 9) that expand across global networks.

Within the literature on global cities, the ubiquity of communication technologies is recognized as central in sustaining trans-urban networks and maximizing the effectiveness of global cities' infrastructure and power (Sassen 2001). Yet communication technologies are primarily discussed as tools, subject to practices and decisions made in corporate headquarters rather than as constitutive elements of the cities' financescapes, ideoscapes and mediascapes (Appadurai 1996). In this same literature, media are totally absent as systems that produce and reaffirm symbolic power by informing practices (Silverstone 1999) and by producing ideas, knowledge and innovation (Hartley 2010). As will be emphasized throughout this book, global cities influence knowledge of the world for the world, constituting media cultures of 'constant virtual mobility' (Jansson 2002: 429). Thus, media do not only find a place to land in the city. They find their realization and capitalize on the specificities of the city and its accumulative power, especially within cultural economy. This duality is rooted in Bourdieu's (1985) concept of symbolic power as having both representational (cultural) and monetary (economic) dimensions. The merging of the leading positions certain cities hold as service centres and media centres turn them into media capitals (Curtin 2003). As Curtin defines these: '[m]edia capitals . . . are sites of mediation, locations where complex forces and flows interact. They are neither bounded nor self-contained entities . . . [they are] meeting places where local specificity arises out of migration, interaction and exchange. As such, media capital is a relational concept, not simply an acknowledgement of dominance' (2003: 205). The power of the media functions through institutional structures and practices, as well as in symbolic forms circulated locally and globally and integrated into everyday life. Couldry argues that 'some concentrations of symbolic power are so great that they dominate the whole social landscape; as a result, they seem so natural that they are misrecognized, and their underlying arbitrariness becomes difficult to see' (2003: 4). There is no better place to observe this over-concentration of the symbolic power of the media than the global city. Here, its naturalization is realized in two ways: in the growing role that cultural industries take in controlling the economy and symbolic forms associated with the city's representations; and, no less importantly, in the diffusion of media and communication technologies across the city's territory, which gives urban dwellers some access to the production of those representations and mediated meanings. Silverstone describes the overwhelming power of the media when he argues that 'the need for doubt falls away, for the invitation is to accept the world as it appears on the screen, an appearance which is, for all its superficial variety, ubiquitous, eternal and, to all intents and purposes, real (although . . . it is nothing of the sort)' (Silverstone 2007: 51). The 'reality' of the urban world is often reproduced in the media: certain cities appear in news and entertainment as having more value than others. The media support global familiarity with 'alpha cities' (GaWC 1998) when they make repeated references to monuments located in these cities, when film studios choose them as settings for their productions and when fashion and other desirable commodities become attributed to certain cities. As a consequence, their symbolic power is both produced and reaffirmed. The global city's hegemony within global systems of representation is regularly marked when Paris, London and New York appear again and again in the media as desirable destinations and commodities, while other cities become either completely invisible or undesirable.

At the same time, the global city's symbolic hegemony is always contextual and linked to history, social life, cultural diversity and economic policies, especially as these are currently expressed in the neoliberal project that promotes urban growth through the commodification of the city. Symbolic forms produced in the media are valuable commodities for the city itself – to promote itself, to construct an identity for itself, to reach out to the world. Powerful representations and the contribution of the cultural industries to the global city's symbolic power build upon long-standing concentrated power, but also on the shifts from manufacturing to a symbolic economy. Historically, long-standing synergies have supported the reputation of certain cities as spectacles and as centres of cultural production (Gordon 2010). Gordon writes about the ways in which communication and transportation technologies have shaped the urban spectator's experience throughout modernity. 'New technologies of vision, specifically the train and the park, produced a windowed perspective on the urban landscape that had never before been experienced' (2010: 15). Amateur photography has also changed the relation of the spectator with the city: a technology which was accessible, promoted by popular magazines and public policy in the United States and 'inexpensive cameras [which] demonstrated that there were no barriers to visually possessing public spaces' (ibid.: 43). In the American context especially, he continues, technological developments played a crucial role in the city's becoming central to the cultural imaginary: '*The American city grew up in parallel to the technologies that enabled its possession*' (ibid.: 3, emphasis in original). But there is also a newness in the synergies of the city and the media. As Hartley (2010) argues, the city has become a 'medium' within innovation culture, with creativity mixed and circulated in its territories and globally distributed through digital networks. As the empirical evidence discussed in the next few chapters will show, mediation also encounters marginality, projects of identity, community and political action.

While the discussion in the pages that follow pays particular attention to the meeting of people, technologies and histories in the city, the proposed analysis would be very different were it not for neoliberalism's advance in media markets. Since the 1990s, major mergers and acquisitions in the global media industries have led to the creation of mega-corporations in media and communications (Thussu 2006) and investment in communication technologies. Transnational media corporations (TNMCs) have benefited from the liberalization of global markets and strategically chosen to base their centres of command in cities which enable, celebrate and symbolically represent the neoliberal project of deregulation (Curtin 2003). TNMCs share some key characteristics with other TNCs (Harvey 2009), two of these being most significant: the core nodes of most global cultural corporations are located in urban financial centres, which themselves represent key places for cultural production. These centres are 'anchoring points' and cultural metropoles (Krätke 2003). Empirical research conducted within the global cities literature, including Hoyler and Watson's (2012) and Krätke's (2011) work on media cities, confirms that there is less decentralization of corporate activities and more concentration of power in key urban centres associated with global networked capitalism (Castells 2009; Sassen 2001). The significant role that cities play in these networks, Hoyler and Watson argue, 'not only allows TNMCs to draw on the creativity that resides in these productions centers, but also results in the global linking of the urban centers of cultural production through established global networks' (2012: 2). In this way, media and communication industries benefit from existing and expanding transnational corporate and communication networks and often merge within larger transnational corporate networks. The mergers of some of these corporations around the mega-media corporations, such as News International, Disney, Time Warner AOL, Reuters, and the peculiar case of the BBC, represent the top tier of a highly concentrated media market. The centres of command of these corporations are most often rooted in cities with long traditions of established media power: primarily New York, London and Los Angeles, with the most recent additions to the map of global media capitals being Singapore and Hong Kong.

The concentration of media power observed in the global city is dependent upon the city's nodality. Both the global city and the cultural industries rely on networks of mobility of people, know-how and products, as much as on concentrated infrastructure, for reproducing their power. Castells (1996), in his concept of networked power, approaches world cities as symbolic centres within networks of cities. 'For Castells, world cities are not simply places, they are processes, hubs through which flows are articulated with power residing in the flows themselves,' note Taylor et al. (2002: 232). These flows are not only regulated through media and communications technologies, as suggested by Short (2004), but are also sustained through their anchoring in powerful centres of command. The economic and symbolic power of cultural industries is as dependent on transnational networks as it is on the concentration of infrastructure, creative and expert resources in the city. Rooted in histories of interdependence with cities and routed through the fluid but persistent interaction with the urban creative classes, political elites and the cultural fabric of the city, the power of cultural industries is partly generated and partly sustained through their synergies with the global city.

Powerful synergies

A city's reputation and symbolic power are increasingly controlled and enhanced through culture, as culture becomes more and more intertwined with capital and identity, argues Zukin (1995) in her analysis of the symbolic economy of cities. 'The symbolic economy unifies material practices of finance, labor, art, performance, and design,' she adds (1995: 9). Zukin (ibid.) defines symbolic economy around three key points: it is urban; it is based on the production of symbols as commodities; and it requires the deliberate production of spaces both as sites and as symbols of the city and of culture. Zukin also emphasizes that culture is no longer a bi-product of wealth, but actually creates wealth. Media and communications represent core components of a symbolic economy, not only because they are great money-making industries, but also because they possess the ability to effectively construct symbolic meanings. A powerful example could be that of the new Guggenheim Urban Lab built from the ashes of an abandoned building in post-recession East Village, New York. Sponsored by BMW, it aims to develop a hybrid community and artistic space, as celebrated in *The New York Times* (Vogel 2011). 'Nothing here is slick. The graffiti-covered brick walls along two sides of the site were left exposed,' writes Vogel (ibid.), contributing to the space meaning making. Between the powerful Guggenheim and BMW brands, the urban crisis of abandoned buildings and the possibility of regeneration through art – largely through its promotion in the media – the post-recession city space is being remade. Powerfully and effectively. Massey argues (2007) that it is primarily through symbolic forms that the meanings of place as unique and global are made.

The narrative of the global city, which Gordon (2003) calls 'globalcitysation', has become in itself a performed identity of certain cities in the global stage. This identity builds not merely on money, but also on urban cultural wealth sustained through histories of imperialism and migration. The global city is a cosmopolitan city, and thus a desirable destination not only for

money, but also for expert labour, tourists and for a range of service industries. The economic benefits to the city, when viewed through the lens of
cultural consumption, are plentiful. This is echoed in Florida's (2002) work,
in which he devises various indicators in order to assess the cultural clout
of cities through a cosmopolitan and creative framework. His indicators
include 'gay', 'bohemian' and 'cool' as gauges of a city's symbolic power.
Florida (ibid.) also puts forward the notion of the 'creative class', which
serves to enhance these alternative indices and works symbiotically with the
construction of a city as symbolically significant. A strong creative sector,
according to Florida, 'signals an environment that attracts other types of tal-
ented or high human capital individuals' (2002: 67). He highlights diversity
and creativity as key factors in the growth and development of a city and
claims that there is a 'tendency for innovative economic activity to cluster in
and around bohemian enclaves' (ibid.: 58). This corresponds to Hitchens's
work, in which he states that: 'every successful society needs its bohemia . . .
[to] regenerate its culture . . . In every age in every successful country, it has
been important that at least a small part of the cityscape is not dominated by
bankers, developers, chain stores, generic restaurants and railway terminals'
(2008: 1–2). Florida (2002) and Hitchens (2008) shift the meanings of the
city from production to consumption and from a neat space of economic
activity to an exciting and diverse space of culture. While this shift importantly captures the growing significance of diversity and of the symbolic
economy in defining the city, most of these analyses deterministically locate
creativity and consumption in an ahistorical and apolitical context. Pratt
(2008: 110) addresses this paradox, claiming that 'with the legacy of past
investment in education, developed countries are likely to do well' in terms
of expanding their creative industries and eventually attracting investment,
tourists and new residents. Bell et al. (2008) add that the city has always
been important as a site of consumption, as well as of production.

Indeed, the notion of consumption has been integral to the development
of the city at least since the nineteenth century, particularly in Europe. Even
city centres were planned with consumption in mind. 'Paris's large networks
of boulevards allowed wide avenues for increased traffic flow and supplied
the stage for spectacular consumption (crucial to an urban plan designed to
enhance the circulation of commodities)' (Highmore 2005: 32). London
and New York have long been the epicentres of the art trading and collect-
ing worlds, containing both numerous auction houses and a vast array of the
world's most prized pieces of artistic output on display in the cities' many
museums and galleries. O'Connor (2007) summarizes the arguments put
forward by Adorno (1991) on the commodification of art, concluding that
'under monopoly capitalism art and culture had now become thoroughly

absorbed by the economy' (O'Connor 2007: 9). Though somewhat pessimistic and highly deterministic, such a view is relevant to the advance of the symbolic economy. It would be overly simplistic to conclude that cultural commodification is an immediate response to mediation and branding. It is unlikely that tourists will automatically flock to 'world cities' renowned for their art collections solely on the basis of an inherent interest in such collections. Instead the issue of taste becomes relevant, in that there is a consensus on those works which constitute 'better' or 'more worthy' forms of artistic production (see Bourdieu 1993). This notion can be applied more broadly to the cities themselves; the success of certain cities as opposed to others in attracting consumers and the creative class is a result not only of a global, collective understanding of what constitutes 'better' culture, but also of an acknowledgement that there are 'better' cities which must attract cultural production and consumption.

Attracting the creative class (Hartley 2010) and 'cultural tourists' to cities 'with the hope that they will be well off and well behaved' has become an important goal for many cities (Pratt 2007: 141). Drawing on Philo and Kearns (1993), Miles and Miles argue that 'the urban form [is] an ideological project and urban culture [is] the active project of the urban bourgeoisie who use a city as a means of asserting their social dominance' (2004: 5). In this light, the city becomes commodified as cultural production and consumption: it is packaged and sold as a cultural product. The symbolic value of the city, then, is closely related to the status of its cultural offerings, which in turn are guided by their economic clout. Thus, unlike Florida's neoliberal celebration of the city as a site of consumption – and creativity as an outcome of consumption's hegemony – it becomes clear that the power of certain cities is accumulated through long-standing economic and cultural hegemony. Consumption and production are thus not opposing forces, but interlinked, both in the ways that the symbolic economy ties them into the neoliberal project and in the ways in which they can define in unpredictable ways urban diversity and the possibilities for communication and identity (for example, in user-generated projects or in the urban cultures of communications discussed in chapter 5).

Selective cosmopolitanism

Urban cultural forms, ranging from food culture to the media, are rich and often contradictory forces, sustaining in their complexity the clout of the global city as a fascinating place and a commodity. In their diversity, cultural industries, alongside other service industries, support the project of the global city as a distinct, desirable and also cosmopolitan place of production and consumption. Restaurateurs and workers in the catering sector have been most often recognized for their contribution to the emergence of cities as cosmopolitan centres; the availability and consumption of food from all over the world is celebrated and cashed in on in the production of the global city's image as a condensed version of the world – a world of culinary delights and pleasures associated with migration. Eade (2000) reviews a number of contemporary tourist guides for London where the 'melting pot' city is celebrated. The concept of the 'melting pot' becomes a way of comparing London to New York and other American cities, thus commodifying difference and turning it into a familiar and recognizable commodity for prospective North American consumers. Certain recognition of difference thus becomes invaluable for some industries' expansion.

Media present no exception. The different kinds of media reflect the richness, but also the repetitive appeal of cultural production and consumption that feed into the symbolic hegemony of the global city. Like other elements of the symbolic economy, ethnic, community and online media are evidence of the city's cosmopolitan credentials. But there is a side to urban cosmopolitanism that is more than the glossy version of cultural diversity. While most studies of media and cultural industries in the city focus on the top-tier media corporations, stratified and multifaceted cultural industries make the city a multi-layered – and thus powerful and unique – cultural space. The less-known element of the cultural industries is that of the smaller media players, often invisible in accounts of the synergies between large cultural industries and global cities. Small-scale media that make little or no profit are as often located in the global cities as are the transnational media mega-corporations (TNMCs). Ethnic media, community media and numerous online media projects are rooted either in global cities or in transnational networks with strong links to global cities. The reasons behind the development of these thriving small players in the cultural industries are many, but the most important are those shared with the larger-scale media corporations. Like major media, small-scale media depend on the concentration of diversity, creativity and innovation in global cities. The large and diverse potential audience located in cities is another important reason, as is the established infrastructure and structures for a functioning industry, ranging from telecommunications infrastructure all the way to industry networks and proximity to advertisers.

The cultural clout of the global city and its ubiquitous media exposure reflect histories of domination, colonialism and capitalist accumulation as much as they reflect new trajectories in urbanization and mediation. Symbolic power is by definition multifaceted, encompassing a wide array of realms and processes. Indeed, Short acknowledges that global cities, which can be seen as symbolically significant, 'act as crucial mediators and translators of the flows of knowledge, capital, people and goods that circulate in the world . . . Inter-city linkages take a variety of forms: economic, political . . . as well as cultural flows including films, television, books and events' (Short 2004: 15). Short's emphasis, along with Castells's (1996) conception of networks of power, highlights the significance of mediated networks and the strategic nodality of cities in the accumulation of both cities' and networks' symbolic power. The strategic place of cities in these networks is of constitutive significance and as such requires further attention. City benchmarking indices like those already discussed praise cities like London, New York, Paris, Hong Kong and Tokyo for their economic and cultural leadership but they rarely praise their 'liveability' vis-à-vis cities that are not on the top tier of urban order. In fact, a recent global liveability survey (Turgis 2011) concluded that, on the contrary, various cities in Canada, Australia and Western Europe were the most 'liveable'. Such measurements demonstrate the diverging systems of recognition of what makes cities powerful and what makes them liveable. The divergence of the two types of benchmarking indices also suggests that the symbolic power of the city remains an intangible force and one that has captured little attention in research on urban cultural and social life. The incorporation of a celebratory recognition of urban cosmopolitanism into city branding reflects corporate and government attempts to narrow the gap between the global city as a place of business and as a place to live. Such cosmopolitan discourses celebrate 'ethnic cuisines', selected benefits of migration and the richness of popular culture. Yet far beyond these celebrations lie the more complex realities of actually existing cosmopolitanism (Robbins 1998).

Corporate and policy celebrations of certain forms of cosmopolitanism are always selective and often imply exclusion. Malpas (2009) writes that city branding may instantiate a tension between a form of cosmopolitanism and a form of 'parochialism', since it prioritizes both the globally shared perspective and the specific perspective associated with a locale. In addition, hegemonic celebrations of cosmopolitanism may conceal tensions between competing projects – between neoliberal cosmopolitanism, which promotes the commodification of the city through a selective 'worldliness', and vernacular cosmopolitanism, which is messy, contradictory and comes out of cultural meetings and hybridity. This is an opposition powerfully expressed in the case of the different consumption cultures discussed in the next chapter. By looking into the everyday life of urban dwellers, in the following chapters I will argue that symbolic power is often *generated* at street level. While the hegemonic synergies between cultural industries and the city

exclude many urban actors, the networked city and the inevitable dependence of the cultural economy upon the city's diversity open up possibilities
for seeing and understanding the self and others within dialectic systems of
communication, coexistence and collaboration. These possibilities and their
limitations will be empirically explored in the following chapters.

Cosmopolitanization: from a top-down to a dialectical viewpoint

Since difference often becomes commodified by tourist and cultural
industries and since it is considered a burden in terms of social control and
cultural homogenization, cosmopolitanism on the top tier of the city is
only possible as a commodified neoliberal project. The limited and selective engagement of corporate and urban leadership with difference in the
city is reflected in the steep reduction of civic engagement among global
corporate leadership, and consequently the crisis of citizenship, Sennett
(2002) argues. The detachment of elites from a city's social life may reflect
a crisis of citizenship, but also indicates that participation in the city's social
and political life is differentiated and stratified. The question is whether
there are other forms of participation that matter, apart from elites' selective
participation. Looking at corporate headquarters and political centres of
established power can only give us a partial insight, although an important
one, into the city as a cultural and social space. The city is not produced
only in global corporate headquarters; rather it is lived in the street, in the
neighbourhoods, where encounters are intense, experienced and present
real dilemmas of how to live with difference and how to make it manageable
through systems of recognition and representation (Fraser 2008).

While corporate global elites may not need urban citizenship, this is not
the case for many other urban dwellers. Refugees, asylum seekers, migrants
and other minorities congregate in the city precisely because it presents
possibilities of citizenship impossible elsewhere. Vis-à-vis Sennett's analysis
of corporate indifference to the city (2002), its specificities, histories and
communicative elements of difference, I propose an exploration of the
possibility of cosmopolitanism at street level: the physical street and the
mediated street, both of which involve exclusions and segregation, but
which also present possibilities for cultural and cosmopolitan citizenship
(Stevenson 2003). Thus, the range of analyses of cosmopolitanism becomes
an important point of reference in the present discussion, as, across their
differences, conceptualizations and applications of cosmopolitanism tend
to recognize a series of changes in agency and communication which have

been either ignored or discussed only peripherally in the globalization literature. Transnational (elite and working-class) mobility, the intensification of transnational politics that challenges the nation-state from below (especially through the activities of social movements), migrant and diasporic cultural and political activities and changing cityscapes have come to centre-stage in analyses of cosmopolitanism. In this context, the transnational and the urban are no longer just side effects or even just the results of globalization (Sandercock 2003; Silverstone 2007; Smith 2001; Stevenson 2003).

Increasingly, diverse cities and the complex social action among migrants, diasporas and other groups marginalized in the national and supranational formations of citizenship and economic engagement are now recognized as fascinating and critical elements of our changing world. Beck's definition of cosmopolitanization (2009) emphasizes the involuntary confrontation with others resulting from the erosion of clear borders separating markets, states, civilizations, cultures and life-worlds. 'This may influence human identity construction, which needs no longer to be shaped in opposition to others, as in the negative, confrontational dichotomy of "we" and "them,"' he argues (Beck 2009: xi–xii). Beck's analysis (Beck 2006, 2009) does not discuss media and the city in any detail, yet it implies their centrality as systems that bring differences closer together. It is precisely in the close interconnection of the media and the city that we can observe most intensely the erosion of clear boundaries and the consequent juxtapositions of difference. The city also allows us to locate cosmopolitanization within a historical and social research context where newness and possibilities are not overemphasized at the cost of continuities and social inequalities. Cosmopolitanization takes place within systems of inequality and within ideological frameworks which still promote nationalisms, Eurocentrism and majoritarianism (Appadurai 2006; Papastergiadis 2012). Thus, solidarity, community and hospitality cannot be directly attributed to processes of cosmopolitanization, but to the possibilities presented by these processes, especially for advancing cosmopolitan agency (Chouliaraki 2006) and for liberatory and democratic politics (Calhoun 2002; Harvey 2009).

Cosmopolitanization represents a starting point for opening a discussion of possibilities for new forms of recognition, representation and redistribution (Fraser 2003), but it does not represent the end point. Cosmopolitanization can be observed in the global city more than in most other places precisely because of the specificities of the place. The global city has always been characterized by transience and openness, with people and ideas flowing into its territory and from it to the world (Amin and Thrift 2002). These flows have intensified and diversified with growing urbanization and mediation. But their outcomes are neither obvious nor predictable. The discussion in chapters 4, 5 and 6 will demonstrate that cosmopolitanization involves ambivalence and that conflict and opposition are part of the dialectics of identity, community and action. It will also demonstrate that Beck's moral undertone, whereby cosmopolitanization is seen as transcending oppositions between *we*-ness and *other*-ness, is always subject to relations of power, not only to mutual exposure. Unlike cosmopolitanism as a philosophy, a vision and a political praxis that implies commitment to human rights and equality (Fine 2007), cosmopolitanization is much messier and more experiential. It neither depends on nor assumes the overcoming (or setting aside) of conflict and opposition. But it makes possible the advance of dialogue and understanding, even if opposition and conflict are still present (as they always are in the city). City life demonstrates, day in, day out, that oppositions persist and that these often become the driving force of the cosmopolitan orientation of urban subjects. Actually existing cosmopolitanism, as described by Robbins (1998), is contextual and historically positioned, particular and grounded, shaped by the meeting of reason and sentiment, of politics and culture. Binnie et al. talk about cosmopolitanism as a practice and a skill acquired through and during encounters with difference:

> involv[ing] the ability to map one's own socio-cultural position vis-à-vis the diversity encountered, and thus require[ing] a degree of reflexive ability whereby the cosmopolite can map and locate such societies and cultures historically and anthropologically. Furthermore, this skilled curiosity towards other societies and cultures often involves a degree of risk by virtue of experiencing diversity and otherness. Thus the skill of the cosmopolite is bound up with moments of uncertainty. (Binnie et al. 2006: 8)

In the city, difference itself – as individuals experience and are exposed to it – feeds into an awareness of uncertainty as well as into reflexivity about one's own limitations, others' limitations and privileges, profound social inequalities and the constraints to which identity and citizenship are subjected. In the urban world, media and communications can become valuable symbolic forms, tools for finding a voice, understanding difference and reaching out to it. Mediation, alongside migration, has 'democratized' cosmopolitan skills and competence, shifting these away from being a monopoly of privileged elites. James Clifford, writing about migrant workers and servants, argues that 'the project of comparing and translating different travelling cultures need not be class- and ethno-centric' (1992: 107). This approach is echoed in Werbner's 'working-class cosmopolitanism' (1999) and Stuart Hall's 'cosmopolitanism from below' (2008). As

Werbner argues, low-income groups develop the same forms of hybridization as elites, but with different consequences. Hall emphasizes migrants' cosmopolitan competence, developed through exposure to difference and through the need to negotiate it on a regular basis. It is in the global city more than anywhere else that this condition becomes inescapable. And it is now, more than ever before, as cities incorporate media and communications in constructing images of themselves – partly in celebrations of difference – and as many urban dwellers embrace media and communications for information, for communication, but also for self-representation and claim making. The unpredictability and openness associated with the diversification of urban life and of the media can help in understanding some of the ways in which those 'in charge' of time and space compression may drive change across boundaries, but also how they may also lose control; how those on the receiving end of power geometry (Massey 1991) may drive elements of change in culture and politics, as observed, for example, in such heterogeneous urban movements as Occupy, and in such creative presence from the margins as urban music discussed in chapters 6 and 3 respectively.

Ethical questions, of course, remain central to the study of a changing world (Chouliaraki 2013; Couldry 2012). Understanding the persistence and complexity of conflict – in its old and new formations, especially as managed in the media – is an imperative of any useful discussion of urban societies. Recording and understanding the ways in which we manage to live together, against each other and with each other, in community or in segregation, is another key area that becomes prominent when we study media and the city. How do the media contribute to living with both these realities – conflict and difference? Not everyone enjoys the media in the same way and the universe of mediated communication is deeply divided along technological, cultural and ideological lines. Not everyone is connected and networked and those who are do not all participate in the same networks. But the city shows us how in difference our fates become intertwined (Sandercock 2003). Mediated geography increasingly defines the limits of communication and participation (and of marginalization and exclusion), bringing distant others close, even if not in equal relationships (Silverstone 2007). In this context, understanding cosmopolitanization becomes a necessary starting point, but not an end point. As suggested by Harvey, there is a need to push the limits of cosmopolitanism as a political project that challenges the world's geography in emancipatory and practical ways (Harvey 2009).

Harvey's conceptual and political proposition presents a break from the dominant liberal social theory on cosmopolitanism. Cosmopolitanism in liberal thought represents a visionary discourse that reflects global change and the possibility of progress within transnational capitalism or a global civil society (cf. Beck's 2006, 2009; Held 2010). Harvey develops a thorough critique of liberal cosmopolitanism (2009), which, as he argues, either ignores inequalities, structures and geography, or integrates these into a utopian vision. The liberal rationalist cosmopolitans, Calhoun (2002) argues, have always been suspicious of religion, tradition and community precisely because these have been seen as anti-modernist forces, thus welcoming mobility of people and circulation of ideas across boundaries. Embracing global change, this scholarship has emphasized the universality of rights and reason vis-à-vis old forms of community that limited individual rights and decision making. Yet, in its origins and in its current incarnations, this social theory's emphasis on the universality of reason, has pathologized the persistence of difference and of particularisms which cannot necessarily fit within liberal or western existing models (and visions) of democracy. Adorno influentially argued that an emancipated society would come through the realization of universality, achieved by overcoming differences (1991). Adorno's call to oppose difference has been followed in different ways, firstly within Marxist writings emphasizing commonality of class interests against other differences, and secondly within a liberal social theory that privileged universality as the reason for western modernity. 'Rationalist universalism is liable not only to shift into the mode of "pure ought" but to approach human diversity as inherited obstacle rather than a resource or a basic result of creativity' (Calhoun 2002: 101). It is at this point that neoliberal and liberal approaches to cosmopolitanism become more difficult to separate. The privileges, Eurocentrism and freedom of movement associated with global elites have become almost natural attributes and conditions of cosmopolitanism; the assumed universality of western liberal democracy's rightfulness and the emphasis on the individual as the primary agent of cosmopolitan values have been equally celebrated across liberal and neoliberal theorizations of cosmopolitanism. Within this kind of universalizing outlook, particularity is acceptable on the individual level, but as soon as it becomes collective, sustained or linked to structural relations in society, it presents uncomfortable and unwelcome realities. In addition, cosmopolitanism's emancipatory potential remains tied to global capitalism and liberal democracy, marginalizing as a result differences and particularities that do not fit or do not accept the rightfulness of this model.

For those embracing, or at least engaging with, the concept from a radical and critical point of view, cosmopolitanism becomes meaningful precisely when it challenges the dehumanization associated with capitalism

– the inequality and fierce individualism that subjects human beings to the powers of the market (Chouliaraki 2013; Harvey 2009; Sennett 2002). In the context of such critical approaches to cosmopolitanism, the neoliberal cosmopolitan vision of multiple flows and progressive individual cosmopolitan consciousness is highlighted as yet another way of legitimating transnational capitalism and its local, regional and global divides. For these critical cosmopolitans, Kant represents both the inspiring starting point and the ultimate limitation of cosmopolitan liberal theory. Among them, Harvey (2009) articulates his critique by juxtaposing Kant's vision of the interconnected world and perpetual peace with his dismissal of 'inferior peoples' – those belonging to regions, classes and settings that do not fit within an organized and ordered cosmopolitanism.

Global cities have been particularly prominent in revealing the messy realities of vernacular cosmopolitanism in contrast to elitist, deterministic and beautified versions of top-down and neoliberal cosmopolitanism. Since the early days of modernity, migrant and diasporic traders and workers and travelling artists and, more recently along with these, trans-urban social movements and transnational media consumers have destabilized the given order of presumed elite cosmopolitanism and working-class parochialism. The empirical tensions between the two cosmopolitan discourses will be discussed in the next chapter, revealing how neoliberal cosmopolitanism may actually represent a much more parochial outlook than working-class cosmopolitanism (Werbner 1999), and how parochialism may now be more attached to class and lifestyle than to location. Alongside vernacular cosmopolitanism in the city, we can see glimpses of emancipatory cosmopolitan politics that challenge neoliberal capitalism, as seen in chapter 6. Such everyday and organized politics challenge the limitations of cosmopolitan theorization of stratified and western-centric rights and competences. In particular, this is revealed in urban dwellers' exposure to the narratives and moralities associated with different locations and cultures, which feed back into identity and into the citizenship skills required in order to communicate and act beyond one's immediate group. This happens as urban geography is increasingly mediated. Multiple mediated networks run across urban territory: they separate existing and new communities and create opportunities for communication beyond pre-existing difference; they link the city to corporate networks of global consumerism and to transnational communities of long-standing or new solidarities. Cosmopolitanization is unsettled and incomplete, and mediated communication plays a key role in opening and destabilizing the city as a political and cultural space.

The mediated city

The media are used by urban dwellers in constructing their sense of their city as a loved as well as an unloved place, as both a shared space and a divided place, as a place providing them with a sense of ontological security against the vastness of the global world they see on their doorstep (Giddens 1991), and as a place associated with global risk (Beck 1999). The media construct a sense of place that is constantly under negotiation. For its people, the city is real, tangible and lived. For these same people, but also for consumers beyond the physical boundaries of the city, it is also a representation positioned in, but also dislocated from, its geographical territory: it is mobile, virtual and intangible. The media not only represent the city as real and virtual; they also appropriate it. Mediated networks link the city to other cities, especially through digital networks, satellite technology and in the production, distribution, and consumption of popular culture such as music and fashion. The city is a media product as well as a real place, but it has become increasingly difficult to separate the *city* from the *image of the city*. As London, Paris and New York, but also New Orleans, Liège and Cork, become largely imagined, branded and lived through their urban and transnational mediated connections, they no longer exist outside mediation. But the shift in the meaning of place has to do with its dual role both as place *and* as process. Burd (2008) uses the concept of the communicative city to bring communication and the city closer together, defining this as 'a medium with an internal geographical locale for interpersonal contacts . . . [that] also communicates an external mediated and virtual image beyond its boundaries' (Burd 2008: 209). Burd's definition links back to Castells's theorization of the city as a process more than a place (1996), but also to Smith's (2001) notion of the distinctiveness of the city. For Smith, the city is not just an empty container for transnational articulations; local cultural understandings mediate and thus mutually constitute the meaning of transnational and networked action.

While mediation is seen as working in different ways, it is Silverstone's articulation that provides me with the most useful framework for understanding the relationship between media and the city:

> Mediation . . . requires us to understand how processes of communication change the social and cultural environments that support them as well as the relationships that participants, both individual and institutional, have to that environment and to each other. At the same time it requires a consideration of the social as in turn a mediator: institutions and technologies as well as the meanings that are delivered by them are mediated in the social processes of reception and consumption. (Silverstone 2005: 189)

Silverstone's conceptualization is particularly important for the present analysis for a number of reasons. In his dialectical model, he explores media's power in social, cultural and political life not as a direct causal relationship, but rather in terms of this power being itself subject to experience and mediation through institutional and social systems and identities. Building upon theorizations of symbolic power, especially Thompson's (1995), he argues that mediation involves inclusions and exclusions, dominant systems of media control and hegemonic representations, but also, precisely because it is a dynamic and dialectical process, resistance, appropriations and counterpoints to the dominant forces (Silverstone and Georgiou 2005). Thus, mediation is political both as a process and in its consequences. Drawing on and linking his analysis to Martín-Barbero's (1993), Silverstone also recognizes the mixed consequences of the media and mass culture. As Martín-Barbero puts it, 'When has there been more cultural circulation than in mass society?' (1993: 35). Along the same lines, Silverstone locates the politics of mediation at the crossroads of the institutional, the symbolic and the experiential. If the everyday is a site of struggle and contestation, then life in the street – the urban and the virtual – is in itself a site of contestation: it reveals the contradictory consequences of media and city synergies for cultural, social and political life.

The street is also the level where the possibility of the ordinary voice (Chouliaraki 2012) becoming part of the narrative of the city emerges. At the moments it does, it can destabilize the set representational and ideological order of what kind of city the global city is. Cultural industries, for once, are increasingly divided and the voices they represent cannot always be assumed to reproduce hegemony. Ranging from the major transnational players to the major national ones and all the way to ethnic and community media, they represent different voices and different systems of representation. The range of media players, as much as their appropriations and uses of communication technologies, represents a fragmented universe. In their diversity, these media players reveal the cultural industries' accumulation of symbolic and economic power, as much as the particular dynamics associated with relations of power in each location. The diversity of players within these industries reflects not only developments in media and communications and the liberalization of markets; it also reflects the urbanity of the symbolic economy that builds upon the internal diversity and globality of media power. In addition, communication practices that take place in the urban street only reach the global radar, both of scholarship and of corporations, when they turn into attractive commodities or when their actors become members of a recognized 'creative class'. Such is the case of urban music, discussed in chapter 4. The under-studied urban symbolic economy is not confined to global and national headquarters, but can be found in the terraced houses and on the council estates that host the less celebrated and recognized ethnic and community elements of cultural industries:

> Minority media may be relatively invisible within a national media culture, just as minorities themselves may be invisible on the screens of the mainstream (other than, as so often, in negative representations), but that invisibility does not erode, and cannot deny, their presence. Both minorities and their media exist as a continuous subtext, occasionally appearing in, and being acknowledged by, occasionally challenging, occasionally defining and transcending, the dominance of the mainstream. (Silverstone 2007: 95)

While ethnic and other non-mainstream media are invisible within the national imaginary, in the streets and neighbourhoods of the city they are real, relevant and ubiquitous actors in cultural production and consumption. It takes only a visit to some of the hundreds of small, independent Turkish or Greek shops in North London to find yourself listening to London Greek Radio (LGR) or London Turkish Radio (LTR) at full volume – often a shared, inter-ethnic listening. It takes only a few minicab journeys anywhere in London to become accustomed to the widespread success of London Asian commercial ethnic radio. And if the ride is at a late hour of the night, and depending on which part of London you find yourself in, pirate radio stations playing reggae or rap reveal themselves as ubiquitous in the ways in which the city is made and lived at certain times and in certain places. Only a handful of the hundreds of producers of these media and only a handful of the artists whose music is played on pirate stations will ever make it to the mainstream media, as will be discussed in chapter 4. Yet, for many urban dwellers and for new cosmopolitan tourists, such sounds become part of what the city is about. Interestingly, such contradictory realities associated with media and the city have recently found a prominent place in tourist guides – those read by the 'new tourists', the *flâneurs* or the new nomads who will be discussed in chapter 5, who become interested in the city as a cosmopolitan destination (and as a commodity, as discussed in the next chapter). It is the complex intermingling of the organic cultural landscape of the city and its brand, created at the very top of the corporate and policy hierarchies, that supports the global city's symbolic power – for itself and for the media that sometimes embraces it, sometimes represents it and sometimes makes it.

3   Consumption: The Hegemonic and the Vernacular

The powerful synergies of media and the city are deeply rooted in the symbolic and physical space that surrounds production and representations, but also in the practice of everyday life. As discussed in the previous chapter, symbolic power is complex, nuanced and diffused and always contested across the different layers of cultural life. Consumer cultures, as core everyday practices, represent some of the most significant leisure activities and organize many aspects of human life, ranging from entertainment to education and health. In the networks where global consumer cultures are constituted, the city is a key node: it is a place to consume and a place to be consumed. The global city is branded as a consumer magnet and is sustained as such through its symbolic economy (Zukin 2011), through the abundance of things (Miller 2010), and through the powerful media representations of commodities that are desirable and which surround many of the representations of the city itself.[1] In many ways, the global city is made through consumption.

Consumer cultures are sites of mediation: they depend on the reproduction of the symbolic value of things; technologies and information are themselves valuable commodities and media consumption informs opinions and decisions about things to be bought, appreciated or rejected. They are also hybrid meeting points, raising questions about the significance of *togetherness* in consumption. Do we communicate more and understand each other better when we consume *together*? To what extent does the materiality of commodities and of the city define meanings of consumption vis-à-vis their symbolic power? And do consumer cultures make a place, or do they push away lived experience and history, turning city space into non-place? This chapter looks at the ways in which consumption contributes to the emergence of the city as a space of communication, as well as of segregation. It does so by counterposing two contradictory cosmopolitan outlooks associated with consumption: top-down cosmopolitanism linked to consumption as the celebrated realization of neoliberalism, and vernacular cosmopolitanism as an embodied, practised and contradictory form of cosmopolitanism that emerges in urban spaces of intense juxtapositions of difference.

The empirical focus of this chapter is East London and, more particularly, two rather different, though not detached, spaces within this part of the global city: Stratford, the radically re-invented – at least symbolically – area of the city that hosted the 2012 Olympics, and Shoreditch, an area of London with a long history of migration and constant flows of newcomers. These places are particular in their local social and cultural histories and recent re-inventions, but are also of global relevance for a number of reasons. First, and while they represent two rather different consumer cultures, they both depend on the flows of tourists and migrants from all over the world for their symbolic use and value. Secondly, the commodified and sterilized space of the mall, as much as the bohemian enclave, represents familiar stories of urban space making from Los Angeles to Shanghai. In counterposing these two different kinds of consumption spaces, I aim to demonstrate that the meanings and consequences of consumer cultures are complex and mixed, revealing two different sides of cosmopolitanization: Stratford's top-down cosmopolitanism, captured in its aggressive and commercial re-invention as a non-place, and Shoreditch's vernacular cosmopolitanism (Papastergiadis 2012; Werbner 2006), reflected in conflicting histories, practices and representations of consumption. Vernacular cosmopolitanism emerges at the fringe of the 'experience economy' (Pine and Gilmore 2011) and of the regenerated city that sustains difference and affect as part of consumer experience. Top-down cosmopolitanism associated with 'safe' consumer spaces of post-gentrification, on the other hand, competes directly with vernacular cosmopolitanism and depends upon hegemonic narratives of global consumption that unites us beyond our differences. This chapter starts by introducing debates about consumption and place, especially those debates that link consumer experience and meanings of place with cosmopolitan imagination. It then moves on to consider these two contrasting projects of place-making and unmaking that reveal some of the most powerful and contradictory realities of cosmopolitanization.

Urban consumption: the placelessness of place

London is a place with a powerful identity, both evidence and product of its concentrated symbolic power. Like all identities, a city's identity is constructed through the juxtaposition of contemporary experience, historicity and the symbolic representations of this identity. The symbolic, political and military power associated with the city has always fed into its identity, but the power of the symbolic has become particularly prominent in global times. With the rise of mass media, transnational mobility and widespread tourism, symbols associated with popular culture and consumption have become widely available and desirable. Consumer culture, Lury argues

(2011: 9), is 'a type of material culture in which the consumer emerges as an identity' – the consumer becomes a master category of identity 'as a consequence of reflexive object worlds' (ibid.: 9). Consumer culture, Lury continues (ibid.), is a result of the materiality of things that count in people's everyday lives, as combined with concerns of the cultural, of the norms, values and meanings of such practices.

In the present discussion, I look at cultures of consumption in plural rather than at a single culture, since I am interested in the convergence and divergence of different logics, practices and meanings associated with consumption within the complex system of symbolic power introduced in the previous chapter. Within the plurality of meanings of consumption, different actors have different levels of access to consumer goods; some of these are largely excluded. Consumers' diverse histories and trajectories play a role when constructing the meanings of their consumption (as mass, rational, selective, ethical, even cosmopolitan). Diversity of meanings is associated with consumer cultures, as well as with inequalities in the ways in which different individuals and groups relate to consumption. As the 2011 urban riots discussed in chapter 6 revealed, even the most excluded groups can participate in consumer cultures, although this participation is of course complex and uneven and, according to Žižek (2011) and Bauman (1998), pathological. Consumer cultures also reflect, perhaps more than any other area of urban life, the hybridization of cultural space, as this emerges at the junction of a place's physicality and its symbolic value – increasingly shaped through media representations. Branding, advertising and consumption represent a continuum within which dwellers and visitors become consumers and mobile appropriators of the city. They do so as the city becomes a brand to be consumed (Malpas 2009) – a unique place, but also a place to consume brands, a placeless container of global consumption (Augé 1995 [2008]). But they also do so as they appropriate the meanings of a 'unique place' and of a 'placeless space' through the practice of everyday life (De Certeau 1984).

The debates on the significance – or even the existence – of place are relevant here. Concepts such as globalization, network society, and particularly cosmopolitanism, have often been used as counterpoints to the notion of place; in such analyses, notions of place and place-ness are sometimes considered parochial and oppositional to cosmopolitanism (Beck 2006), or challenged for their uniqueness within the network society (Castells 2009). Consumer cultures have often been interpreted within such frameworks, especially in works influenced by Augé (1995 [2008]). At the same time as place has been under attack, it has also been re-invented. Robins (2001) emphasizes the materiality of place and the significance of its actual co-presence with difference, which, while not necessarily chosen or desired (Georgiou 2008), gives meaning to the practice of everyday life. Massey (2005) argues for 'nature' as relevant to social constructivism and against its dismissal, especially by those preoccupied with the immateriality of new technologies: 'If the mantras around new technology have evoked an infinite instantaneity of dematerialised mobility, those around nature have proposed the opposite,' she writes (2005: 97), calling for research that looks at both the material and the immaterial, the grounded and the abstract in their dialectic relation to one another. Massey, along with Robins (2001), Werbner (2006), and Couldry and McCarthy (2004), emphasizes the significance of place and its ecology in revealing the dynamics of globalization, its coalitions and collisions, which are particularly relevant in understanding the ways we live together in difference.

Ecological approaches have had some influence in media and communications research, drawing on geographical and sociological approaches, especially the Chicago School of Sociology. The Chicago School's urban scholars, Park, Burgess and McKenzie (1925), recognized the city as an organic space, an ecosystem where individuals and communities develop social relations and strive for survival, largely through systems of urban communication and grounded in the space of the city. For the Chicago School, the tensions and the possibilities for participation in social and economic life were largely dependent on the ability of city dwellers to see themselves represented in public life, to a significant extent through the diverse mediascapes of the city. Ball-Rokeach and her long-standing Metamorphosis project at the University of Southern California (cf. Lin, Song and Ball-Rokeach 2010; Matsaganis, Katz and Ball-Rokeach 2011) have built upon and sustained the relevance of the Chicago School's ecological approach within communication studies. For the Metamorphosis scholars, it is the communication infrastructure within the city and the relations that develop among city dwellers that make it an organic space of community and citizenship. Lin, Song and Ball-Rokeach (2010) argue that ethnic communities in the city of Los Angeles manage their lives in the city within a system of interpersonal, community and urban communication networks. Yet the city is always an incomplete place. London, like all cities, is not a stable, coherent or pacified space. 'A place is a constellation of processes rather than a thing,' argues Massey (2005: 141). Place is open and internally multiple and not intrinsically coherent, a locus of 'the generation of new trajectories and new configurations' (ibid.: 141). Place is constituted through practices and through representations.

The emphasis on the co-constitution of place and symbolic forms is prevalent within media studies, learning extensively from urban and social geography. Couldry and McCarthy (2004) use the hybrid concept of MediaSpace to capture the co-constitution of space and social relations through mediation: 'MediaSpace, then, at once defines the artefactual existence of media forms within social space, the links that media objects forge *between* spaces, and the (no less real) cultural visions of a physical space transcended by technology and emergent virtual pathways of communication' (2004: 2). In this context, media do not just represent city space, but also contribute to its formation. Representing a significant tradition within media and communications research, mediation as an analytical framework recognizes the emergence of the spaces of identity and of the meanings of *self* and *other*, not only through social relations but also through representational systems of social relations. Thus the city is not a contained place, and it not only hosts but constitutes its own dynamics of identity and representation. Mediation brings a Heideggerian emphasis on experience closer to a social constructivist analysis – experience is as much subject to social relations as it is subject to location in space and to access to and use of technologies and representational systems. In this context, the city is organic and unique because it brings together individuals to share consumer experiences associated with the specific dynamics of a place. Moreover, a city as a place is always a networked place, a representational space, and a place that is always represented, not just through language and its symbols, but significantly through mediated representations available within and across the city's territory: a representational apparatus of its symbolic power. Within this system, advertising and media representations of commodities promote hegemonic narratives and images of the city's identity, yet they never fully homogenize it, as will be seen below: the city is also a complicated and a practised place.

Unlike everyday practices, representations are selective, often one-dimensional and always ideological: the advertising of places, of commodities and of places as commodities are the most typical cases of this. Meyrowitz's (1985) influential thesis argues for the collapse of place through media representations and media consumption. Media, he argues, have changed everyday experience in such a way that place – *where people are* – has become less relevant than *who people are with*. As media connections challenge limitations of physical space, the limits of social relations also shift and the boundedness of social groups and identities (e.g. men and women) is also challenged. Augé (1995 [2008]) has pushed the notion of the 'attack' on place even further in his analysis of 'supermodernity'. Places of consumption, associated in modernity with the uniqueness of the city centre as a place for meeting and for shopping, have turned into places with an unidentifiable identity. Supermarkets and high streets have been taken over by chains of shops that look the same in every city, and increasingly popular virtual places of consumption, such as Amazon.com, have replaced the uniqueness of place. Augé (1995 [2008]) refers to the move away from identifiable places which carry histories and are associated with processes of identity construction as non-places. Spaces of circulation, communication and consumption are non-places privileged by supermodernity, Augé continues:

> If a place can be defined as relational, historical and concerned with identity, then a space which cannot be defined as relational, or historical, or concerned with identity will be a non-place. The hypothesis advanced here is that supermodernity produces non-places, spaces which are not themselves anthropological places and which, unlike the Baudelairean modernity, do not integrate the earlier places. (Augé 2008 [1995]: 63)

The neat divisions that Augé proposes do not translate into the practised, even the represented, place. In fact, it is the way in which practices and representations merge and converge to produce and challenge meanings of place as stable and contained that redefined places as dialogical (and uneasy) spaces of communication. In this context, Meyrowitz's work may be the most important, not in his attempt to dismiss place, but in his emphasis on *who people are with* as largely shaping communication. The current discussion aims to understand *who people are with*, as well as *where (they are with others)*, and with what consequence for communication and for the understanding of difference.

The East End: between the place and non-place of consumption

The cases discussed here show two different forms of convergence and divergence of place and placelessness and reflect the internal contradictions of cosmopolitanization: in the case of top-down cosmopolitanism, the non-place of consumption becomes cosmopolitan through the dilution of placeness (which inevitably is conditioned to placed experience); in the case of vernacular cosmopolitanism, experience is tied to the place of consumption, but also to proactive articulations of the place as a location of 'thrownto-getherness' (Massey 2005). Two contrasting shopping destinations in East London present powerful empirical evidence: the first has become a globally recognized brand – Westfield Stratford City – especially as part of the 2012 Olympics regeneration of Stratford. The second – Shoreditch – is a hip and bohemian destination, hosting many independent local designers and vintage shops, night clubs and restaurants, alongside pre-existing ethnic minority economies representing the cultures of consumption of the area's culturally diverse population. Shoreditch represents an amalgam of alternative, urban and culturally diverse lifestyles that depend on a long history of place as a destination for newcomers. Stratford, in similar ways to Shoreditch, has a long history of attracting newcomers, but has a very different current trajectory, especially since part of the area has been entirely redesigned and redefined in its uses and meanings during the countdown to the 2012 Olympics. Drawing on ethnographic observations, I shall demonstrate the interplay between the powerful symbolic meanings associated with each of those locations as consumer destinations and as places with (or without) a history. These locations are constructed as places to attract different kinds of consumers. Representations through branding, advertising and other media narratives inform their identities as places or non-places, as locations where encounters of difference can take on different meanings.

The re-invention of East London, which includes both Shoreditch and Stratford, as an attractive destination had started well before the 'regeneration' plans associated with the London Olympics (Brown 2006). Since the 1990s, East London has slowly become gentrified, attracting first the bohemian creative classes and then the affluent youth working in the financial sectors, located in geographical proximity to the deprived neighbourhoods of Newham, Tower Hamlets and Hackney, which are discussed in the next chapter. These areas represent some of the most culturally diverse locations in the world. Gentrification has been a contested project, often a reflection of the neoliberal redefinition of working-class and culturally diverse urban neighbourhoods. But, in itself, gentrification does not erase place; rather it can advance different conceptualizations of place: on the one hand, the cosmopolitan middle classes become locals while, on the other, working-class inhabitants can find themselves trapped in a place because they cannot go anywhere else. For Harvey (1989), the problem does not lie in pushing placelessness, but in pushing place-ness through social divisions of space. He argues that policies of place emphasize its image and its uniqueness, unlike those examining the needs of territories and of their inhabitants (ibid.). While Massey agrees that place is made and is political, she argues that it is also and always incomplete and a space of junctures, thus presenting possibilities for our living together (2005).

While there is no doubt that place is experienced differently as a result of the unevenness in the economic and cultural experiences associated with its territory, consumer cultures represent cultural frameworks that bridge some urban and social divides. There is no doubt that mass tourism has advanced mobility beyond single locales, providing, through mobility, different perspectives on place (Urry 2007). Even more than physical mobility, mediated exposure to different commodities and advertising has altered relations to place. The constant presence of transnational elites and tourists in most sections of the global city's consumer hubs makes it difficult to separate these places from their global representations. Place branding, along with commodity branding, shapes the city's meanings, argues Malpas:

> The city is that in which we live, and through which our lives are often articulated and shaped, and yet, as expressed in the ideology of the city brand, it is little different from the relationship we have with any other commodity – that we are citizens of this city is little different from the fact that we consume this variety of soft drink or that make of sports shoe. (Malpas 2009: 196)

Shopping areas, especially as increasingly associated with globally recognizable forms of consumption and spatial organization, are fields where struggles about the present and future trajectories of the city can be observed in all their intensity: is the global city primarily a space for living (together) or for maximizing profit? The two case studies discussed below reveal some of the difficulties of giving simple answers to this question. These case studies, like the discussions that unravel in the following chapters, show that in the city such questions are always open-ended. But this open-endedness is not unconditional: since urban encounters and their consequences always take place in environments of inequality and enormous unevenness, they are subject to the conditions associated with economic and symbolic power. This is the story of Stratford's mega-mall and of the street level consumption cultures of Shoreditch.

Constructing the mega-mall: a city within a city

'This is the future: a whole indoor city,' a visitor to the latest addition to the shopping world of London, the mega-mall of Westfield Stratford City, said in describing his fascination with his new experience. Indeed Westfield Stratford City, an enormous shopping and entertainment area built on land previously occupied by industrial remnants of the old East End, has changed the topography and the symbolic meaning of Stratford. Until the turn of the century an area symbolizing the unattractive *other* London, Stratford is now the gateway to the Olympic Village and to a whole shopping 'city within a city', offering an enormous range of shopping and entertainment opportunities.

Westfield Stratford City, the biggest shopping centre in Europe, opened its doors to the public in 2011, representing a milestone in the transformation of East London in the countdown to the London Olympics. The mall identifies itself in a way which was also adopted by many of the visitors I spoke to: 'Westfield Stratford City is a new metropolitan capital for East London, a city within a city, an innovative and dynamic place for a new generation of consumers to shop, to eat, to meet, to be entertained and to stay' (Westfield Stratford City 2011). The mall's online self-representation builds upon the recognizable global brand of Westfield attractive to tourists, but also on the promotion of what is presented as social responsibility through participation in projects with local charities and schools. The mall represents one of the major plans for the transformation of a historically deprived area of London which, until recently, was located outside the imaginary boundaries of the cosmopolitan city and its mental and printed maps of a tourist's and consumer's heaven. The ideology behind this enormous plan for the regeneration of East London is visible in the realization of the changing city: consumption and entertainment in a glamorous, surveyed and controlled environment is linked not only to pleasure, but also to a better quality of life. Local and political voices that resisted the direction followed by the grand regeneration plan for East London have long been marginalized. The 'new' Stratford, coming out of the East London Regeneration plan and initiated with £9 billion in public investment (London First 2008), represents literally and metaphorically a vast element in the neoliberal ideological orientation of regeneration: what regenerates an area are businesses, tourists and consumers. The direction of the plan is vividly captured and celebrated by London First, the influential business lobby that put development and investment at the heart of the project (2008), while the Department of Culture, Media and Sport has made special reference to the new mega-mall as a core element of regeneration and job opportunities for locals (Department of Culture, Media and Sport 2011).

There is no doubt that the new shopping centre provides new opportunities, as argued above. But what kinds of opportunity are these? Celebrated in their abstraction by businesses and politicians, opportunities here become directly linked to consumer cultures: the presumption is that the locals get jobs in shops and restaurants and the visitors bring in precious economic capital. The mere size of the mega-mall and its busy space confirm this vision. The scenario of opportunities to be celebrated reinforces a global imaginary of a shared consumer culture while organizing social divides in a coherent and managerial manner that brings as much control as possible to this space. Order runs through the symbolic and geographical organization of the mall's space. Security cameras are strategically positioned, as are private security guards; media advertisements for the mall as the self-evident reason for visiting Stratford, and a neat and strategic incorporation of narratives of diversity in the self-representation of the mall, create a calculated, rational and repetitive system of urban order (Rose 2000) associated with consumption.

Both the brand and the geography of the mall are familiar and global. Westfield is a transnational corporation owning 48 malls in the United States (westfield.com) and dozens of malls in Australia, New Zealand and the United Kingdom. The celebrated globality of the mall builds on the growing familiarity of brands and space-making associated with consumption which spreads from North America to East Asia. The mall is branded but the space is branded too through widely recognizable global labels: Disney, Apple, Armani Jeans, Forever 21. The dozens of restaurants represent an eclectic selection of recognizable 'ethnic' cuisines, reflecting 'commodified spaces of alterity and difference which, rather than generating new or challenging encounters, potentially result in a homogenization and domestication of difference' (Binnie et al. 2006: 18). The parade of ethnic restaurants in the main restaurant and fast-food areas is almost comical in its intended variety, the 'box-ticking' of diversity well captured: Cabana Brazilian Barbecue, The Real Greek, Chicago Rib Shack, Comptoir Libanais, Tortilla, Lotus Leaf, Pizzeria Franco Manca and more. The area surrounding the mall, like so many places to be found around the world, is also strategically organized around a safe and familiar geography of consumption. On arrival at Stratford station, visitors are guided by signage that makes the mall their almost obligatory destination. Should they nonetheless find themselves outside in the street, prominent signs and billboards give them a second chance to choose the 'right' way. A sculpture of a metallic tree both helps to direct visitors to the mega-mall and conceals the entrance to an older, outdated local mall representing a different Stratford. Familiarity associated with consumption is the most prominent narrative here: a cosmopolitan imaginary of sharing across difference is aggressively tied to a communal experience of consumption.

One of the most intense experiences in this mega-mall, as in many of its kind seen rising in cities around the world, is a sense of disorientation as a result of the artificiality of the organization of space. This is a feeling that I had myself and which many of its visitors described when asked. The disorienting effect of the 'futuristic' space is not coincidental and is both enabled and managed through mediation. Large screens with advertisements constantly remind the visitors of brands: specific brands found in the shops, but also the brand of the shopping mall itself. The mall is not just a container for shopping, but a brand in its own right that needs to be reaffirmed to its multiple users: both the potential visitors who are bombarded with advertisements for Westfield on many of London's and Britain's media and the actual visitors already in the branded space. Whilst it might appear to be 'preaching to the converted', this ongoing advertising is not redundant, but it represents a strategy of reminding visitors that their physical presence makes them part of the brand, that they have the embodied experience of it and should make a commitment to the mall, or the brand, or the merging of the two. No wonder the experience becomes intense and disorienting for visitors bombarded by beaming vibrant colours, music and advertising. This is why there are maps all around the mall showing visitors where they are at every step of the way. These maps that remind them of a conventional and familiar geography counterbalance the abstract and mediated experience of the many screens, billboards and shop windows.

Futuristic and highly mediated, as well as largely familiar to most of its visitors because of its similarity to other places of consumption, this is also a stratified and classed place. The mall has three main levels, representing a symbolic and physical stratification that are perhaps appropriate to its neo-liberal vision: a single space where difference is organized in a securitized, safe and non-conflictual manner. The top two floors host the best-known brands, most of these representing transnational corporations. The bottom floor, at lower-ground level, hosts stores offering commodities mostly of the same kind as those on the top two floors but as a rule at a lower cost. The eating places reflect the same kind of stratification. The top-floor mezzanine hosts the best-known restaurants (almost all of these belonging to upmarket chains). While the second floor offers the parade of ethnic, but gentrified, restaurants, the food hall on the lower ground floor brings together the usual fast-food chains: McDonalds, KFC and local chains offering choices in a similar price range. Even in this ultimate global commodified space, homogeneity is not an option or even a desire. The diversification of experience reflects the social divides presumed to characterize the visitors and is reflected in the social geography of this space. This is why a place is never fully definable as a non-place, but is always a lived space. As Zukin puts it: 'Shopping spaces are a valuable prism for viewing public culture. The types of goods that are sold, at what prices, and in what forms – these are the everyday experiences in which physical spaces are "conceived" in the light of social structure' (1995: 257).

Yet Westfield, like all malls, is the closest we can get to a non-place – largely mediated, controlled, commodified. Westfield Stratford City is both indistinguishable from other spaces of global consumption and a very specific place: a shopping destination for urban dwellers, a new London landmark for tourists, a space where locals (as long as they carry some buying capital) can meet, spend their leisure time and have fun. It is a place designed for recreation and enjoyment around consumption. However, like all consumption, these activities, organized neatly and against the unpredictabilities associated with place, are still made sense of through the actual experience – experience which is both physical and is mediated. Zukin (1995) reminds us that shopping and places of consumption are also places of public culture. A local family posing for a photo in front of a lower-range sports shop is a particular element of public life here – an image and a practice observed across the mall. The concentrated symbolic power of an apparatus of power, in this case captured in the meeting of the global city, the global brands and the globally recognizable shopping mall, becomes diffused and confirmed in the way consumption becomes personalized and experiential, as in the case of taking photos. But the power of the experience is crucial here: consumption is not just repetitive, mechanical and subject to the rules of profit. The place of consumption becomes a part of experience, of pleasure, and when captured in a family photo it becomes part of a family's history, a point in shared memory and identity. For a moment, at least, it is a way to put the self and the family into the larger picture of a shared world. The mediation of experience in the mall is everywhere. Indeed, a surprising number of people take photos and make videos in the mall, turning the commodified non-place into a special, unique place of their own. Coming closer, in this environment, to difference becomes a peculiar amalgam of the physical proximity to other consumers and the negotiated and conditional proximity that personal technologies allow. The faceless, 'cosmopolitan' space of consumption becomes unique and one's own through the production of personal representations of Westfield. Putting oneself or a loved one 'in the picture' immediately appropriates the commodified space. Creating personal memories through captions on photographs or video that place one's self in the centre of the mall's global story is just one of the many ways in which Westfield is mediated.

The city space as a place of consumption or a place to be consumed is not available to all shoppers in the same way, since each carries different cultural and economic capital. However, the social stratification which is visible in Westfield Stratford City, as in most public spaces, is not entirely divisive. Observing the consumers of the lower-ground floor food hall, it becomes immediately apparent that, even within this relatively small territory, the clientele does not represent a fully homogenous classed group. The cross-class and cross-cultural appeal of fast food is evident here. And, while inside some shops the clientele appears clearly filtered by class, the public spaces in the mall are shared by many different people. No doubt this is a space of close encounters of difference. But does the encounter matter?

The coexistence of difference within the new idealized environment of the mega-mall destabilizes the singular narrative of the cosmopolitan city. Yes, most visitors come here as consumers but, within this singular context of consumption, their appropriation of the space varies: some respond to the media 'call' to visit a new global centre of consumerism, while others come here because there is little else to do in their locality. The irony is that this controlled space offers more opportunities to encounter local, urban and global difference than most other local places in the city, which tend to be much more homogenous in terms of their ethnic and, to an even greater extent, their cultural composition. The striking opposition of the encounter becomes visible when one visits the Stratford Centre, the old Stratford mall next door to Westfield, which has been there for decades. There is little doubt that the old Stratford mall is a place that carries years of social experience and corresponds to the social history of this area. The Stratford Centre attracts the local working class, primarily a British Asian and British Caribbean clientele. In the centre of this old shopping area, market stalls mark the merging of the street and the mall in a mundane and less 'cool' and constructed manner. At the same time, this shopping centre corresponds much more neatly to a stratified, top-down conceptualization of cosmopolitanism. Here, minorities are at home, performing mundane, non-conflictual practices of particularity, while remaining at a distance from the white middle class. In a peculiar and contradictory way, there are moments when elite cosmopolitanism is disturbed precisely by the enormously diversified consumption taking place in the new mega-mall next door. The mere co-presence of people from different backgrounds reaffirms that even the most controlled space cannot be sufficiently sanitized to exclude all flavour of the real city that surrounds it.

The visibility of minorities and of the urban working class in the glamorous neoliberal cosmopolitan environment of Westfield has some significant policy implications. Working-class visitors do not just shop. They also live in the city. Their presence raises questions around social inclusion and recognition. Are social and ethnic minorities contained within a culture that reproduces their marginalization, or do they become recognized as active makers of a local culture (that includes shopping)? The mall, no matter how disorienting and faceless, offers to many living in the surrounding deprived areas of London one of the very few safe and public spaces for recreation. As government cuts reduce even further available public spaces, such as youth centres and libraries, for local people, the commodified space of the mall remains a relatively accessible public space. Surveillance plays a double and contradictory role here. On the one hand, it prevents some of the most deprived people from entering this controlled territory, but on the other it offers a safe space. As I was writing this chapter, police announced a 10 per cent increase in knifepoint robberies in the United Kingdom. Many of these take place in London, especially in deprived areas of the city (BBC Online 2012a).

The city's and the country's political leadership and the business world have praised this space as evidence of regeneration. Consumption is praised at every step of the way as evidence of well-being and a good quality of life. While we know little about how consumption advances Westfield visitors' sense of happiness, the appropriation of the meanings both of consumption and of the space itself has a powerful role to play in shaping urban life. As visitors produce their memories in this space, and as they personify the mediated and commercial experience associated with the mall, they become part of the global story of the city. 'Places are consumed and, hence, they are fantasized, travelled to, stayed in, experienced through purchases of goods and especially services, and then remembered, often in the company of others,' write Elliott and Urry (2010: 116).

This story unfolds at the meeting of the top-down and commodified cosmopolitanization of the city through the reproduction of globally recognized spaces of consumption and the tensions associated with the surrounding urban regeneration. The brand of the cosmopolitan city becomes embodied and reaffirmed in redefinitions of places as global spaces, but also in the embodied experience of the people who occupy this space. The 'new' East End becomes, through commodification and the global brand of the Olympics this embodies, a place of consumption and a place of global appeal. The 'new' East End is a place of promise, glamour and desirable commodities. Consumption and the powerful images that surround it in non-places, in billboards and in advertising partly produce cities as simulacra (Baudrillard 1994); the representational value of consumption is so aggressively reproduced that meanings of urban spaces, from Singapore to London's 'new' East End, cannot be imagined outside the system of representations that produce it.

The socially stratified place made inside and around Westfield Stratford City builds upon narratives of difference and togetherness: different commodities, characterized by different prices and styles and catering to different tastes, are inviting varied patterns of consumption within the same space; customers of all different backgrounds are supported in their navigation of the shopping area – previous knowledge of the place and of the local geography is not required since visual tools help the customer at every step of the way; the transnational clientele scarcely need a shared language since the visuality and price tags of powerful images of food and clothes become the prime system of communication between the service providers and the customers. A safe imagined cosmopolitan experience

(Binnie and Skeggs 2006) encapsulates and celebrates togetherness and conviviality. What is missing from this togetherness, from this cosmopolitan
imaginary? Security guards, but also the very geography of the space, make
it clear that this is not a place for everyone. A non-place is a familiar location for the middle classes and for international travellers, but is alienating
and even threatening for many working-class locals. In his ethnographic
account, Lindsay (2012) repeatedly recorded a sense of total exclusion from
the Olympic regeneration experience. Most people living on estates close
by have never even considered visiting this mega-mall because they saw it
from the start as an alien and unwelcoming space (ibid.). In a peculiar way,
the mega-mall's togetherness is subject to very clearly defined geographical and symbolic boundaries. Visual markers separate Westfield from the
old Stratford mall, associated with the classed and migrant histories of the
place; inside, Westfield's stratification of the consumption experience, with
each floor offering commodities to different consumers, reaffirms divisions
within togetherness. A liberal notion of cosmopolitanism as an exposure to
other people and other cultures is well in place here. Even the choice of East
London for the Olympic Park has been a project developed within a cosmopolitan framework (Occupy London 2012: 2012), celebrating London's
diversity. Westfield Stratford City became part of this narrative and cosmopolitan consumption has become part of what this space is about, not least
as visitors to the Olympic Park had to go through the mall to reach it: did
the mega-mall and its brands mediate the celebration of the Olympics and
its brand's global togetherness or the other way around?

Urban alterity: the placeness of place

The hegemonic narratives of cosmopolitan togetherness might prevail in
the intensely controlled symbolic and physical spaces of a mall but the city's
terrain and practices are inevitably multiple. They come with different histories and diverting trajectories, especially in those parts of the city that have
developed through mobility, migration and intense juxtapositions of difference. Locations marked as different precisely on the basis of their alterity are
found in all cities, certainly in all global cities. Shoreditch, East London, is
such a place. It brings together two alterities: the East London Bangladeshi
community and the bohemian youth occupying artistic and gender identities on the border of mainstream urban public life. An area with a high
concentration of artists' studios, numerous Bangladeshi restaurants and
hubs of gay culture, Shoreditch reflects both the amalgamation of the inner
city through intense contact between alterities and a hip destination for

consumption and entertainment. The tensions between different imaginaries and claims to the symbolic and physical space of Shoreditch have certain particular characteristics associated with its history and spatiality. At the same time, they represent familiar tensions for many cities: histories of mobility and settlement, changing demography and uses of space and, most importantly, in the context of this discussion, different claims to the symbolic making of the urban space reflect struggles that take place in most urban societies.

A space of alterity, such as Shoreditch, is an uneven place, an impure place, a place always in the making. De Certeau argues that all urban experience is structured around the phenomenological encounter – the practice of occupying the urban street – and the overarching logic of the concept of the city (1984). Thus walking, buying and talking in the streets of London become practices filtered through the concept of London as a city (global, dangerous and cosmopolitan). The very concept of the city is dependent on government and corporate strategies for the organization of city life. When it comes to street-level life, De Certeau argues, the city is navigated in multiple tactical ways and not necessarily by fully following the planned city strategy, or, for that matter, hegemonic meanings of coming together in consumption and leaving difference aside. In focusing on neighbourhoods that carry powerful signifiers of the city concept, we can observe the complex tactics of navigating it at street level and the ways in which city space is practised (ibid.) and made. Shoreditch carries a long history of struggles between strategic plans for the role of the area within London and its ubiquitous appropriations and readjustments of the meanings of this area's histories and trajectories at street level. Partly through its consumption cultures, Shoreditch has come to represent a powerful example of vernacular cosmopolitanism (Papastergiadis 2012; Werbner 2006, 2008).

Cosmopolitanism – an underlying reality of place-making throughout the twentieth century in inner-city locations – has now become a powerful narrative, expressed especially in consumption cultures. Importantly, there is no single cosmopolitan narrative that runs across the organization of space and public life in this area of the city. Place-making in this case contrasts with the sleek, top-down cosmopolitanism promoted and safeguarded in Westfield Stratford City. Instead, Shoreditch's cosmopolitanism is lived, historical and diverting in its different articulations between the groups that occupy its territory as inhabitants, consumers and visitors. Place-making in this case is as much a story of migration and of class as it is of consumption.

The Shoreditch area, with Brick Lane at its core, represents the heart of the East London Bangladeshi community, established in this part of the city after a long migration initiated in the 1930s (Eade 2000). Shoreditch is located within Tower Hamlets, the borough with the highest number of children living in poverty in the United Kingdom (Tower Hamlets Borough 2010). It has long been a migrant destination, but its history was not always one of poverty, though it has always been one of close encounters. During the 1880s and 1890s, East European Jews settled in this area and by the inter-war period Shoreditch was a relatively prosperous part of London. In the mid-twentieth century, the Abercrombie Plan moved people and jobs to new cities, and the new arrivals from Bangladesh took the space of the old Jewish population who were moving out (Eade 2000). It is important to note that, as its demography, Shoreditch has historically attracted attention as a desirable destination. Eade (2000) quotes a 1926 travel guide which demonstrates the fascination of its author with the *other*-ness of this part of London. It is another city altogether, he writes (ibid.)

Jacobs (1996), who studied East London's Brick Lane, discusses the ways in which Brick Lane's branding reinforced a racialized discourse of multi-cultural consumerism through its celebration as London's 'Banglatown'. This kind of representation, write Shaw, Bagwell and Karmowska (2004), has been reinforced by public policy which focused on the creation of a space for touristic consumption and voyeurism of *other*-ness. It is also evident in the media, which casually, and sometimes in an endearing way, refer to the area as Banglatown. While the name has become a recogniz-able brand, it has also become a contested one. A local British Bangladeshi councillor campaigned in 2008 to name a local station Banglatown (BBC Online 2008). Yet the hipsters of Shoreditch claim a different representa-tion of the area, which focuses on avant-garde art and fashion, while the gay community actively promotes the area as the core of gay-friendly London. The radio station Hoxton FM and the magazine *Made in Shoreditch* are two local media initiatives among many, reflecting the artistic avant-garde's claims to Shoreditch. As Hoxton FM put it: 'Hoxton Forward Movement (FM) is more than just a fresh new internet radio station broadcasting all genres of music, art, fashion and culture 24/7. Focusing on diversity and high quality, Hoxton FM is instigating a creative meritocracy in London and beyond' (Hoxton FM 2011). The ironic, yet very real, instigation of a 'creative meritocracy' demonstrates the rather polished discourse that cul-tures of diversity can turn to. In the global city, difference can become terri-torialized, placed and also commodified. It becomes territorialized when the attractiveness of an 'exciting' locale is clearly defined by its physicality and the concentrated symbolic power it carries. For Shoreditch, the local con-centration of symbolic power is not abstract and imagined: it is reflected in art produced and exhibited on the streets, and in a commerce around enter-tainment and culture that is profitable and makes links between the very specific locale and key nodes of production and consumption of popular culture in global networks. Networks of culture, as the self-identification of Hoxton FM above demonstrates, represent elements of the story of Hoxton that make links between London 'and beyond'. These networks are also becoming increasingly influential in fashion and food cultures in the city and beyond as local and international media now recognize and legitimate such bohemian locales' claims to cosmopolitan identity and their global leadership in setting fashion, music or culinary trends. This is a place where property becomes attractive, where nightlife is enjoyed at some cost, where a range of cuisines parade in hip high-street restaurants, where restaurants, boutiques, clubs and galleries whose names are widely recognized compete for an elite, cosmopolitan and creative clientele.

Such a place becomes deterritorialized, however, when the cultural symbols associated with the specific locale are detached from its histories of migration, poverty, family fortunes and community. This results in the commodification of cultural difference and the production of sets of *other*-ness that involve people who share territories but not histories or, for that matter, systems of communication. Interestingly, through and within the territoriality of urban difference, the *other* is not necessarily the socially marginalized city-dweller. Cultural capital owned by the pre-gentrification residents is valuable in navigating not only the locality, but also the cultural landscape that makes the locality a desirable destination and a symbol of 'fascinating' and cosmopolitan city life.

Importantly, such inner-city spaces have both commonalities with and differences from those aggressively controlled symbolic and physical spaces discussed earlier in the chapter. It is not only geographical proximity that makes Shoreditch and Westfield Stratford City relevant to each other, but also the element of transformation and 'change' implied by the symbolic (re-)invention of both places, especially through consumption cultures. There is something about change and the buzz associated with change that becomes incorporated in the ways these places are imagined and consumed. People go to both places to spend money, to be entertained and to shop. That is the case at least for visitors, who are the primary users of shops and restaurants in both places. It is interesting, though, to see the contrasts between the two kinds of place-making in the representational value of Shoreditch and Stratford: old/new; continuous/discontinuous; historical/ahistorical. For the gentrified and transformed 'new' East End, the image of the new, global, clean and safe space of the mall is counterposed to the deprived and undesirable past (which, of course, you need only turn a corner to return to). For the other East End of Shoreditch, it is the continuity and richness of the past, feeding into the present and future of an area that is constantly under construction that makes up its image as a desirable destination, a symbol of urban cool. In this way, we can observe how work-ing-class histories and histories of migration into the city become separated in a selective articulation of their historical and representational value.

This is a struggle for symbolic power. In Shoreditch, it was the rich histories of migration that established food industries and tailoring as the main elements of the local economy. This heritage, which has always built on transnational networks, has fed into the symbolic economy of the place and its recognizable image as a cosmopolitan cultural location; its long transnationality has been central to the place's attractiveness for the young, cool, creative classes. The top-down cosmopolitan project of Stratford, on the other hand, has focused on stripping the place of the specificities of its histories. The powerful and aggressive stripping of a place of its historical and demographic histories and its representational re-invention has become a familiar story of the redefinition of many city spaces around the world, through strategic redefinitions of space for consumers, visitors and inves-tors. The overarching project of the global form of the mall leaves little space for reflection on histories, continuities or the messy journeys associated with migration (itself linked to a significant extent to the history of the urban working class and the divides between zones of prosperity and poverty).

Experimentation is also a distinct element in the vernacular cultures of the impure inner city – a grounded element of urban openness. Dress codes among squatters in East London have been taken over and reproduced by the boutiques in the gentrified parts of these same areas of the city and displayed in trend-setting magazines and blogs that reaffirm urban openness and transience, but also the economic conditionality of experimentation. The acclaimed fashion trends of Shoreditch have become not only desired commodities among Londoners who can afford them, but also an attraction for visitors, tourists and fashion-watchers across the world. The attractive-ness of these trends to urban and global consumers is not detached from the history of difference associated with the location of their emergence. In vernacular cosmopolitanism, difference merges with practices and represen-tations in complex ways. The symbolic power of urban fashion builds upon difference. Yet recognition of difference, the forms of its materialization and consequences, is not always the same. More often than not, histories of difference and the struggles behind some forms of urban creativity and expression become decorative elements of the actual commodity. Not unlike Westfield's cosmopolitanism, difference can become a repetitive form of controlled narrative (Rose 2000). Innovative economic activity has a tendency to cluster in and around bohemian enclaves, as Florida writes (2002) in celebration of neoliberal cosmopolitanism. This clustering is associated with the identity of the city as a place of consumption and as a place to be consumed: 'Every successful society needs its bohemia . . . [to] regenerate its culture. . . . In every age in every successful country, it has been important that at least a small part of the cityscape is not dominated by bankers, developers, chain stores, generic restaurants and railway terminals' (Hitchens 2008: 1–2). The logic of the commodification of place and its stripping of historical complexities is celebrated in such discourses, which turn consumption and creativity into placeless realities. These can be associated with cosmopolitan consumption, but not with mutual understanding. 'Rather than learning from and truly engaging with difference, cosmopolitan consumption entails the consumption of the non-cosmopolitan "Other",' writes Bodaar (2006: 172).

The difference between inner city's vernacular cosmopolitanism and a controlled space of consumption's neoliberal cosmopolitanism is not a clear opposition. However the difference between neoliberal cosmopolitanism and vernacular cosmopolitanism is oppositional in many ways. In the project of a global mega-mall, we see aggressive efforts to erase the histories of working-class and migrant cosmopolitanism and replace them with commodified and securitized plateaus of difference. Moving to the global city's street-level cosmopolitanism, as seen in Shoreditch, we can observe the representational struggles in the city. The mobility of the middle classes in the culturally diverse inner-city meets working-class cosmopolitan practices (Werbner 1999), not just erasing them. The present and past markers of migration spill into consumer cultures that become distinctly associated with a place precisely because of its difference. Vernacular cosmopolitanism is not visionary and pure, but it is the closest to a willingness to engage with *others* (Hannerz 1990). There is a communicative dimension to the desire to cross the boundary, a process of *reaching out* that comes with growing knowledge and sometimes with a growing moral sense of respect for others and their histories. The moral dimension of the coming together of difference in a place and in (its) consumption is reflected in numerous projects in Shoreditch. Many of the commodities available in the area, for example, are branded through the logic of ethical business; in many restaurants and boutiques, sustainability and fair trade in the use of materials and resources are promoted; the artistic and literary creativity associated with this place very often builds upon narratives and imageries of mutual respect of the area's different communities. Hoxton Apprentice, a restaurant in Shoreditch, is a vivid example of promoting an *ethical togetherness* around consumer cultures. The interplay between liberal values and a cosmopolitan morality is revealed in its self-representation on its website. The restaurant aimed: 'to give its diners a top quality but affordable eating experience and to prepare unemployed people for jobs in the hospitality industry. Hoxton Apprentice cooks modern European food to a standard that has won Michelin recommendation. . . . What makes Hoxton Apprentice stand out is that 100% of all its profits – your money – is reinvested to help unemployed people.' This case shows that the vision of a viable shared future has a strong classist aspect – not all participants in this narrative take an equal position within the vision that makes of some demanding consumers and of others competent servers. The limits of liberal cosmopolitan morality are apparent in this case and across many realities of a place that is caught between a branded trendy place and a lived deprived space. Bursting with high-quality restaurants and trendy bars, many of which promote an ethical business model, Shoreditch, like so many other bohemian locations in powerful cities' inner city, is also torn by poverty. The real tensions between liberal cosmopolitanism and neoliberal politics were even more vividly revealed when the charity-run restaurant was forced to close after government cuts to charity funding. As this case shows, the viability of projects of conviviality that recognize and celebrate difference and mutual commitment to a shared future is always conditional on neoliberalism's aggressive grasp of the city.

Consumers united?

In *World City*, Massey (2007) argues '*against* localism but for a politics of place'. And she explains: 'There is a need to rethink the "place" of the local and to explore how we can rearticulate a politics of place that both meets the challenges of a space of flows and addresses head-on the responsibilities of "powerful places" such as global cities. . . . What is needed is a politics of place beyond place' (Massey 2007: 15). What Massey argues is that the local politics of global cities cannot be understood within the framework of a global/local opposition because the local is framed through the participation of urban activities in global flows, while its particularity is at the same time not lost. Powell adds the element of technology, and not only global economic flows, as being intrinsically linked into the way a city is shaped as a space of communication and as a place of action (2004). Consumer cultures represent one of the domains where place is articulated at the junction of global narratives and technologies of practice and representation. Consumer cultures make the city a place, a place which is neither stable and self-contained nor totally taken over by powerful global culture narratives. It is a place which finds its meanings in dialogue and in conflict between the various narratives and experiences of being urban and global, and in the unstable narratives of cosmopolitanism that emerge around these. Global narratives and practices of consumption shape the different ways in which a place can be cosmopolitan: through neoliberal and stratified cosmopolitan celebrations where consumption itself becomes an end point; in contradictory 'niche' consumption cultures that reflect urban dwellers' efforts to find a place in the city and a place next to one another; and in the diversion of meanings of difference, which in the case of top-down cosmopolitanism becomes overridden by the shared experience of consumption, and which in vernacular cosmopolitanism drives practices and contact. Complex and uneven consumer cultures help us to understand some of the elements of *togetherness* which unsettle given social and cultural order in the city, but without always changing it.

Top-down cosmopolitanism represents the project of the neoliberal city (Miles 2012), enabled through the close collaboration of local and national government and corporate interests. This project incorporates and celebrates a cosmopolitan neoliberal ethos widely visible in projects of branding, rebranding and redefining meanings of places. Neoliberal cosmopolitanism incorporates such values as hospitality towards the newcomer, but conditions hospitality upon the newcomer's buying power. Commodities and spectacle, as captured by the Olympic Park and the mega-mall of Westfield Stratford City, redefine the meanings of a place like Stratford through powerful representations that brand it as a recognizable, familiar and securitized non-place. The hospitality and recognition of difference and the possibility of a shared experience depend on emptying Stratford of particularistic meanings and complex histories, unless these are adapted to global consumerist conventions. Thus this project uses cosmopolitanism as a tool for building the neoliberal city while being blind to real power divides associated with place and history. The second kind of cosmopolitanism, vernacular cosmopolitanism, is much messier and less harmonious. It emerges out of the history of East London as a meeting place and out of the contradictions of consumer cultures that both reinforce divides and create shared symbolic spaces of experience. Vernacular cosmopolitanism is about hospitality, which, though conditional (Chan 2006), makes the urban landscape's history and present always a history-in-the-making, a history of newcomers. It is also a story of urban habitus (Binnie et al. 2006: 23) that intersects and contrasts with other forms of habitus, especially as associated with class, creating internal tensions between different claimants to particular cityscapes. Vernacular cosmopolitanism is about the never-ending story of place-making, its particularities and the struggles that constantly take place around claims to the city's symbolic and physical resources, to identity (see next chapter), community (see chapter 5) and action (see chapter 6).

4 Identity: Popular Culture and Self-Making

Looking at the city from street level, we can observe the contradictory expressions and consequences of cosmopolitan discourses in the practice of everyday life, as in the case of consumer cultures discussed in the previous chapter. Staying at street level, another compelling yet ordinary element of urban life is constantly observed: creativity. From drawing on walls to making urban soundscapes through music, urban dwellers constantly use the city as a canvas to mark their identities: signs, symbols and sounds of the self are produced and circulated in everyday life, revealing many urban dwellers' struggles to find a place in the city and a place in the world. At the meeting of mediation and the city, popular culture turns the city into an experimental space of identity: making music and consuming music; drawing graffiti; looking at graffiti on walls, advertisements, films and the internet; drawing new graffiti over old ones, demanding blank walls without them and defining them as either 'art' or 'vandalism' are only some of the continuities and fractures in the cultural landscape that reflect its dwellers' identities and their struggles to see themselves in the city. I discuss here the practices of creative production and consumption and their convergence[1] under the umbrella concept of urban cultures of communication. Urban cultures of communication contain production and consumption practices which have often converged within popular culture. These cultures are as urban as they are mediated and they are powerful domains, bringing the city's cultural histories and trajectories into shared spaces of communication. Complex and diverse, urban cultures of communication are relevant to this discussion as they become tools in urban dwellers' attempts to mark their identities in their city and in an urban world which is increasingly mediated and made sense of through powerful symbolic forms. Urban cultures of communication also present a counterpoint to the hegemonic representations of the city's identity, persistently and aggressively promoted at the centre of its global story.

Conquerors, powerful leaders and visionary artists are represented in every part of the global city's core – in museums, in statues and in the names of streets, squares and buildings. Alongside these, contemporary urban celebrities regularly parade on television screens, magazine pages and trendy high streets. Prevailing symbols in the streets and in the media, they become selective imprints of a city's history, its reputation, its people. The working class and most migrants and women are almost invisible in those powerful representations of the city; their identities are strategically absent from the global city's hegemonic identity. But they are not altogether absent from the city's cultural interface. The identities of social and cultural minorities have long been made and recorded in marginal quarters and deprived inner-city neighbourhoods. Literature and poetry, music, oral history and public art have written histories of urban identities outside palaces and museums. Excluded from official urban and national history, creativity within popular culture has long provided a medium for the representation of diverse identities and a tool for making the city a place of belonging.

While creativity within popular culture has been a powerful, if not unique, way of preserving presence and history from the margin within modernity, contemporary culture has intensified the significance of the popular as a space where identity struggles take place (Gilroy 1997; Hall 1990), to a great extent by making difference an ordinary ingredient. At the same time, digital culture, alongside the rising power of cultural industries (Hesmondhalgh 2007), has opened up new spaces for the (self-) representation of identity, often through the commodification of cultural products originating on the social margins. Confronting and reproducing mainstream culture at the same time, creativity on the margins of the city becomes more than mere everyday practice; it becomes a practice of identity by sustaining the symbolic power of (selective) recognition of difference.

This chapter focuses on urban music and graffiti[2] as powerful symbolic forms which play a key role in the representation of socially and culturally marginal identities in the global city and in the context of global culture. Graffiti and urban music – rap, hip hop, R&B, grime and other hybrid genres referred to as urban music – represent powerful urban cultures of communication, originating on the margins and carrying elements of the cosmopolitan histories and trajectories associated with the city.[3] In their histories, conflictual narratives and imagery, but also in their association with wider systems of global culture, urban music and graffiti represent symbolic elements of ongoing struggles against exclusion, as well as complex and sometimes alienating continuities between the marginal and the core and between the urban and the global. Popular culture, as Williams (1997) has powerfully argued, can be a site of contestation and resistance. Following Silverstone (2007), it can be argued that popular culture presents the possibility for different voices to emerge within a single discourse, even when some of these voices are 'sub-dominant' (ibid.: 83). Is this discourse liberating or alienating? Does it advance mutual understanding or does it advance profit making within a single, but stratified, system of symbolic forms? And does it create spaces of identity which are not mutually exclusive, but dialogical? It is in the context of an overarching and powerful popular culture that urban music and graffiti become prolific. Needless to say, urban music and graffiti do not cover the range of cultural production, let alone the richness of urban cultures of communication. Yet they represent key points of reference since they gain prevalence in representations of urban identities through the juxtapositions of the global and the local, of the urban marginal and the mainstream.

The discussion below starts by locating the analysis of urban cultures of communication in dialogue with Silverstone's contrapuntal cultures (2007) and Derrida's *différance* (2001a [1972]). It continues by providing an entry point to the urban landscape that empirically informs this analysis: the transformed and contested space of the inner city. Hackney, East London, is the main empirical point of reference as it offers a powerful case for understanding inner city as a space of identity: with histories of migration, marginality but also of creativity, it is currently in the processes of gentrification like many inner city locations across Europe and North America. Inner city becomes a dynamic location of struggle for self-representation and identity where hegemonic and counter-hegemonic narratives of class, race and the nation clash and feed into each other. What will be discussed below is the making of the inner city alongside the making of the self through mediated encounter through music and graffiti – the most widely seen elements of urban cultures of communication. In music and graffiti, identifiers of marginality become storytellers of the core narrative of the city. As music and graffiti become systems of self-representation from the margins, they challenge the distribution of symbolic power while advancing opening up symbolic spaces for the recognition of difference. But they also demonstrate the limitations that such possibilities are subject to, especially since they are always confronted by commodification and the global city's inequalities.

Beyond binaries: contrapuntal cultures of communication

In Benjamin's travel journal of Naples (1997 [1925]), working-class life is described as torn by poverty, crime and religious repression. But some of Benjamin's best descriptions of life in Naples focus on street music, nightlife, the theatricality of street life and the aesthetics of public life. These crucial fragments of the landscape of Naples bring the city to life as a space of identity, as well as of struggle:

Music parades about – not mournful music for the courtyards, but brilliant music for the streets. A broad cart, a kind of xylophone, is colourfully hung with song texts. Here they can be bought . . . So everything joyful is mobile: music, toys, ice cream circulate through the streets. This music is both a residue of the last and a prelude to the next feast day. Irresistibly, the festival penetrates each and every working day. Porosity is the inexhaustible law of life in this city, reappearing everywhere. A grain of Sunday is hidden in each weekday. And how much weekday there is in this Sunday! (Benjamin 1997 [1925]: 171)

Not unlike Benjamin's Naples, the global city's landscape is a space of contradictions as well as of possibilities. The city's structured and symbolic landscape captures and reflects its numerous, and often brutal, inequalities. Yet, and in part because of this, as Benjamin argues (ibid.), it also reflects its porosity, where meanings are constructed through the spillover of different practices into one another. Derrida's analysis of *différance* becomes a useful point of reference in theorizing urban porosity and transience. Derrida initially introduced the notion of *différance* as a way of understanding relational meanings within language (2001a [1972]). As he argues, all meanings are constructed within a broader system where there are no fixed binaries; meaning is always in process and in translation and it becomes relevant within a spectrum of other meanings (or events or practices). 'In language there are only differences' (ibid.: 63), he argues, emphasizing that neither the signifier nor the signified exist before or outside the linguistic system. Along these same lines, Isin (2002) argues that neither citizens nor non-citizens exist outside a system of citizenship; certain groups become the city's *others* within a system that defines a *we,* and the *we* is defined through defining *others.* '[T]he important thing about *différance* is that it prevents any system at all from stabilizing itself as a fully sutured and finished totality,' argues Hall (2001: 11) in his interpretation of Derrida's *différance.* It is within the context of such conceptual claims that the present discussion takes place.

Focusing on the particular field of minority media, Silverstone develops his thesis on contrapuntal cultures, arguing for the continuity of meanings between minority and mainstream mediascapes. With direct reference to Said (1994), Silverstone talks about the contrapuntal as speaking 'to the inevitable, continuous and significant juxtaposition of elements and threads in a life, a text, a history, and to the necessity for an analytic which confronts that juxtaposition and deconstructs it' (Silverstone 2007: 85). The contrapuntal becomes both a point of meeting and also a point of confrontation and of struggle between different elements within a context of 'diversity between, and necessarily within' (ibid.: 83). The contrapuntal recognizes diversity within media culture in terms of different 'strands of reporting, storytelling and representation' (ibid.: 84), as well as in terms of the technologies and kinds of institutions that constitute it (ibid.). But the contrapuntal also invites us to consider the integrity of media culture as a result of all its different elements. This single media ecology, Silverstone continues, makes minority media an element, and not an outsider, in dominant media culture, advancing understanding as much as segregation.

The wide circulation in global markets of urban music and graffiti, increasingly referred to as 'street art', reflects the political economy of what Silverstone (2007) calls integrated media ecology. The commodification of urban music and graffiti represents a key element in the meanings of these cultural forms that take shape between urban creativity and global markets, between projects of representation and alienation. The association of music and graffiti with questions of identity is linked to their urbanity. The city is a space of identity: people's identity and its own identity. For some of the new urban middle classes, the city provides a space for global identities seeking connections outside the nation (Binnie et al. 2006). For other urban groups, such as migrants, the city is a space of identity because it represents a key node in transnational cultural networks (Georgiou 2006). For many new and old urban groups, the city becomes a space for the emergence of defensive parochialism (Binnie et al. 2006), especially in the face of constant exposure to diversity. The never-ending difference Hall talks about (2001) also gives rise to certain systems of morality primarily associated with the city: hospitality for one, as Derrida writes (2001b), or a humanistic vision that links city life to global narratives (Cheah 2007; Keith 2005). Bell and de-Shalit (2011) write about the morality of cities as an element of their identity. Each city's morality, they argue, relates to the predominant values that enable us to recognize and evaluate it: 'Typically speaking, an evaluation of a city's desirability is not just an aesthetic judgment; it is also a judgment about the moral ways of life of people in that city. Such judgments are often more strongly held than judgments about countries, which tend to be more abstract and imagined entities than cities are' (Bell and de-Shalit 2011: 4). Global cities in general, and London in particular, are recognized in systems of global representation as sociocultural spaces built through histories of difference, mobility and openness (as well, of course, as of concentrated power). These qualities often provide evaluative frameworks for the cities themselves, but also for their people and their cultural production. Looking at this from the bottom up, from street level, identity is constructed in dialogue, in negotiation and in conflict, against and next to other identities. There is no place where proximity with other identities is more intense than in the inner city; in this context, self-making cannot but be a constant process of being reminded of difference, of other cultural and social identities. In this way, the inner city becomes a space of intense cosmopolitanization. The inner city brings together unending systems of difference, as well as conflicting claims to physical and symbolic ownership of the place and its resources. Urban cultures of communication emerging in the rich and contested space of the inner city's need to be understood within a contrapuntal culture: popular culture.

Claiming the inner city

Popular culture is ubiquitous in the city. Music blasting out of cars is as much associated with the urban soundscapes of the city as are concert halls. Graffiti on walls are as much associated with the 'problematic' neighbourhoods of the city as they are with branded youth clothing and, increasingly, with desirable art pieces shown in galleries and global auction houses.[4] The city is a space of sensory overload (Bull 2007) and of struggles for the management and control of cityscapes – both are associated with popular culture as a terrain where struggles for the distribution and control of symbolic power take place. Urban dwellers find different ways to perform within the rich sensory landscapes and use these landscapes strategically to either communicate with or isolate themselves from the sounds and images of other occupants of the city space. Binnie et al. (2006) talk of the cosmopolitan skills that urban dwellers develop in managing the city's diverse landscapes and of the tensions around defining who or what actually 'belongs' in each part of the city. The visual, oral and aural intensity of city life reflects points of contact and separation that define it as a space of identity. The city territory is often negotiated through the senses. While the city is for everyone a space of inevitable proximity to difference, city dwellers, visitors and consumers use their senses to sustain proximity or distance from others: by avoiding or seeking out places that look and sound very different; or by learning how to navigate city spaces through auditory and visual experiences, for example through music (Bull 2007). Setting or negotiating boundaries becomes both sensory and performative – especially as sounds and visuals are used by different groups to demonstrate their symbolic power in parts of the city – from music sounds to house alarms, from graffiti to security cameras.

Urban borderlands are integral cultural and physical elements of the inner city. While the inner city has always been a transient place, with newcomers replacing old populations throughout history (Eade 2000), in recent years it has become a much messier place. Twentieth-century middle-class suburbanization has shifted with the deindustrialization of the city. The transformation of urban economies from manufacturing to services (Massey 2007) and from production to consumption (Hayward and Yar 2006) also redefined the city as a living space and as a space of contested identities. The changes in the economy and environment of the city made it yet again a desirable destination for the middle classes, especially those working in the service industries, but also those in the creative sector. The creative classes, Florida (2002) writes, have been attracted to cities with histories of creativity and of diversity, establishing their presence in areas that have always been destinations for newcomers and bohemians. As attractive poles for new urbanites, places in the core of the global city have become zones for living, recreation and consumption (Zukin 1995). The shift in the demographic composition of the inner city and in its symbolic value has been accompanied by a contestation of space ownership and of access to resources, including housing, jobs and education. While the creative classes have benefited from quick access to the service industries located close by, the old residents have been increasingly marginalized. 'The people who seemed so rooted in these neighbourhoods are disappearing,' writes Zukin (2011: 8). The sustained and new divides in the inner city have reinforced its role as a symbolic urban borderland – the inner city is associated with fuelled and powerful representations of a migrant and poverty-ridden place, as much as with representations of a promising and exciting destination.

There are two kinds of boundaries in the city and a third kind of boundary that is a merger of the previous two, exemplified around mediated communication. Physical boundaries surround landscapes and allow or restrict mobility and access to natural resources. But there are also symbolic boundaries, which either coincide with physical boundaries, or create perceptions that boundaries are natural and given, even when they are not. Boundaries dividing the city into classed neighbourhoods, for example, may coincide with geographical features. 'Boundary is not a spatial fact with sociological consequences, but a sociological fact that forms itself spatially,' writes Simmel (1997: 143). 'Boundaries often present themselves to us in cities as if they are natural, physical entities . . . a city of finite spatial facts that carefully and seemingly unambiguously delineate the spaces either side . . . dictating what we can do and when,' adds Borden (2000a: 20). Borden defines the borders of the city in two ways: as barriers and walls, which vertically constrain horizontal movement, and as doors, bridges and turnstiles, which can be both exclusionary and conjunctural, allowing us 'to travel from one space to another (maybe)' (Borden 2000a: 21). In their capacity to transcend, but also in restricting mobility, these borders tend to be controlled and to define social movement, as well as rights to mobility.

Bridges may provide access to places, but crossing them may also require car ownership or the payment of a fee. Turnstiles give access to stadia and museums, but they come with costs which are restrictive to some and not to others. But there is also a third kind of boundary, one which is ambivalent in meaning: a boundary which those outside desire to cross, although those inside may detest it or despair of it. This is the boundary that allows consumers to cross to the culture of the *other*, especially the *other* who is socially marginalized but culturally attractive. The despair captured in hip-hop lyrics written by young black men in the ghettoized estates of Parisian suburbs fascinates the affluent clientele of nightclubs in Paris and across the world. Urban black youth in the United States is socially and economically excluded, writes Nightingale (1993), but, when it comes to advertising and music, it is culturally and economically *included* (emphasis in the original).

Life and control of the inner city become increasingly managed within a representational apparatus that reaffirms and at times challenges bounded identities. Within this apparatus, the inner city is defined through a range of representational systems: as the nation's *other*; as home to the *other*; as home to the new urbanites; as aspirational and 'different'; as a place with increasing symbolic value. Difference is a quality recognized across diverse representational systems, providing a continuum in the construction of meanings of the inner city (and its people and cultures). This continuum comes with its own internal asymmetries, invisibilities and polarizations. The case of Hackney captures these in their intensity. Hackney, East London, is one of the poorest areas in Britain. It also represents one of the nation's most 'impure' areas, with 41 per cent of its population belonging to ethnic minorities (Borough of Hackney 2010). A television documentary on a major national channel, Channel 4, described Hackney as 'the worst place to live in the UK' (Butt 2006). As emphasized in the press release announcing the programme: 'Phil and Sofie have used rigorous criteria to reveal the trends that make for the must-have postcodes and no-go neighbourhoods. They've number-crunched crime stats, education tables, employment rates, and environment and lifestyle factors, to find out where you should be moving to, or escaping from' (Harris 2006).

The discourse of this programme exemplifies a national imaginary of purity, whiteness, securitization and predictability. Within this discourse, there is no doubt that the inner city represents the nation's *other* and the dystopia of the white middle class. Yet, this discourse competes with an urban and global discourse advanced in the media where impurity and difference are indicators of high symbolic value. Within this discourse, the interplay between the idealized non-urban and the new urban is constantly shifting, as projects of regeneration and gentrification demonstrate. The politics of language – and even more of practice – in terms of what constitutes regeneration and degeneration also reveals the tense and powerful politics of marking the symbolic value of a territory as pure or impure. The Dalston Square regeneration project in Hackney aimed to attract the creative classes and financial district workers by redefining the meaning of the area primarily through its proximity to the city centre and its 'buzz'. In the marketing of the project, the key phrases were 'all change' and '10 minutes from the City'. The message here is clear: for the existing inhabitants, a reminder of change; for newcomers, an invitation to redefine the area through its links to the financial district (and presumably its human capital).

Unlike the national imaginary reflected in the Channel 4 programme mentioned above, the urban imaginary is much more complex and less binary. In times of austerity, measures largely targeting welfare services, levels of poverty and marginalization are yet again on the rise. At the same time, global events such as the London Olympics and the expansion of urban cultural industries led to a peak in gentrification in many parts of East London, including Hackney. Gentrification and debates around it capture the divisive power of space control for the identities of urban dwellers, linked to what Zukin (2011) calls 'crisis of definition' of black neighbourhoods in the United States. In 2008, the well-known children's author Michael Rosen attacked the New Labour-controlled council of Hackney for marginalizing its inhabitants in favour of the profit-making business of new developments in the name of regeneration. In response, the local council attacked him, saying that Rosen, like many Leftists, wanted to keep Hackney 'crap'. Rosen's response was that he had never thought Hackney was crap, just that the council's policies were. Following that war of words, a local project, entitled Walking Tour of Gentrification, used a mixture of *flânerie*, ethnography and interviews with locals to explore the realities of gentrification. The tour, organized by a local group, the Hackney Solidarity Network, was both virtual and physical and has established its longevity through its online still and moving format, including a YouTube video. Attacking the split of the area between the new affluent and the 'deliberately run down and neglected by a mixture of council corruption and developers' greed' (Hackney Solidarity Network 2008), such activism invites questions that are relevant to projects of transformation of many cityscapes, from London to New York and Beijing: how much of the histories and the journeys associated with modern inner-city making is lost in the name of change? In fact, recent statistics show a decline in the migrant population compared with the data from the 2001 Census (Borough of Hackney 2010), possibly as a result of gentrification.

As poverty is attacked through the widespread celebration of change, which however is not accompanied by serious public investment in bringing people out of poverty, the human face of the inner city changes. As old inhabitants become further marginalized, affordable housing and the symbolic value of diversity offer the bohemian and creative classes opportunities to perform a cosmopolitan lifestyle and to articulate a global sense of identity (Bridge 2004). Rofe's (2003) study of middle-class residents in gentrified areas in Australian cities showed that 74 per cent of them experienced themselves as members of global communities with a cosmopolitan orientation. Their lives in specific parts of the city led to a performance of distinction and a pathologization of the local, Rofe continues (ibid.), and to the 'othering' of parts of the city and of people who would identify primarily with the nation, especially the suburbs. Butler and Lees (2006), writing on the gentrification at Barnsbury, North London, argue that gentrification has changed over time, reflecting differentiation within the middle class. As increasingly gentrified parts of global cities like London and New York take on a unique character, it becomes important to move beyond the homogenizing assumptions of the effects of gentrification on the inner city. As Butler and Lees write, the 'super-gentrifier' employees of the global financial industries have no interest in social involvement in the inner city, unlike other middle-class gentrifiers, such as teachers, academics and young artists, whose commitment to the inner city goes beyond an individualistic lifestyle. While, for the middle classes, gentrification represents a global habitus and cosmopolitan-orientation credential (Binnie et al. 2006), it can be more than that: gentrifiers will commit to local education and to quality of life in their locale, often becoming attached to the place where they live.

Inner-city locales undergoing gentrification represent not only urban complexity, but also the asymmetries of power. My argument here is that part of the struggle in the inner city is as much about access to basic amenities like housing, schooling and health as it is representational – the ability to see the self in one's own city. I would push this argument further by claiming that, yet again and like other moments in history when marginalized groups had almost no access to centres of political power, creativity and self-representation become two of the very few tools for gaining visibility and a voice.

Representational claims are currently intensifying. The urban poor have almost no political representation and recognition. However, they have some presence within symbolic forms associated with popular culture. At the same time, these same symbolic forms and the symbolic economy of the city that is partly sustained through the commodification of urban difference are sources of wealth and prosperity. How much do the different groups – the new and old inhabitants of the inner city; the creative classes and the marginalized urban poor – meet in symbolic and physical spaces in the city? How much and which among them find spaces for identity and presence? As will be discussed below, popular culture provides momentary opportunities for the different groups occupying the inner city to communicate; these are the moments when urban cultures of communication become products of the encounter and reflections of identities constructed at the point of the encounter.

Marginality and creativity: a project of identity?

Cities are unequal places. Between 1993 and 2002, 50 million poor were added to cities around the world (Burdett and Rode 2013). In London, the richest 10 per cent is worth 273 times more than the poorest 10 per cent (Jones 2012), while American cities represent some of the most unequal places in the world, with concentrated poverty in old inner-city areas (Reuters 2011a). In such divided urban societies, the opportunities for communication between different social sectors are minimal – their close physical proximity notwithstanding. Popular culture represents one of the few domains where urban dwellers find shared spaces of communication. The contradictory realities of the city as a space of divisions and of communication are reflected in its internal divides, but also in the complex interconnections between one city and others and between London's urban culture and other parts of the world. As urban and global networks become increasingly central to the making of culture (Hartley 2010), not just to circulating it, a city's culture becomes less and less dependent on a centripetal organization of cultural production and consumption. While stratified, and to some extent controlled, urban cultures are also multi-nodal, organic and dispersed. The agency of urban subjects is expressed in different ways, not least in creativity. Where there is no other capital, popular culture – either through creativity or through consumption – becomes cultural capital for marginalized urban dwellers.

Urban music and graffiti become elements of the oral and visual history of the creator's *own* city, a voice and a presence both inside and outside a territory, somewhere between poverty and claims to the symbolic power of the global city. Intentionally or unintentionally, urban music and graffiti become expressions of urban identities from the margins. For cultural industries, they also become invaluable commodities, precisely because they are considered to be authentic (Krims 2007) and globally desirable commodities. Needless to say, as cultural forms, graffiti and music have many distinct characteristics. However, they both represent powerful forms of urban creativity associated with the histories of urban marginality. For example, many globally recognized musical genres carry with them histories of migration to American and European cities. Hackney, like many American inner cities, has had a powerful and long-standing tradition of urban music. Initially, as a result of the concentration of Jamaican migrants in the area who brought the sound system clash culture to the city, Hackney is also considered as the origin of jungle (Bennett 2011). Along with other deprived inner-city areas, that part of London is considered as the origin of grime – an urban music genre that has recently gained great global success (Coomes 2011). This music is produced and consumed locally, but also exported to transnational cultural networks and to global audiences primarily through the cultural industries' distribution systems. Music and graffiti give some visibility to the most marginalized groups, while at the same time providing some possibilities for communication across the enormous social divides from a very rare and (symbolically) privileged position that destabilizes hegemonic relations and cosmopolitanizes popular culture. As the *others' others* become attracted to their cultural production and its mediation (as well as to the neighbourhoods where these emerge), their difference ceases, at least momentarily, to be problematic or marginal. Thus, what appears as a self-enclosed system of communication is linked directly to territories beyond, and to the rest of the world. The author and graffitist King Adz captures the powerful intermingling of creative agency, the urban street and global popular culture in his definition of street culture:

> [Street culture is] an unconscious creative collective (in the fields of art, food, music, fashion, etc) that is borne from the streets of the urban environment. It has its own visual language: a multi-ethnic, multi-disciplined, multi-media stream of consciousness that has a unique look and feel which cannot be faked. The audio/visual is god in street knowledge. As is frequently suggested, sound and image is (almost) everything, and it is an integral part of its DNA. This visual language is an ever-changing montage of retro and futuristic images. The cyclic nature of the culture means that looking back is just as important as looking forward. (King Adz 2010: 6)

The street is a powerful space with rich cultural connotations and historical appropriations that reveal some of the ways in which urban creativity has become associated with the project of identity. In the case of graffiti, the street is both a physical place for displaying a message and a space that is inclusive and welcoming to certain forms of marginalized expression. No less, through graffiti, the urban street and its walls become reclaimed platforms used to defy certain rules of urban order and hegemonic aesthetics from the margin. For music, the street is a space of multiple trajectories.

Historically, in the modern city the street has provided a public space of mobility and visibility for migrants and the working class who are excluded from other public and private spaces. The inner-city street has also provided an extension of other public spaces, such as churches, as well as the private space of the home for generations of people growing up in the American and European inner city. In addition, the inner-city street has been a space associated with poverty and crime in national imagination and, perhaps in response to that, it has been reclaimed from the social margins as a space associated with presence, as many forms of urban music demonstrate. The powerful and influential hip-hop scene coming from Detroit and the folk Mexican-American music of San Antonio are as much associated with histories of marginality as of urbanity.

At the meeting of marginality and urbanity, one can observe powerful musical products that bring together urban marginal experience, identity and knowledge into powerful symbolic forms. Ms Dynamite, who grew up in north London, like many other urban musicians wrote numerous songs that reflexively explore life and identity from the social margins of the global city. The realism and universalism of many of her song lyrics, looking at the dilemmas of growing up and struggling with coming of age, make them accessible to global audiences. At the same time, lyrics about the difficulties of living with poverty and trying to make the best of oneself in tough social and familial contexts make her songs tools for communication from and to a community that many urban artists identify with. That urban, working-class and (multi-)ethnic community remains central in the narrative and imaginary of urban creativity beyond the global success.

Ms Dynamite, one of the few female artists to have found global recognition, comes like many urban artists from the urban world that generates inequalities and differences. In this world, intense juxtapositions of difference make each actor well aware of other realities, and consequently well aware of limitations in their own realities and of the inequalities, in this case of class and gender, that surround their own identities. Songs and graffiti popularize urban experience from the margin: by being named and shared with global audiences, this experience becomes a global story and also a story told by its actors, who are most often deprived of a public voice: urban cultures of communication become moments for making agency.

Urban cultures of communication are most powerful when bringing to the foreground of popular culture the voices of the unheard margins. But, since they are contrapuntal cultures, the boundaries between those heard and unheard are blurred. Banksy, perhaps the most globally recognized graffitist, used his creativity to speak on behalf of the urban subaltern (hooks 1994) to depict the urban agency of resistance and presence against its silent marginality (Ellsworth-Jones 2012). In a similar way, a number of middle-class graffitists have added to the urban presence of the marginal. A trademark example of the graffiti made by Stik, now globally known, grounds particular gendered and ethnic identities in the urban global experience of London. On Princelet Street, East London, Stik's work represents a Muslim woman wearing a niqab and holding hands with a man, in a positive and loving representation of a fully covered Muslim woman very rarely seen in the public domain. The publicly invisible local Muslim woman finds an unexpected space of representation on the urban street (and at the same time, through the digital archiving and circulation of graffiti, through the global mediated spaces of representation). The urban meeting of identities is encapsulated in the marked presence of the invisible *other* on the city's wall, embraced by passers-by and by the global cultural networks that incorporate it into their appropriation and circulation of urban popular culture. As Isin argues, the city makes identities and represents them:

> The city is not a container where differences encounter each other; the city generates difference and assembles identities. The city is a difference machine insofar as it is understood as that space which is constituted by the dialogical encounter of groups formed and generated immanently in the process of talking up positions, orienting themselves for and against each other, inventing and assembling capital, and making claims to that space that is objectified as 'the city'. (Isin 2002: 283)

Urban cultures of communication reveal the intertwined fates of urban subjects (Sandercock 2003). As they become symbolic forms of expressivity and identity, urban cultures of communication destabilize, even if momentarily, exclusionary systems of symbolic power in the city and in global culture. For both consumers and producers of these forms, the representational systems constitute a space of flows of meanings and of agency. The identities of the marginalized urban working class do not exist outside the mainstream cultures of consumption; they are not self-contained, since no identity in the city is. Hall (2003) notes how calypsos, the songs associated with the West Indian carnivalesque traditions, travelled with the migrants to Britain and were used to mark their participation in national events, such as the coronation, or local events, such as riding the underground. He refers to one of those calypsos, *London Is the Place for Me*, as a 'witty and joyous testament of the creative power of popular culture and a document of more innocent times. It constitutes one of the best starting points for that rich, unfinished history of the black British diaspora and its intricate interweaving with British life that remains to be written' (Hall 2003: 425). Musical forms, norms and genres associated with migration (such as the reggae

79

sound system associated with black migration, bangra associated with South Asian migration and tejano associated with Mexican migration to the United States) have been writing different stories of what it means to be an urban subject and what the city itself represents to its marginalized dwellers and for its neglected territories. McClary (2003) talks about desire and pleasure being articulated by black female singers at times of intense marginalization of black people and of women in particular. She calls the rise of 'blues queens' in the classic blues period an unparalleled moment in the history of cultural representation. This was the moment when black female artists broke through the norm of regularly having others speak for them to develop their own voice (ibid.). The long and complex history of music that came out of migration and cities of difference is ongoing and remains to be written. But it is also a history with chapters written by different actors, not always included in history books, but nevertheless marking popular culture. The grime musician Professor Green reflects on the interplay between repression, resistance, desperation and solidarity that have contributed to the history of identity in the city:

> London is a wonderful place to grow up. The fact it's multicultural, the fact we aren't segregated, there's a lot of good that comes from this. The other side to it, is that for many people it is a tough and cold place to grow up. As a kid on Northwood Estate [in Hackney] for the most part we had to make our own fun. Nobody had much, and the olders [*sic*] we looked up to and spent time under the wings of were already some way involved in what most of us youngers [*sic*] one day would be (in Hancox 2011).

Mechanisms of community support through creativity are many but are also often invisible to the mainstream. A now gallery owner and former gang member for whom involvement in graffiti art was a turning point is interviewed by Ellsworth-Jones: 'It sounds so corny, but graffiti saved my life' (2012: 36). He explains how, for a teenager in the inner city, street life is central to identity construction and acceptance by peers. Graffiti provided an alternative to gang crime, he explains. East Londoner Lethal Bizzle, involved in a project to support young people through musical production, expressed his outrage about the attack on rap by the prime minister-to-be as an attack on urban youth and the urban poor:

> Open your eyes to UK society David Cameron. By making comments like this you're taking yourself further from the young British society. I'm a young black British music artist and I'm the voice for the streets; you should be working with us instead of laying the blame on us. A lot of what I do is on a positive tip for the community, but that all gets ignored. I've signed 14 young rappers from east London to my own label; that's taken them off the

streets and given them something positive to look forward to. . . . Work with us and you will reach the kids. Artists like me should be used as street MPs, to empower the kids to get more involved with government and give them a voice. (Lethal Bizzle 2006)

Street and politics come together in the words of the musician, for whom the transience of the city is expressed not only in the musical connection of the marginal and the mainstream, but also in the links between the street and representational politics – only this link is hegemonically produced as oppositional. In his response to the prime minister, the urban music producer speaks of the alienation of young people from politics, but he also proposes dialogue and communication, 'a voice' for disenfranchised urban youth. Rap becomes politics. As Lott argues: '[R]ap music articulates the perspective of a black lumpenproletariat. For this reason, class lines have been drawn around it within the black community. This "underclass" status of rap, however, tends to conceal the fact that it has certain social and political dimensions that suggest that something other than pathology is occurring in black youth culture' (Lott 1999: 120). In the context of intense representational struggles, urban music is counterposed as a possible element of intercultural dialogue and of participation in the mainstream. As Silverstone (2007) argues, subordinate voices can still be part of the narrative of a story within contrapuntal cultures – in this case, the narrative of urban identity from the margins but against marginality.

Reclaiming self-representation against marginality

The mainstream media have often used artists associated with urban cultures of communication as spokespersons for marginalized urban communities, demonstrating the appeal of popular culture in both cultural and political public life. Depending on the ideological orientation of these mainstream media, these voices appear as either 'apologists' for violence and alienation among the urban working classes or as interpreters of their realities. Urban cultures of communication have often been targeted as encapsulating everything that is wrong with the urban working class (Jones 2012). As discussed in chapter 6, politicians and public commentators held urban music partly to blame for the actions of looters during the 2011 urban riots. Since urban cultures of communication represent some of the very few platforms for the social margins to be heard and seen in the mainstream, sometimes their narratives bring to the fore urban experiences otherwise alien to the mainstream. Some of the cases where urban creativity turns into a bridging mechanism and a dialogical point of reference between the particular and the universal were discussed on pp. 61–3. Below, another expression of contrapuntal culture is introduced: that which represents the opposition between the marginal and the mainstream.

Grime lyrics often describe a world of poverty, crime and local pride, as much detached from as unseen in the mainstream. One of the most globally recognized grime artists, Dizzee Rascal, repeatedly represents grim and hopeless situations associated with urban marginality in his lyrics. Unlike Ms Dynamite's case briefly discussed above, where reflexivity, hope and change challenge despair and poverty, Dizzee Rascal's musical world is the world of urban streets and neighbourhoods of despair and loss. In his musical narrative, the artist's agency, and that of his urban subjects, is everpresent. But it is deprived of happiness and hope and suppressed within a policed system of controlled life. As the actual experience described in the song is as far removed from mainstream society's experience as possible, the role of urban creativity becomes crucial to its communication beyond particularity. The artist behind the song becomes the voice of the voiceless and the presence of the unseen. The power of popular culture in representing the invisible in the urban media ecology was also seen during the urban riots of 2011. Some of the grime artists desperately tried to explain the urban riots (Hancox 2011), providing not only reflexive accounts, but also a political language for understanding inequality in the city. In other cases, urban cultures of communication have been used as representations of identity outside systems of identification and addiction that reproduce deprivation and crime, especially as this is associated with gangs. Projects for former and potential gang members, such as the Gunz Down project (www.gunzdown.moonfruit.com/), used music and imagery associated with graffiti as tools for self-expression and identification for young people in inner-city neighbourhoods.

Urban creativity has also become a political site of contestation, revealing tensions and clashes around identity and community which both encompass and go beyond issues of class and inter-ethnic relations. A poem written by Dean Atta went viral in its rap version and in the aftermath of the trial of Stephen Lawrence's killers. The Stephen Lawrence case was a landmark case in racial crime and revealed institutional racism in London's police force. Two of the teenager's killers were only convicted in 2012, eighteen years after Lawrence's murder in London by a racist gang. With this event as a key reference, Dean Atta protested against the wide use of the word 'nigger' in rap in his poem, 'I Am Nobody's Nigger' (2012). In this poem, Dean Atta makes urban music a domain of clashing ideologies around identity, not just their representation:

Rappers when you use the word 'nigger'
remember that's one of the last words Stephen Lawrence heard,
so don't tell me it's a reclaimed word.

I am nobody's nigger
So please, let my ancestors rest in peace
Not turn in their graves in Jamaica plantations
Or the watery graves of the slave trade
Thrown overboard into middle passage
Just for insurance claims
They were chained up on a boat
As many as they could manage and stay afloat
Stripped of dignity and all hope
Awaiting their masters and European names
But the sick and the injured were dead weight to toss
And Lloyds of London would cover that cost.

I am nobody's nigger
So you can tell Weezy and Drake
That they made a mistake
I am nobody's nigger now
So you can tell Kanye and Jigga
I am not a nigger . . . in Paris
I'm not a nigger in London
I'm not a nigger in New York
I'm not a nigger in Kingston
I'm not a nigger in Accra
Or a nigger with attitude in Compton
Cos 'I don't wanna be called yo nigga'

How were you raised on Public Enemy
And still became your own worst enemy?
You killed Hip Hop and resurrected headless zombies
That can't think for themselves or see where they're going
Or quench the blood lust because there's no blood flowing
In their hearts, just in the streets
They don't give a damn as long as they eating
Their hearts ain't beating, they're cold as ice (bling)
Because they would put money over everything
Money over self respect or self esteem
Or empowering the youth to follow their dreams
Stacking paper cos it's greater than love it seems
Call me 'nigger' cos you're scared of what 'brother' means

To know that we share something unspeakable
To know that as high as we rise we are not seen as equal

To know that racism is institutional thinking
And that 'nigger' is the last word you heard before a lynching. (Atta 2012)

Full of powerful discourses of identity, the poem links the history of slavery, resistance and transnational agency but also trans-urban popular culture. It is a political point of reference that reclaims a space of identity beyond demeaning language, by indeed refusing to 'reclaim' a word that in itself carries a painful history of repression. In 2012, rapper-turned-director Ben Drew (aka Plan B) produced the equally powerful film *Ill Manors*, which he introduced as an explanation of the urban riots a few months earlier. An equally political statement about crime, drugs and police violence, the film ends with an optimistic message of cosmopolitan agency, perhaps not different to that seen in a number of Spike Lee's films. In *Ill Manors*, the fates of a young British Asian man, a prostitute, a drug addict of uncertain ethnic background and a young Eastern European mother held in captivity by traffickers coincidentally meet. Their painful individual journeys reach resolution when they come together to escape deprived inner-city London by catching a train to Cardiff. Benjamin (1997 [1925]) talks of stations as capturing the transience of the city, as being points that sustain the city's openness, porosity and its position as a point of destination and departure. In the case of the film, it is the city itself that brings the four characters together to discover each other and, through each other, to discover them-selves. And it is the city's transience, through its 'throwntogetherness' (Massey 2005), that links their fates, providing an opportunity and hope of escaping marginality and destruction. Importantly, this happens through their togetherness in difference.

Creativity from the margins, as in the case above, and as observed in the case of rap and pirate radio, has become the contrapuntal (Silverstone 2007) within media culture. As Hancox writes (2011): 'Two decades ago Chuck D famously described rap music as "the Black CNN" – a means of describ-ing the kind of daily lives which the real news network would never care to investigate; by this token, grime and UK rap is the BBC News 24 of the British urban working-class – not necessarily black, not necessarily young, but mostly so.' As discussed in chapter 6, urban music has most often been attacked for inciting violence and a 'culture of entitlement' rather than seen as a tool of expression and identity. Yet it is pirate radio stations, often broadcasting from council estate flats, which have made rap, grime and hip hop the music of the locale for the locals. In the same way, it was the walls of the inner city that brought graffiti into popular culture, not the galleries and websites where these works were later exposed. It would, of course, be naive not to acknowledge the continuities and co-dependence of the marginal and the mainstream, and of the 'authentic' and the commodified, that reaffirm the prevalence of urban music and graffiti as creative forms beyond the boundaries of marginality. These continuities between production and consumption and between otherwise clashing social groups are not smooth and predictable. They reflect the internal contradictions of cosmopolitanization that bring difference to the centre of the city's story, but which also limit its effectiveness in terms of social change, especially for groups torn by poverty and marginality.

Commodification: against identity?

Urban music and graffiti mark specific territories and reveal conflicting claims to place, identity and resources. These struggles are expressed in the growing desirability of these creative forms. They have also become widely recognized symbolic forms, demonstrating the interplay between marginalized and excluded experiences of the city and the mainstream of global popular culture. The globalization of popular culture through the growth of cultural industries (Hesmondhalgh 2007), the expansion of the consumption of cultural products across global markets (Thussu 2006) and the diversification of cultural production as a result of migration (Georgiou 2006) have advanced the presence of these forms of cultural production within global cultural markets. At the same time, the exclusion of certain social and cultural groups from the mainstream of city life has reinforced the importance of such symbolic forms as tools of visibility and of symbolic power (or the illusion of symbolic power). Urban cultures of communication are both reflections of and forms of opposition to the power of the global cultural industries: while urban music and graffiti originate from the margins and global cultural industries from the core of the global city, both depend on the merging of symbolic power and symbolic cultural forms. Like other media products coming out of the cultural industries' headquarters, urban music and increasingly graffiti are circulated globally in cultural and corporate networks. The global, primarily middle-class and largely white consumers of urban music and graffiti paraphernalia gaze into marginal urban lifestyles, consuming in this way the city's 'authenticity'[5] as much as its globality. Musical genres originating in African-American urban musical traditions – rap, hip hop, R&B – represent approximately a quarter of all music sales in the United States (The Recording Industry Association of America 2007), while the East Asian market for hip hop and rap is enormous.

There is no doubt that the commercial success of urban cultural products has unsettled the binaries of vandalism vs. art and vulgarity vs. music. The enormous success of hip hop and rap and the 'street art' phenomenon celebrated in recognized artists like Banksy have changed the rules of the game. Graffiti and music made on the urban street provide starting points, but not end points, within systems of cultural meanings. Awareness of a potential global audience, and possibly of a market, is evident in the words of various musicians and graffitists.

The Graffiti Life team, a corporation of artists, talks about graffiti not just as a form of communication, but also as a form of mediated and global communication:

> We can now bring the graffiti out, rather than just leave it for only few people to see it on the wall. With our studio we can now bring out work to the general public. As long as you have a camera, as long as you record it that is the only thing you can do to preserve your work, you cannot expect the graffiti to be there tomorrow. (Koutroumpa 2012)

In the same interview, another graffitist, Darren Cullen, talks about a recent shift in graffitists' identity, not as a cause but as a consequence of the commercial success and growing media success of visual forms of urban expression: 'If it wasn't for Banksy, graffiti would still be about vandalism. He inspires people to be more artistic with graffiti, he is creating artists. I don't call myself an artist, because at the moment I am a businessman. If I wasn't a businessman I would be a graffiti vandal' (Koutroumpa 2012). The interviewee's cynicism is evident when he makes a clear link between graffiti as a project of identity and as vandalism, on the one hand, and between art and business on the other. Since it is creators of graffiti associated with the city's social margins who are usually prosecuted, there is some truth in this cynicism, which reflects the shifting space of cultural production and consumption. Commercially and artistically recognized graffiti tend to be associated with middle-class street artists, as shown in the appropriately titled film made by Banksy, *Exit Through the Gift Shop* (2010). The aesthetics of other graffiti primarily associated with deprived inner-city youth groups may be recognized and valued in certain youth subcultures, but they are also prosecuted and rated as inferior within high-art markets.

As discussed above, and following on from chapters 2 and 3, city and urban culture can turn into products sold to tourists and to global audiences. Dizzee Rascal may be a music symbol associated with East London's inner city and his songs may bring to the fore the realities of living on the social margins, but he became a celebrated global icon when he sang in the opening ceremony of the 2012 Olympics in London. The commodification of difference, in its hegemonic incarnations, itself threatens difference, locking 'such dizzyingly varied experiences into tight, highly controlled, and intensively structured packets' (Krims 2007: xxxiv). Two recent advertisements for cars provide interesting cases of the appropriation of graffiti by one of the most mainstream industries – the car industry. The advertisements for the Nissan Qashqai and the Vauxhall Corsa follow remarkably similar visual narratives. In both sets of advertisements, the city is represented as a beautified urban terrain. The beauty of the urban landscapes lies not in greenery, but in the range of graffiti that decorate the city's walls. In the case of Nissan Qashqai, the graffiti travel with the car through clean, safe, empty streets, which are otherwise urban. The advertisement represents the car as an urban car and everything about the advertisement shouts 'urban'. The car advertised – an expensive four-wheel drive – is conventionally associated with rural life and suburbia. Its rebranding as urban is aesthetically organized around one of the most powerful imageries associated with the city: graffiti. The symbolic value of graffiti here is more than merely artistic – it is also a value associated with urban identity and urban difference, though strategically stripped of the complexities of difference (not unlike the top-down cosmopolitan discourses discussed in the previous chapter). Unsurprisingly perhaps, this same car, the Nissan Qashqai, was the sponsor of the *Street Art* exhibition at Tate Modern in the summer of 2008. As graffiti move out from the walls of the inner city, they become a commodity and an artistic form. Do they become less relevant to urban identity as a result?

From global auction houses where Banksy's works are sold at astronomical prices to graffiti tours that are now offered in cities like Berlin, London and New York but also Bogota and Buenos Aires, graffiti become an attractive commodity and a symbolic product associated with the image of the city. Alongside these, websites such as Global Street Art (2012) bring together urban and media platforms as global fora. On the internet, graffiti is shared and preserved beyond the ephemerality and physicality of the urban street, supporting perhaps a more sustainable space of identity, but also a more selective one. As the cityscape expands into the virtual and the global, the authenticity of urban culture is sustained virtually, well after it disappears from the physical locale.

The merging of the virtual and the urban street within the context of popular culture has in part redefined urban cultures themselves. Some graffitists start out on the web, or they post images of their graffiti on the web almost immediately after exposing these on the street. As the web becomes increasingly central to exposing and sharing urban cultural production, one wonders if the street is the original and central location for this form of creativity and identity representation or if the global virtual environment has in part replaced physicality. For example, the Mexico City-based *The*

City Loves You (www.thecitylovesyou.com) produces graffiti primarily for the internet's global audiences (King Adz 2010). 'I love it: street culture Mexican style. This is what the culture is all about, taking something global and giving it a local twist!', continues King Adz (2010: 45). The interplay here of the local and the global is fascinating and captures an outlook that sees the street less as a particular physical place than as an element of a symbolic and global space of subcultural identities. The expansion of urban creativity online has also provided a hybrid space of intercultural meetings, a dialogical space for communicating across distance and difference – a cosmopolitan, though nonetheless elite, space.

These virtual incarnations of urban cultures of communication come with contradictory consequences, not unlike those of their street-level success. Sharing urban cultural products online can advance the collective claims of communities on these as much as it can attract buyers and sellers. Digital media have also reinforced an internal order in urban cultural production, reproducing systems of celebrity and hierarchies of 'worthy' and 'less worthy' music and graffiti. Celebrities of the graffiti world, like urban music stars, flit from city to city and themselves represent powerful brands. When the *Space Invaders* trademark of the graffitist Invader appeared on Brixton walls, lively discussions about the arrival of the graffitist in London took place in online graffiti fora. When Banksy used his trademark stencils for a graffiti in Turnpike Lane, North London, the local station staff had to produce a map indicating directions to the new 'site' for the urban tourists who flocked into an area usually unattractive to visitors. When later the graffiti mysteriously disappeared from the wall to reappear in a Miami art auction catalogue, the level of interest the event caused led to the withdrawal of the sale and the involvement of the FBI (Champion 2013). Commodification contributes as much as experience and the process of creativity to the way in which urban cultures and places take on their meanings. Thus the interplay between identity, *other*-ness, place and the desirability of the city takes place *within* a complex system of cultural meanings with many players: urban dwellers, artists, consumers, networks of distribution and cultural industries. Cultural industries promote urban cultures that build on the fascination with the urban and the exoticization of the urban *other* as they offer variation in products within popular culture (Zukin 2011). In music that celebrates gun crime, violence against women, money and bling, and in graffiti that push the limit between legality and illegality, the urban subject becomes 'authentic' and desirable to a global gaze. Yet, while cultural industries promote the formulaic reproduction of certain versions of urban culture, we can hear and see, on the margin of the music and graffiti that make it through, some alternative narratives of identity in the urban world: powerful representations of poverty, deprivation and despair, but also of aspiration and hope for change. Also, while many of the cultural products consumed across the globe may often reproduce stereotypes about the urban subaltern, by their mere popularity they create a space for the marginal *others* to be seen (even through the stereotype). It is in this complex and contradictory space that urban music becomes important as a medium of self-representation, agency and identity. As Barthes puts it, 'we ourselves are other', consuming the music of the *other*, who becomes the primary producer of the desirable product. According to Barthes, the city is the 'place where the other is and where we ourselves are other, as the place where we play the other' (1997: 171).

Identity and transient urban cultures

Urban cultures of communication deconstruct, at least momentarily, meanings of *we*-ness and *other*-ness as binary oppositions creating spaces for cosmopolitan reflexivity, even celebration, within the context of popular culture. As these cultures emerge at the meeting point of difference, they demonstrate that no cultural meaning is fixed and complete. Neither are identities, including those that appear to be the most oppositional. In fact, it is through cultures associated with urban cultural expressivity, creativity and diversity that oppositions are made sense of and made manageable for urban subjects. As noted above, social inequalities are powerfully and violently revealed in the social geography associated with the advance of neoliberalism in the city (Harvey 2001; Miles 2012). As a consequence, the physical and symbolic terrains of the city have become increasingly divided (Jones 2012; Zukin 2011). What remains less clearly divided and bounded is the cultural interface of the global city. Symbolic forms, such as graffiti and music, bring producers and stories from the margins into the mainstream global culture. Their consumers are as likely to be located in the inner city as they are to be in other cities around the world. These same popular culture genres muddle the city as a space of oppositions and divides as, more and more, graffitists and musicians have different identities and histories. The urban wall and online music and graffiti fora are more likely to bring urban dwellers with different social and cultural backgrounds into a common space of communication than most educational, cultural and political spaces, which are increasingly and rigidly divided. The latter spaces become instrumental in the neoliberal policies in culture, education and politics that reinforce divides in the city. Yet, in their production, distribution, representation and consumption, music and graffiti, like other genres within popular culture, both reinforce the neoliberal city (Miles 2012) and contest it (Binnie et al. 2006; Hall 2003). Both possibilities are part of the spectrum of meanings associated with urban *différance* (Derrida (2001a [1972]) and the continuity of meanings associated with popular culture, its origins, diffusion and commodification.

Media play a key role as they enable the production and the wide circulation of symbolic forms such as music and graffiti. In this way, urban creativity turns its symbolic products into powerful markers of identity. On the one hand, popular cultural forms – and inevitably the agents behind them – are recognized locally and globally as identifiers of the city. On the other hand, through their circulation, graffiti and music enable and support continuities between the city and transnational cultural networks. In this way, they constantly expand the significance of urban culture beyond the nation, confirming its openness and transience. I argue that these are both key points with relevance to identity projects for marginalized groups: those who can only seek and possibly find recognition in the city (and certainly not in the nation or its institutions), and who themselves sustain connections with transnational cultural networks, especially through histories of migration.

The meanings of urban cultures of communication are always dialogical, mirroring the struggles for identity and representation within transient, porous and uneven urban terrains. The aesthetic value of graffiti is not separate from the illegality of the act, and its representational significance is not separate from its creators' and viewers' agency. The success of urban music and graffiti is located in the interplay of young people's aspirations and the commodification of 'urban authenticity'. The powerfulness of these symbolic forms is located at the juncture of social marginalization and the possibilities for self-representation. Urban cultures of communication remind the producer, the consumer, the walker and the listener that the urban margins do not fall outside the story of the city. They are part of it. This is one city, with many struggles, many inequalities, but also with continuities that run across the flows of local and global mediascapes.

In the urban cultures of communication discussed above, we can observe different narratives of identity, which, in different ways, recognize the co-presence of the *self* and the *other* within larger urban cultural systems. The containment of difference in this urban universe is in many ways a recognition of the continuities of symbols and meanings associated with contrapuntal urban cultures: continuities that link social margins with global industries, *we*-ness with *other*-ness, and racial politics with the making of urban identities. The sub-dominant, which is still present within a larger cultural system that Silverstone (2007) talks about, is the creative agency behind many graffiti and musical projects. The asymmetrical flows that link it to the dominant players within popular culture's networks of distribution and consumption show that the social margins and their creativity represent a 'continuous subtext' (ibid.: 95) of the city's identity and of the city as a space of identity.

In many ways, these forms of urban expression represent a way of seeing oneself as a storyteller – *to speak, not just to be spoken to and spoken about*. The story of the city is written again and again, in history books, in national policies, in local policies and in the media. But urban cultures of communication from the margins bring within them claims to the city and to the world through self-representation and self-authoring. Oppositional meanings are inherent in the urban cultures of communication, since none of their parts makes sense without the others, not unlike text, as Derrida argues in his analysis of *différance* (2001a [1972]). It is partly through the popularization of urban cultures of communication that genres and agents become recognized. Recognition becomes a possibility, but not an end point, for marginal groups. Recognition without redistribution, argues Fraser (2003), may make marginalized groups turn against their own interests. Urban cultures of communication represent a powerful, to an extent reflexive, urban project of identity making from the margins. The celebration of the *this and that* (Beck 2006) in the graffitist's words above projects cosmopolitan discourses and aesthetics, but says little about what takes place within the wider spectrum of meanings of urban culture beyond the domain of popular culture: the continuities between the mainstream and the marginal remain conditional, the divides of the city remain unresolved and become reinforced through neoliberal policies and securitization. The urban wall, the pirate radio station, the moment of the 'breakthrough' to the mainstream become spaces for hope as, at the same time, they become spaces of identity. But these are also symbolic spaces associated with contestation and with struggle; they are platforms for observing urban identities, but also, and through these identities, for reflecting on the asymmetries of power.

5   Community: Transnational Solidarities

Projects of creativity and self-representation, as discussed in the previous chapter, can occasionally destabilize the unequal distribution of symbolic power in the city. However, these projects represent more than individuals' experimentation with identity; very often, they are linked to projects of community. Community – as imagined, sustained, lost and re-invented – takes on particular forms and meanings in the city: this is a space where people find each other, where they find a home, but also where they encounter intense, sometimes intimidating, difference. It is in this context that meanings of community in the city need to be understood: as emerging at the meeting of urban placeness and urban transience. The city has always been open and incomplete, Benjamin (1997 [1925]) reminds us, and it has also been a place of community. But the city has also become increasingly transient, more so with technologies of transportation and communication that open it up to rich and diverse flows of people, ideas and information (Appadurai 1996). It is migration that has most influentially, throughout its history, defined particular qualities of the city as a space of community: as a destination, a refuge, a place where different ideas and experiences meet. The establishment of diasporic communities as a consequence of migration has demographically and culturally marked the global city internally, but also expanded its outward connectivity. Community networks which expand across space, communication between dispersed families and the establishment of transnational, diasporic and ethnic media make the city a space of belonging, but also a node that belongs to transnational networks.

The constitutive role of migration in making the global city is widely but conditionally recognized. For once, the neoliberal urban rhetoric coming out of corporate headquarters and urban government praises migration and diaspora: in city branding as evidence of a city's cosmopolitan identity; in the discourse of cultural industries as a core element in urban creativity; in financial circles as a source of valuable human capital. Yet the neoliberal recognition of migration's benefits for the city's symbolic power and economy has strategically undermined transnationalism's complexities. Unlike neoliberal cosmopolitan celebrations of 'ethnic colour' in the city and utilitarian interpretations of migration as serving economic growth, migration and diasporas have marked the city's symbolic space in nuanced and contradictory ways, as a space of community, solidarity, segregation and communication. Demographic and cultural changes associated with migration regularly challenge ideologies of contained and hierarchal cultural, racial and social order. As a location of different trajectories, the city has also challenged the rightfulness of liberal democracy as universal truth: from Sharia law practised in urban neighbourhoods to radical politics of dissent, the city has become a site of experimentation, reflection and rejection of the hegemonic cultural, gender and political order. The city of meetings and mixings within its territory and beyond, the city of different forms of agency and community, is a transnational city.

This chapter focuses on the global city as a space of community, constantly redefined through transnationalism, and on the role of media and communications in this process. Conceptually, the discussion aims to relocate community within a universalism-particularism continuum (Robertson 1992) and against claims that community tends to reproduce anti-cosmopolitan parochialism. Instead, multiple particularisms, it will be argued, complicate systems of hospitality and citizenship and redefine these for urban and transnational times. Empirically, this chapter draws on three cases in which the synergies between media and the city redefine and expand meanings of community by bringing together communalist and cosmopolitan discourses in the messy realities of cosmopolitanization. The first case is that of the Arab diaspora in Europe, with a primary but not exclusive focus on London. Diasporas are long-standing transnational communities that keep changing, partly as a result of growing mediation. The second case is that of inner city's multi-ethnic communities. Regular encounters with migrant difference both inform the formation of local communities and link local communitarianism to global solidarity. The third case is that of urban nomadism, a new kind of trans-urban community consisting of elite migrants moving between cities. Global cities represent key nodes in this networked community, which celebrates cosmopolitan values while still being characterized by communitarianism, albeit an elite version. As argued below, the synergies between the media and the city reveal some of the ways in which community persists, but changes, at the meeting of grounded urban experience and mediated transnational connectivity, especially through mediated connections between here and there, diaspora and *homeland*, identity and difference. The persistence of community reveals some of the ways in which certain groups establish themselves in the city (and claim some symbolic power), alongside the challenges of sustaining the city's transience and openness. In concluding this chapter, I address these challenges by referring to and expanding Derrida's (2001b) call for cosmopolitan hospitality.

Between particularism and universalism

In defining what he calls migrants' inevitable cosmopolitanism, Stuart Hall explains that migrants often have no choice but to be cosmopolitans: 'They have to learn to live in two countries, to speak a new language and make a life in another place, not by choice but as a condition of survival . . . So, culturally, they're living "in translation" every day of their lives' (2008: 347). Along the same lines, Werbner has coined the description 'working-class cosmopolitanism' (1999), explaining that migrants broaden their horizons as they come across different cultural groups, in work environments or as they move and rely on and themselves offer hospitality. While their cosmopolitanism remains rooted within specific orders (e.g. the transnational Sufi order centred in Pakistan, as Werbner (1999) writes with reference to a Pakistani migrant to the Gulf), migrants are exposed and often embrace universalistic values of humanism (Papastergiadis 2012). Needless to say, they do not all share cosmopolitan consciousness in the same way that transnational elites do not.

In these writings, cosmopolitanism is discussed in relation to ideology, consciousness and practice among those who move, but also, and importantly, in relation to those who may not move but are exposed to cultural and social change associated with transnationalism. Exposure to different particularities changes not only each of these particularities, but also the universalist trajectories of a society in its different sections and as a whole. I find Robertson's (1992) universalism–particularism continuum inspiring in terms of understanding what happens as particularism and universalism meet, which is constantly the case in the global city. This is the case for many reasons. For once, global cities represent core nodes of liberal democracy, a system closely associated with universalist trajectories of equality, fairness and justice (even if the system's inherent flaws attack those same values). The global city is also a node in numerous transnational networks, linking the local to other parts of the world. And, of course, the global city is a location where people of different backgrounds and destinations congregate. Robertson's (ibid.) concepts of the universalization of particularism and the particularization of universalism are a useful analytical reference for understanding the consequences of the universalism–particularism continuum in the global city since they deconstruct the oppositions of particularistic experience and universalistic values. Against such oppositions, he argues:

> [t]hey have become united in terms of the universality of the experience and, increasingly, the *expectation* of particularity on the one hand, and the experience and, increasingly, the *expectation* of universality, on the other. The latter – the particularization of universalism – involves the idea of the universal being given global-human concreteness; while the former – the

universalization of particularism – involves the extensive diffusion of the idea that there is virtually no limit to particularity, to uniqueness, to difference and to otherness. (Robertson 1992: 102)

Robertson's analysis emphasizes the dialectic of difference and commonality and their interpenetration. This process has to do, on the one hand, with the human condition, and, on the other, with the specific formation and intensification of cultural interpenetration in the present. This analysis highlights many of the ideological intensities and consequences of the universalism-particularism continuum. Diffusion of such ideologies allows space for projects such as, for example, diasporic media, which are global in their reach, but particular in their cultural role. The vast majority of such projects celebrate particularism within universalism and rely on the assumption that they can function as particular, different and unique because the present condition (of universalism) allows space for all different and unique projects to emerge and develop (Georgiou 2006). At the same time, diasporic media serve the universalization of particularism in the city since they represent one of the many particularities that form the urban communication landscape. In addition, they are expressions of the particularization of universalism, precisely because, like other media, they follow certain patterns of production, representation and distribution characteristic of the wider media industries. It is within this dialectic that diasporic media, local interpersonal communication and trans-urban, networked communication are discussed in this chapter: in reproducing their particularity, they intentionally or unintentionally enhance universalistic values of recognition of shared humanity; at the same time as they engage with universalistic values, they filter these through the particularities of diasporic, migrant and urban experience. Thinking of cultural difference and ideologies of particularism as interwoven with universalistic ideologies can help us to understand cultural tensions and conflicts as the inevitable struggles that take place in the process of surpassing exclusive and neoliberal universalisms and exclusive and insular particularisms. Thinking about solidarity in urban contexts becomes an invitation to break with the romanticism and the pathologization of particularism, as well as the fear and the demonization of universalism as an ideology of western domination of the *other* and the subaltern.

Transnationalizing the story

Cities have been studied in their significance as key nodes of transnational communities and action within studies of transnationalism more than in any other scholarly tradition (cf. Portes 2001; Smith 2001; Vertovec 2009). While this scholarship has been important in revealing continuities and connections between spaces of community across space, mediation has mostly been discussed as a background to or as a consequence of transnationalism. Vertovec put networked communication at the core of transnationalism's conceptualization, arguing that relationships have been 'globally intensified and now take place paradoxically in a planet-spanning yet common – however – virtual arena of activity' (Vertovec 2009: 3). While he emphasizes change in the quality of relationships formed in transnational mediated networks, he still considers virtuality a paradox. In most research on transnationalism and in research on the reconfiguration of time and space relations (cf. most influentially Giddens 1991 and Harvey 1989), the constitutive role of mediation for relations, practices and values is either underplayed or dismissed. Most significantly, it is research in media and communications that has empirically demonstrated the intensity, simultaneity and interactivity of communication within and across local and national spaces with consequences for community and identity (cf. Bernal 2006; Georgiou 2012; Karanfil 2009). Diminescu writes that the transnational continuum in spaces of communication and practice among migrants forces us to think about whether our societies have shifted from predominant sedentarity to a prominence of hyper-mobility (2008). Yet, while media and communications scholarship has more consistently theorized the role of mediation, the city has been surprisingly marginal in this same scholarship, with few exceptions (cf. Georgiou 2008; Gumpert and Drucker 2008; Kosnick 2009; Robins 2001). Robins (2001) argues that we need to think through the city rather than through the nation because it is an existential and experimental space. Elsewhere, I suggested (Georgiou 2006) that we need to locate our understanding of diasporic identity within a spatial matrix that includes the home, the city, the nation and the transnational space, i.e. the components of the diasporic communicative and community space.

A spatial understanding of media and identity is necessary to understand the city as a space of agency. The city constitutes a core element of transnational community, as much as transnationalism represents a framework for understanding how community is communicated, sustained and transformed within and across cities. Transnationalism becomes grounded in urban life and in the city's ability to provide some continuity in the insecure life of the mobile subject. At the same time, the city is supported by transnational communities (Appadurai 2006). This happens particularly in two ways: as migrants and diasporas contribute to urban economies, including cultural economy; and, importantly, as migration brings to life the realities of cosmopolitanism when communities emerge next to and against one another. The city itself represents the movement of the *other* from the periphery of the Empire to its core (the metropolis – the city), argues Eade (2000), thus destabilizing and redefining global hierarchies. Sassen (2003) discussed extensively the ways in which migrants have contributed to the development of global cities from the bottom up and while remaining largely unrecognized and unrewarded, especially when taking difficult and undesirable jobs. Agency, a necessary ingredient for building symbolic spaces of community, is less often discussed and recognized, not only in national systems of citizenship (ibid.; Benhabib 2008), but also in many academic debates about migration and neoliberalism. As migrants and diasporas move to the core of global capitalism – the global city – they occupy a symbolic and physical space that is powerful in its presence and in the active alteration of what it used to be. Both for global capital and for migrants, the global city is a strategic site of economic, cultural and political operations. Michael Peter Smith (2001) coined the concept of transnational urbanism as a response to this condition, arguing that this is 'a cultural metaphor that captures the criss-crossing transnational circuits of communication and cross-cutting local, translocal, and transnational social practices' (Smith 2001: 5). His analysis is particularly useful in surpassing the binary division between those who move (and thus are transnational and cosmopolitan) and those who stay (and thus are outside cosmopolitanism). Smith argues that we can refer to transnational social actors either if these are connected to the city through practices and networks which have at some points been found in the city and in their transnational communication circuit, or if they maintain transnational connections by using advanced means of communication and travel that are historically attached to the orbit of urban culture.

The dialectical matrix introduced above emphasizes the continuities between transnational communication and urban life, the tensions between the project of the neoliberal city that depended on migration and the project of community in the city as a result of migration, and the ways in which both these significant sociocultural conditions inform discourses of community, solidarity and hospitality which will be empirically explored below.

City and community

Within the analytical framework proposed above, migration and transnational communication represent elements in a wider system of communication that links the city to global capitalism, but also to fragile but persistent projects of community. Williams (1961) suggests that the process of communication is itself a process of community. This is precisely why communication practices reveal the possibilities and constraints of togetherness, of dialogue and of understanding between differences in and across cities. Mobility within and outside the city, and shifts in the demographic composition of urban neighbourhoods, have made community both possible and impossible. One of the main elements of the city's attractiveness as a destination has always been the possibility of finding hospitality and community among difference when fleeing conflict, prosecution and marginalization. At the same time, the city has always been a place where the limits and the meanings of community have been challenged and redefined. To a great extent this happens through the media: in many media representations, community is lost in the big city; in such narratives of urban nightmares (Macek 2006), the city exemplifies the collapse of 'community' and its values. Alongside these powerful representations, other very different narratives have supported projects of community among old and new transnational groups. Diasporic media, and more recently trans-urban digital networks, have been supporting the city as a space of community, not least in its complexities that result from processes of cosmopolitanization: the multiplication and diversification of migrant congregation and the expansion of media communication as systems for communicating within and beyond particularities.

As the city has historically grown into a complex organism, an amalgam of many micro-worlds, with neighbourhoods composed of populations that bring with them particular cultural and social histories, it has presented a challenge to any vision of a singular and contained community. As argued here, community in the city can only be understood in its symbolic meanings and as it emerges through the juxtaposition of particularism and universalism. Migration and diaspora may sustain the prominence of particularisms in the global city, but they also confront Eurocentric, nation-centric and elitist articulations of universalism that are often re-dressed as cosmopolitanism. While the contradictory realities of cosmopolitanization resist any unconditional celebration of togetherness, this chapter is an attempt to investigate the different ways in which community is sustained and rearticulated through difference. Mediascapes, ethnoscapes and ideoscapes have been changing cities (Appadurai 1996), bringing different versions of particularism and universalism closer together and presenting new challenges to the sustaining of a balance between them.

In cities, and especially in global cities, particularities exist next to one another, but are also negotiated through the realities of urban life. Recent census data show that minorities are now majorities in a number of cities: for the first time the 2011 census showed this to be the case for London

(BBC Online 2012b), while the 2010 US census showed that minorities are now numerical majorities in 22 of the 100 largest metropolitan areas in the country (Reuters 2011b). Population mobility and demographic change significantly impact on the way urban dwellers imagine community and polity as urban subjects. In a 2011 poll of 1,507 Londoners, eight out of ten declared their pride in being Londoners (IPPR 2011), prioritizing their city as a space of community and belonging. But the city is also divided as a result of histories of racial and social divides (Wilson 2008). It was London's cosmopolitanism that found itself at the centre of populist attacks concerning the collapse of communities in the wake of the 2011 urban riots. It was the illegal immigrants who were demonized in the popular press during the urban riots in Athens in 2008. Media representations in both cases, as will be discussed in the next chapter, blamed consumerism and urban diversity for violence and rioting. But the story behind the media events surpasses popular fears of the city's *others* as a possible source of the problem. Topping (2011), writing in the *Guardian* only days before the London riots, raised questions about the effect of widespread cuts in social services on individuals and communities. A 15-year-old interviewee explained in his own way how the mass shutdown of youth centres was an attack on community: 'When we are all together with our hoodies up, no one wants to be around us. The youth club was just a place we could all go and have fun, at least we had somewhere to go. Now we walk down the streets, we get pulled over by police. There is nothing here for us' (ibid.). It is no coincidence that the urban riots took place a few days later and in both Athens and London at times of growing deprivation. Austerity measures across cities of the global North hit services directed at young people, leaving many of them in search of new community spaces, or simply with a sense of loss. The performativity of destitution demonstrated the ways in which community is sensed, practised and lost in the city. Importantly, the words of the young person quoted by Topping reveal the insecurity among those treated as a threat in the unequal and securitized city because of their performed particularity – embodied, for example, in the 'hoodie'.

A space of contestation, loss and fear, but also of co-presence, the global city hosts transnational working classes and transnational elites. Migrants are most often located at the bottom of the national social and ideological order, but they often represent the most visible communities in the city. The over-concentration of minorities in urban centres, and particularly in certain areas within urban centres, has extended problems of ghettoization, poverty and racism, with long-term consequences of social exclusion and segregation (Massey 2005, 2007). Research in Germany, France and the Netherlands shows that Muslims are over-represented among the unemployed, while they are under-represented in executive positions and in higher education (Demant, Maussen and Rath 2007; Muhe 2007; Tebbakh 2007). In Denmark, unemployment rates for people with origins in Somalia, Iraq and Morocco reached levels of more than 65 per cent, as compared to 18 per cent among the Danish native population (Hussein 2007). Research in different locations across Western Europe also shows that migrant families disproportionately turn to social housing, and thus continue to occupy socially and ethnically segregated parts of the city for longer periods (Muhe 2007; Tebbakh 2007).

The socio-economic marginalization of migrants partly reflects the social consequences of neoliberalism and partly results from national-ist and majoritarian ideologies which perceive difference as threatening. Majoritarianism, Appadurai argues (2006), sees migrants and minorities as a threat precisely when some minorities remind majorities of the small gap which lies between their condition as majorities and the horizon of an unsullied, pure national whole. Appadurai writes about transnational change, which has media at its core: 'The global flow of mass-mediated, sometimes commoditized, images of self and others creates a growing archive of hybridities that unsettle the hard lines at the edges of large-scale identities' (Appadurai 2006: 83). Media and communication bring together the intense oppositions associated with the control of symbolic power and the space of community. While, as Appadurai rightly argues, transnational and urban media flows destabilize the rigid boundaries of community spaces, national media still reproduce majoritarian ideologies. In a study we conducted for the EU Fundamental Rights Agency (FRA) (Firmstone et al. 2009), on the representation of minorities in the UK national press, the most important finding was that only 7.5% of stories in the national press sample made reference to minorities. Among articles with minority content, the thematic areas most referred to were: politics (19%), terrorism (10%), sports (10%), violence and crime (8%), war (9%) and immigration (8%). When it came to Muslims, in 56% of cases these were associated with a ter-rorist organization, and in only 3% of cases with a religious organization/ institution. Ferjani (2007) notes a similar situation in France, with minori-ties rarely shown in the media as ordinary members of French society.

Hegemonic representations of minorities, or their mere invisibility in national media, make the possibility of solidarity among different groups at national level almost impossible: the construction of rigid *we*-ness and *other*-ness is so prominent that it leaves little space for interaction and com-munication. This is precisely where the space of the city – both physical and mediated – matters. The hegemonic majoritarian discourses which predom-inate in national political and cultural narratives of community are directly challenged in the city. As shown by the three cases discussed below, mediated and physical encounters with difference are so ubiquitous in the city that they inevitably challenge the ideological framework of majoritarianism. These are not cases where majoritarianism and parochialism cease to exist in the city; rather, we shall see that the city presents increased possibilities for alternatives to the majoritarian conceptions of community and moments for solidarity and action across difference.

Diasporic communalism with cosmopolitanism

With the migration of people, alongside the transmigration of capital, places which are not geographically proximate become tied into intense and sustained connections, argues Vertovec (2009). In the case of migrant transnationalism, such networks are primarily and historically associated with identity and community, yet also, and increasingly, associated with political action and engagement that take place locally (in the place where migrants live), translocally (in actions that link places of origin and of destination) and transnationally (in sustained transnational digital networks that reproduce by their existence cultural, social and political connections). These multi-spatial systems of communication reconfigure the organization and qualities of community life, as demonstrated by the explosion of social media, the vast popularity of satellite television and the effectiveness of political niche media. Sassen (2004) argues that such politics is not cosmopolitan, but primarily a particular way of building on local and translocal agendas and interests. But I would argue that it is precisely in the persistence of particularism through transnational communication that we can understand cosmopolitanization: not as an oppositional force to transnational community, but as articulated within it.

In explaining the delicate, often contradictory, but often reflexive interplay between communalism, cosmopolitan vision and practice, I draw on work with focus groups of diasporic Arab audiences of transnational television.[1] The Arab diaspora in Europe represents a very diverse and fragmented but established community. In the seven European capital cities where the study was conducted, many Arabs spoke of the ways in which they have found themselves in the turmoil of the politics of fear and surveillance associated with the 'war on terror'. This is also a group that has access to a wide range of transnational media, with Arabic-language television representing a medium consumed by more than 90 per cent of all survey participants.[2] The focus groups, conducted in each city with adult men and women from three different age groups, brought together a diverse group of individuals occupying a range of ideological, political and religious positions. While diversity of experiences, practices and uses of media and communications within these heterogeneous groups was enormous, certain patterns in participants' identification with community, media use and interpretation were significantly persistent and important for the present discussion. Below, I draw from data collected from London's Arab diaspora in order to sustain a focused discussion. All participants identified as Arab (and self-identification was also the basis for their recruitment) and none of them distanced themselves from other Arabs – though many expressed an uneasy relationship with what they referred to as the Arab community. A significant proportion of them identified both with a transnational Arab community and as Londoners, alongside other identifications. Identification with their city was also projected among participants in other capitals, such as in Madrid for example. In fact, for many, commitment to a transnational and urban community was much more dominant than their commitment to a nation, demonstrating an unspoken attachment to communitarian identities that carry a certain symbolic power in the form of pride, recognition and globality. Importantly, some linked their sense of belonging to local politics and action and their transnational sense of belonging to the media: 'I do affiliate with this concept of the global Ummah, through the media and I never used to have that type of affiliation or association. I think that has developed recently' (male, 18–25). Among younger participants a sense of multiple belonging was repeatedly proposed against singular belonging: 'I say I'm Lebanese Palestinian living in London, but not I'm Lebanese and not Palestinian or not from London. Nowadays, a person can be a million things at the same time, a million citizenships, have more than one job, no more this or that' (female, 18–25). In other cases, it was the rejection of identification with a singular national community that was projected, especially as this was seen as a form of majoritarian rule over minorities: 'Why do I have to say I'm British or Sudanese? I don't want to be nothing. I'm a citizen of Mars, nobody can say anything. I don't think we should be being asked. Why don't they go and ask some British people' (male, 18–25). Identification with different communities or just rejection of forced identification appeared in this study as reflexive cosmopolitan narratives that many of these same people used to refer to their commitment to knowing what's going on in the world. These participants by no means fit within a neat category of a 'cosmopolitan elite', but rather represent mostly, but not exclusively, a young group with mixed social backgrounds. But what is important here is the high level of media literacy they share.

While this was far from being the case for everyone within this group, most participants spoke about a range of media they used regularly. The richer and more diverse the media world of individual participants, the more they appeared to resist parochialism. In their diverse media consumption, many participants evaluated and controlled the abundance of information available to them while becoming increasingly aware of the different interests and ideologies that surrounded them. 'I don't trust Western nor Arabic media 100%. Every channel wants me to see events as it is considered by its agenda, every channel is reflecting its own politics' (female, 26–45). What can be argued here is that this group's cultural practices reaffirm some of the qualities associated with cosmopolitan subjectivity, such as regular participation in transnational networks and access to diverse media worlds. At the same time, and while following some cultural practices usually attributed to elites, such as multilingualism, frequent travel and ownership of many different media, this group did not possess the financial capital of cosmopolitan elites. Importantly, the articulations of cosmopolitanism among participants had their own specificities. While far from a homogenous ideological space, the diasporic space has distinct characteristics. For example, in this study many of the participants referred to Islam as a source of their own values of justice or charity; others repeatedly referred to suffering among Arabs – especially in Palestine and Iraq – as evidence of injustice in the world and of the West's selective morality. Thus, and while demonstrating a reflexive individualism (Bauman 1998), the discourse of community remained powerful in this case. Narratives and values associated with particularism and universalism in this case have a distinct diasporic slant. They both carry histories of migration and awareness of current politics and, very importantly, they are grounded in the city where participants live. When many of them emphasized their identification with their city rather than the nation, they located their particularity in a specific space, which, against the national framework, might allow them to establish a sense of community, of presence, and even some recognition of their contribution to the city's symbolic power. The daily encounters with difference among urban subjects in the inner city demonstrates the mundane ways in which migrants contribute to making the city a space of community, but also a space for cosmopolitan visions.

Local communalism with cosmopolitanism

The particularism–universalism continuum (Robertson 1992) could not be more obvious than in the case of culturally diverse communities, especially those organically emerging out of inner city's encounters. In the previous section, the role of television was discussed as sustaining the commitment of members of a transnational diaspora to communities, but also to filtering their engagement with community and global affairs through media literacy. Television, alongside online media, not only expands transnationalism outside the city and into transnational networks. It also brings transnationalism into the city and feeds into the life and communication practices of new, diverse communities. Living in culturally diverse cities constantly exposes urban subjects to numerous particularisms. In many ways, particularism is the universal reality of urban life; the city is a place of constant encounters with difference (Amin and Thrift 2002). The public life of the city especially, as it expands from the street to the school, from shopping to work, makes difference banal and ordinary. It also makes it a quality of everyday life, perhaps a source of the symbolic power – as argued in the previous chapter – of urban dwellers. At least, this is the case for those who are not completely excluded from these shared realities (or for those elites that choose to withdraw from them).

Television, as the most popular medium across generations (Ofcom 2010), represents an element of public life inasmuch as it plays a key role in informing knowledge and understanding of the world close by and far away. The symbolic power of television, associated with televisual imagery and its wide diffusion, makes it a still relevant medium in times of digitalization. Since its early days, television has been discussed as a 'window on the world', but, as the global city brings us 'the world in a city' (Anisef and Lanphier 2003), the spaces of interpersonal and mediated communication merge. In the case of the inner city, this merger presents possibilities for new communities that build upon the difference which may not be shared through common histories but is shared in two ways: through the common urban present and through shared exposure to the media.

This was especially what we observed among young people who constructed local, grounded but not parochial community discourses in London's inner city. In a study we conducted for the International Broadcasting Trust (IBT) (Georgiou and Coleman 2008), we recorded powerful discourses of community among young people (aged between 18 and 25) that emerged through their exposure to one another's particularity and their shared engagement with media narratives and technologies. Participants in focus groups in Lewisham, South London, and Islington, North London, demonstrated much higher levels of empathy towards distant sufferers (Chouliaraki 2006) and engagement with international affairs than their suburban counterparts. Many of those participants projected common identities associated with narratives of shared humanity, but also with their urban and neighbourhood experience – both seem to be mediated through urban and media synergies as these constantly feed into each other. A participant who said that he watched Al Jazeera to better understand his Muslim friends talked about the channel as widening his perspective on the world: 'Al Jazeera doesn't only cover wars. They cover places and events, say in Congo. They will take you in a village and show you how people live. People should be shown that sort of thing, maybe more people would then want to help if they saw others' life. It might make the world a better place' (male, 18–25).

Among the inner-city focus groups, living with diversity was repeatedly referred to as a key element in what made them Londoners but also individuals in an interconnected world. This was the case for most participants of both migrant and non-migrant backgrounds. The members of the focus groups, while not previously known to one another, constantly cross-referenced material from the media they were all exposed to (especially films and global media events), but also from friendships with locals from different cultural backgrounds. Their wide exposure to the media, as well as their local but diverse friendships, were referred to by many as evidence of their 'legitimate' understanding and interpretation of distant events.

The particularization of universalism was repeatedly observed in the discourses of community among these young participants. For example, many of them identified with diasporic cultural discourses, for example celebrating certain musical subcultures, even when they had no direct diasporic family links to these. Their city is a transnational city and as such their understanding of both the city and the world is filtered through this transnationality. It probably comes as no surprise to see diasporic discourses adopted by some of those young people, even when they do not themselves have family diasporic connections. The diasporic exposure may come not through family, but through friends. This intense interest in parts of the world that their friends come from was shared among many young urban subjects and repeatedly observed in all the London focus groups. For many of these young people, cultural divides from non-Londoners (especially people living in rural areas) were more important than those between Londoners from different parts of the world: 'You get racist and ignorant people wherever you are but perhaps someone from outside London might know less about the world. Someone who sticks to the countryside won't have the same friends like me. Their only contact with Indian and Chinese people will be through the media' (male, 18–25). The nuanced and banal reality of the global city's diversity was used by many of the participants in this series of focus groups as an interpretative framework when talking about poverty and corruption in the developing world. Some of these participants quoted their friends who had links to specific regions of the world as reliable sources and mediators who helped them to understand the international affairs they saw reported on the news.

The transnationality of everyday encounters in the global city defines to a great extent the borders of community and the emergence of new communities. Especially among young people and young families, one can observe new, locally based communities. The local communities emerging in many parts of the city, for many families around schools, are filtered through transnationality. An element of this transnationality relates to the redefinition of networks of kin in the global city. Since most people migrating to the global city have experienced the disruption of many family relations, they redefine their system of support in their new locale. Many of the other people living around them have experienced the same kind of disruption and, especially when it comes to family life, these networks have to be re-established and re-invented – the global city becomes a collection of particularities. Bilingualism and multilingualism also become mundane realities of transnational urban life. Multilingualism, which expands from intergenerational diasporic family encounters to school environments and local shopping areas, mediates understandings of community which are framed within the broader context of close proximity to difference. This is not to say that there is no retreat to sameness. But retreat to sameness is primarily a response to close encounters with difference, rather than a reproduction of earlier forms of bounded communities. No community exists here outside its exposure to difference. And no community exists outside exposure to the world stage, which both filters and is filtered by exposure to the neighbour, as shown in the words of one female participant: 'The media give the impression that Muslim women are forced to wear their veils, when that is not the case' (female, 18–25). She justified her statement by making reference to her contact with Muslim women in London and on her travels around the world. Living in the global city and travelling around the globe were referred to as a continuum of experience, rather than as diverting practices. A humanistic outlook that links life in the global city, travel to new places, engagement with international affairs and empathy with those suffering close by or in distant places is regularly adopted by many young inner-city dwellers.

While the reflexive space that emerges around the diversification of mediated urban spaces is notably and repeatedly recorded, both among local urban youth communities and the London diasporic community, it comes with significant limitations. For urban dwellers living in extreme marginality, primarily as a result of lack of, or very limited access to, basic education, employment and housing on the one hand, or as a result of stigmatization that pushes them further to the margins, on the other, encounters with the city's diversity are also constrained and limited. These are the voices that are rarely heard in research or policy; these are the experiences mostly spoken about and recorded not through people's own agency, but primarily within discourses that locate migrant and diasporic communities within frameworks of marginality and *other*-ness. Against the voices that are missing and the voices that are contradictory and balance between old discourses and practices of communalism and new narratives of cosmopolitanism are some new ones, resting upon high levels of media literacy, pre-existing wealth, but also new urban experiences – this is the case of the urban nomads discussed below.

Cosmopolitan individualism vs. community? The limits of solidarity

The city has always been a location full of contested meanings. While for Simmel (1997) it exemplifies strangeness, for others it has been a location of freedom and resistance. According to Bell and de-Shalit, the city is the location of resistance to the homogenizing powers of globalization, often investing in opposing 'globalization and its tendency to flatten cultures into sameness' (2011: 5). The city has attracted the most dystopic academic and literary analyses of loneliness and rampant individualism. Sennett (1990) wrote about the strangeness of city life, where individuals possess the right to 'invisible shields', the right to be left alone. Simmel (1997) writes that the urban subject's strategy for managing the chaos, intensity and over-concentration of the city is to become blasé: 'things themselves are experienced as insubstantial. They appear to the blasé person in an evenly grey tone, no one object deserves preference over any other' (1997: 179). As Bull writes, for Simmel, 'urban life becomes a dialectical process of freedom and insecurity in which the urban citizen progressively retreats into their own cognitive or physical shell whilst simultaneously neutralising the public spaces of the city' (2007: 27). It is the mechanisms of distancing from the *other* (ibid.) that are at the core of urban dystopia, or arguably at the core of urban life in post-communitarian times. The uses of technologies, especially of personal media (Du Gay 1997; Bull 2007), and of the car (Sheller and Urry 2003; Thrift 2004) have often been discussed in terms of their oppositional role to community: enabling mobility, personal freedom and control of space, they are also seen as advancing alienation, distance from others, and hierarchical and individualistic uses of the public space within urban domains: 'Automobility indeed constitutes a civil society of hybridized "cardrivers", dwelling privately-within-their-cars, and excluding those without cars or without the "licence" to drive from the car-dominated public realm. Such a civil society of automobility transforms public spaces into public roads, in which to a significant extent the hybrids of pedestrians, cyclists and even public transport users are marginalized' (Sheller and Urry 2003: 118). Almost inevitably, such debates concerning the advance of individualism against community and solidarity marginalize debates about cosmopolitanism. Yet, and paradoxically, the centrality of the individual within these debates complements the cosmopolitan ethos in at least one way. Within the cosmopolitan rhetoric – or the cosmopolitan ethos – individuals are the driving force of human rights and equality, not of states or nations, or for that matter of any kind of community (Hannerz 1996; Stevenson 2003). Bull writes about iPod owners in the city as using these to 'close their ears to the multifaceted sound world of the city' (2007: 28). As iPod users construct privatized soundscapes and individualistic enclaves within the public urban space, they isolate themselves from difference but, as Bull continues, they adopt an 'interiorised cosmopolitanism' (2007: 37), expressed in the variety of their playlists. One of the groups gaining prevalence within transnationalism – urban nomads – has emerged out of the advance of individuality in late modernity. Representing one of the new trans-urban communities, urban nomads are people who choose to move from city to city and not to settle anywhere in particular. Their prime identifiers are the urbanity of their lifestyle, their mobility across cities and the hyper-mediation of all elements of their lives. And there is one qualitative identifier: the fact that they move not only across cities, but also across nomadic communities. These groups, representing new forms of mobile and trans-urban communities, live highly mediated lives and, at least in part, find fulfilment and continuity by sustaining transnational mediated connections. As defined in the *Urban Dictionary* (urbandictionary.com), urban nomads are: 'A small but diverse section of society that lives and works in an urban area, yet does not rent, own or otherwise reside permanently in any one location. "Nomad" suggests a chosen lifestyle, as opposed to "refugee", and it also suggests that nomads feel they have a home, as opposed to the "homeless"' (2012). The elements of choice and mobility are central here: a sense of home through movement. Besides its self-definition through mobility, this group has not only mobile and virtual, but of course also embodied, experiences. The embodied experience of the urban nomads is most often, but not exclusively as will be shown below, encountered in cities like London, Berlin and New York. Certain parts of these cities, such as Hackney in London or Kreuzberg in Berlin, which are in the process of gentrification, represent temporary homes for urban nomads. Seen in a number of local cafés, often recognized through the very sleek technology they carry with them, they are regularly encountered in the hybrid space of work, leisure and socialization that moves with them in the city space and the trans-urban space of their travels.

Numerous blogs written under titles which are variations of the phrase 'urban nomad', and which are often written in the local urban cafés offering free Wi-Fi, provide different insights into these emerging and vibrant trans-urban communities. The virtual self-representation varies from self-indulgence and narcissistic exploration of a trans-urban lifestyle to travel and resettlement advice, all the way to denouncing corporate values, excessive salaries and consumerism. Many of the urban nomads appear to change their lifestyle by leaving behind highly paid jobs, which are associated, as one blogger writes, with 'evil' big-city law firms. Challenging dominant values and the status quo through individual lifestyles and choices is a recurring theme in many of the online spaces shared by nomads. Living Radically (www.livingradically.com) proposes a list of 'things to do' in order to become an urban nomad. These include two main categories: 'getting rid of stuff' and 'no location dependency'. Under 'getting rid of stuff', prospective urban nomads are advised to get rid of subscriptions to newspapers and magazines, of books that are not in electronic format, as well as of plastic bags and plastic bottles. Under 'no location dependency', the advice includes getting rid of property and aiming for short-term rentals that allow the nomads to move freely between places. The author of the list is a freelance writer and consultant and, similarly to other people in the knowledge economy, is able to work while on the move.

Literature on expert migrants and cyborgs (Berker 2005) and Castells's concept of communication power (2009) have focused on the emergence of communities in and through digital networks as giving rise to hybrid spaces between individualism and communalism. As Castells (2009) argues, networked individualism meets communalism, especially in project-oriented social movements that build on the sharing of new values among individuals. In his analysis, reflexive modernity has been advanced through communication and, consequently, identity and community are filtered through reflexivity. Urban nomadism can be viewed within the dialectic of individualism and communalism proposed above. A lifestyle choice made by individuals, it also represents an identification with communities of like-minded cosmopolitan urban globetrotters. The knowledge economy and the urban symbolic economy increasingly build their functions, and even their identity, around those new trans-urban communities. As *The Economist* writes:

> Urban nomads have started appearing only in the past few years. Like their antecedents in the desert, they are defined not by what they carry but by what they leave behind, knowing that the environment will provide it. Thus, Bedouins do not carry their own water, because they know where the oases are. Modern nomads carry almost no paper because they access

their documents on their laptop computers, mobile phones or online. Increasingly, they don't even bring laptops. (*The Economist* 2008)

Work, life, love and, in consequence, place change with nomadic lifestyle. Media and communications, especially as represented by the forms of urban creativity and expressivity discussed in the previous chapter, become organic and dynamic systems for advancing new identities, but also in the practices of new communities. King Adz (2010) describes the creativity and morality associated with culture jamming, a practice found in new (trans) urban cultures. According to him, culture jamming is a reaction and a form of resistance to mass culture. It can be manifested in street art and graffiti, in alternative media production, especially online, and occasionally in forms of public protest associated with other social movements. Culture jamming is about action. And action is about community. A merger of resistance with mass culture and a system of self-representation become a movement linked to lifestyle, cosmopolitan identities and creativity. Areyougeneric.org represents itself as a community of culture jammers, the nemesis of unethical corporations, censorship and biased media, maintaining a global presence through its sleek and open website (ibid.). The call to community through a discourse of resistance to mass culture is apparent in the case of this team and of many other culture jammers. Naomi Klein, in *No Logo* (1999), writes about the incorporation of the techniques of culture jamming by corporations themselves which twist these anti-corporate, anti-advertising aesthetics into actual advertising. Levi's 2011 *Go Forth* campaign used an anti-capitalist discourse and images of demonstrators and rioters to sell its jeans. While the purity lacking in every element of urban culture is expressed here in the incorporation of resistance advertising, culture jammers reclaimed their imagery in an adopted version of the campaign (re)called 'Go Forth and Revolt'. In the video advertisement, the text over the original Levi's advertisement reads: 'Capitalists have stolen the whole world. . . . Even riots can become advertisements for products. Our moments of joy are flattened into images that impoverish our lives. Now their system is collapsing. Let's tear it down. Go forth and destroy capitalism' (Creative Activism 2012).

Such practices use transnational media spaces to call to community and to action. The unifying discourse of different cultural-jamming projects has the city and digital media at its core:

> I am an urbanist. Okay, so I'm from the green suburbs of London but that is just the point. It's not about where you are from it's about what you are into . . . We are well into the twenty-first century and we are down with the latest in everything. Nothing is hidden, everything is instantly accessible.

Urban street culture has influenced everything you can touch, smell, watch, buy, wear, listen to, download, upload, TIVO, record and burn. (King Adz 2010: 6)

While nomadic communities are more likely to be encountered in global cities, the mobility and lifestyle that they represent has been transforming a number of cities and pockets of cities, from Portland to São Paolo and Sydney. The mediated semi-fictional interpretation of new urban cosmopolitan communities represented in the American sitcom *Portlandia* reflects the emergence of cities of refuge out of nomadic mobility. A comedy series on American television, *Portlandia*, produced by the Independent Film Channel (IFC), was enormously successful in 2011 and 2012. A humorous celebration of Portland's tattooed, organic, and alternative culture, the series creates a fictional version of the city of Portland. 'The city is now the unofficial world capital of a hyper-liberal, artsy and environmentally conscious hipster lifestyle . . . Its denizens are heavily tattooed, excessively pierced, and obsessed with local brands. They shop in co-ops and hate corporations,' writes Harris (2012: 29). In many ways a city of refuge, Portland provides impressive levels of access to public life and sustainable living for minorities and environmentalists. The appeal of *Portlandia*'s nomadic and urban lifestyle reflects global patterns of urban living: '*Portlandia*'s success relies much on a hipster boom worldwide. In areas like Hoxton in London, Williamsburg in New York, Silver Lake in Los Angeles, and cities like Austin in Texas, a recognisable culture has sprung up' (Harris 2012: 29). The series presents an example of the attractiveness of new nomadic communities that flourish around cultures of hospitality, openness and cosmopolitanism, but which nevertheless tend to remain bound by moralities and politics tied to western modernity and liberal democracy. It thus should come as no surprise that the mediated version of such a lifestyle has such a wide appeal in its televisual version.

These are communities of choice, trans-urban communities associated with youth culture, alternative middle-class lifestyles and patterns of exploration of urban living that spread across the cities of the urban North – and are glimpsed in the emerging global cities of the global South. The association of urban nomadism with the city and the street with urban and global systems of self-representation are tools for advancing symbolic power that can travel with individuals (partly necessary to sustain its members' employability). These are communities of individuals sharing a sense of awareness of the city and their own subjectivity in the city. Often individualistic and narcissistic, they are about the lived experience in the urban street and about its merging with virtual spaces of communication and self-representation.

Self-representation feeds a subjectivity which is composed in order to be in control of the city, of consumption and of time and space, as King Adz writes above: 'we are down with the latest of everything.' It is also a culture of mediation. The street moves to the screen and the link between experience and a mediated (representation of) community grounds these communities within the realities and virtualities of transnational urbanism. Like the two cases of urban communities discussed above, urban nomadism is an ambivalent community. However, unlike these two other communities – the diasporic and the local urban – its ambivalence lies in the fine balance, not between communitarianism and cosmopolitan orientation but between individualism and its cosmopolitan orientation. There is no doubt that the practice of urban nomads reveals cosmopolitan competence – travelling across the world, challenging the limits of identity on the basis of national belonging, engaging with strangers encountered in virtual and urban life. But just as diasporic particularism can always lead to segregation and closure, so can the cosmopolitan vision of urban nomads. Inasmuch as individualism is celebrated within an elite cosmopolitan lifestyle, this community represents no more than a parochial and inward-looking neoliberal cosmopolitanism – the stranger being another techno-savvy nomad, the engagement with the city being one that limits responsibility and commitment to others. This is precisely the challenge for these new communities: the choice between a politics of nomadism that challenges neoliberalism and the politics of nomadism that enjoys mobility selectively secured for some through neoliberalism. The consequences of these different versions of cosmopolitan practice and vision presented in the three different communities are discussed in the last section of this chapter.

Hospitality and the city of refuge

The three cases above represent different formations of community, as well as different ways to articulate the ideal of 'the citizen of the world' at the meeting of the city and the media, the particular and the universal. Do the formation and persistence of different communities in the city reveal distinct qualities of the city and urban values? Derrida (2001b) writes about the city of refuge and the value of hospitality as key elements of a cosmopolitan ethics. Solidarity represents another key element of this. If we think about the three communities described above, do they advance cosmopolitan solidarity, and if so, solidarity between which actors and with what consequences? Calhoun (2002) is concerned with new forms of attenuated global solidarity, which may lack the qualities of old forms of solidarity. If we think of a thick concept of solidarity through empathy, support, commitment and fraternity, what are the different forms of solidarity that we can observe in each case?

In the case of diasporas, it is perhaps the long-standing values of community that present a mixed and contradictory picture: in the transnational and highly mediated everyday life of the diasporic group discussed above – Arabs in London – discourses of communitarian solidarity and cosmopolitan solidarity constantly compete. In this case, mediated communication becomes a tool for expanding the meaning of community, but also for reflecting on its limitations. Urban and diasporic mediated communication present two different expressions of the universalism–particularism continuum. When it comes to diasporic media, these emerge precisely because there are people, institutions and communities which feel the need to sustain particularistic spaces of communication vis-à-vis other spaces of communication (universalistic or homogenizing). The mere existence of particularistic communication depends on different forms, content and meanings of communication to which diasporic people respond or from which they turn away. The relation between particularistic and universalistic discourses is inevitable here, as each becomes a response to the other; thus it is more of a dialectic relation than an opposition; indeed, it is a continuum (Robertson 1992).

In the case of urban communities, what we see emerging most vividly is the universalization of particularism (ibid.), i.e. the acceptance and celebration of and, importantly, the engagement with and moral commitment to understanding and supporting particularities. This is perhaps the most vibrant case of grounded cosmopolitanism: formed in the constant interplay of interpersonal and mediated exposure to difference, it represents a reflexive and lived form of solidarity, aware of difference as inherent in the city and directly linked to hospitality as a shared responsibility of urban subjects.

In the case of the urban nomads, we can see a constant shift between discourses of particularism and universalism, although assumptions about the universal rightfulness of the selected lifestyle and the individualistic trajectories that accompany their cosmopolitan vision also show the limitations of their cosmopolitan solidarity. Expecting to benefit from urban hospitality, there is little evidence that this group contributes to expanding it to those who need it the most. In this case, solidarity tends to be much more inward-looking, directed towards other nomads and particular life choices associated with nomadism. The centrality of mediated communication for this community reinforces its boundedness, as it secures the flows of communication and the reaffirmation of what constitutes shared values. It does this in the way that elite cosmopolitanism always has, by reinforcing privileges – in this case by expanding them through digital and trans-urban networks.

If we return to Derrida's concept of hospitality (2001b), it is important to consider whether new formations of community in the city advance hospitality and reinforce the city of refuge. In the way that Derrida spoke about hospitality in the city, Silverstone (2007) argued for its central symbolic significance of hospitality for media spaces – the obligation to create space for *others* in the *mediapolis*. I argue that the global city, which is also a transnational city, represents the hybrid space between the symbolic and the physical, where hospitality becomes subject to the exposure to difference and negotiated through different claims for presence, recognition and refuge. In drawing on Arendt, Derrida and Silverstone, I recognize the need to protect stateless people and those suffering persecution as the nemesis of the nation-state. The right to asylum, Arendt argues, has a sacred history (in Derrida 2001b), a history that is currently yet again under attack. Asylum seekers and migrants are increasingly pathologized as bogus and greedy outsiders seeking access to the wealth of the West while having no rights to it (Georgiou 2010; Lentin and Titley 2012). In the contradictory, top-down ideological framework that defines the global city, elite and expert migration is celebrated while the migration of people who really need to move is pathologized. This is precisely the point where community needs to be also associated with the values of hospitality and solidarity.

Marginalization and deprivation in global cities also show the fragility of community and of the discourse of hospitality in culturally diverse societies. The ethos and morality associated with living with difference are crucial elements for understanding the realities of and the possibilities for community in these societies. The case of creative, trans-urban, middle-class nomads is as different as it could be from that of persecuted people who face suspicion, if not hostility, when they cross borders. Representing the top tier of cities of refuge, urban nomads usually have enough economic capital and symbolic capital to support their trans-urban mobility. While not the persecuted people Derrida talks about, they reflect the sustained and growing complexity of the city as a space of hospitality, as well as a space where symbolic power is partly diffused. Even in their limitations, elite appropriations of the city are important precisely because they confirm the existence of the city of refuge and because they demonstrate its limits. Migrants from the global North find little hostility in the cities they land. Ideological frameworks of Eurocentrism have long mediated the meanings of different *others* (some of whom we might see as like ourselves and welcome within an elite cosmopolitan discourse). The experience of these new communities represents a vision and a hope that cities today have a renewed ability to become cities of refuge. In these cities, newcomers have agency and tell their own stories of their journeys and communities; they tell the story of the city itself. But the hospitality extended to these new transnational and nomadic communities also reflects the biases of cosmopolitan hospitality that reproduce western ideals of individuality and subjectivity as self-efficient, ideally white and middle-class. More than anything, the case of these new communities confronts the limitations of a cosmopolitan imaginary when this is self-referential rather than reflexive and open.

Derrida (2001b) argues that the forms of solidarity required to support cities of refuge have not yet been invented. He is not quite right. The publicness of everyday life, and the constant expansion of that publicness through the criss-crossing of different narratives, imaginaries and ideologies in transnational and urban mediascapes, demonstrates that these forms of solidarity and community exist, although they are still marginal. 'It is the exposure to difference that in time becomes the major factor in happy cohabitation by causing the urban roots of fear to wilt and fade,' argues Bauman (2005: 78). Cohabitation and publicness create spaces for recognition and for agency, for claiming the right to a voice and a responsibility to engage in dialogical encounters.

The narratives of universalism, of justice, freedom and access to the city need to be understood precisely in their dialogical interdependence with the various particularisms that also shape the conditionality and level of hospitality: the particularisms of those elites that are not willing to see, let alone accept, newcomers; the politicians who reproduce moral panics around *other*-ness; but also the particularities of the urban and transnational subjects who seek refuge and a home, a space for community. For Silverstone, the obligation of hospitality to a stranger in a symbolic space is 'a precondition for media justice . . . Hospitality then becomes intertwined with the requirement not just to let the other speak but the requirement that the stranger should be heard' (2007: 139) – both speakers and listeners have agency and a right to a voice.

Fraser's 'three Rs' (2003) – recognition, representation and redistribution – invite us to think of hospitality in relation to citizenship and equality alongside recognition of difference. Sassen's (2002) analysis of migrants' claims to citizenship could be seen as emerging through the juxtaposition of recognition and representation (that should expand to include self-representation alongside political representation).

The daily practices by undocumented immigrants as part of their daily life in the community where they reside – such as raising a family, schooling children, holding a job – earn them citizenship claims in the US even as the formal status and, more narrowly, legalization may continue to evade them. There are dimensions of citizenship, such as strong community ties and participation in civic activities, which are being enacted informally through these practices. These practices produce an at least partial recognition of them as full social beings. (Sassen 2002: 12)

Sassen proposes a dynamic and agonistic analysis which can be of relevance to an analysis of hospitality not as *offered* by majorities to minorities, but as a dialogical process engaging different actors. A moral responsibility, as proposed by Derrida (2001b), hospitality is more than that. It is also political action through the recognition of the presence and contribution of groups who may lack political rights and economic capital, but which, in their cultural presence, in their civic participation and in their community life not only ask for but demand rightful recognition. Where better to see this than in the media worlds of diasporic and diverse urban communities? To Derrida's and Silverstone's theses above, then, I add an element of hospitality, which concerns the responsibility to enable and recognize participation for all its communities – new and old, transnational and local. In this context, the universalistic values that inform hospitality cannot but be limited and conditional on acceptance of difference, unless they incorporate different particularisms. Particularisms complicate hospitality, but they are not impossible to incorporate in systems of recognition, of citizenship. The mere emergence of diverse community spaces in the global city presents powerful evidence of this. Particularities that range between class, gender and generation, all the way to the variety of ethnic and cultural community histories, need to be not only acknowledged but also enabled in order to target inequalities of wealth, representation and recognition.

6   Action: Presence and Marginality

Social inequalities in the city have redefined not only community, but also politics and action. In the midst of the global financial crisis, social unrest and revolt rolled out around the world. 2011 became the year of the protester. So said *Time* magazine, naming the protester as their Person of the Year. And that year's events are a catalogue of this. It was the year that the marginal and the invisible took centre stage in political affairs. The 'Arab Spring' brought the global margins to the centre of politics and representations of revolt. The urban riots of 2011 in Britain brought the social margins to the centre of the urban social space. And the global Occupy movement brought the political margins to the centre of the global political discourse. There are many and complex reasons explaining why the margins became part of the core narrative and of a reflexive discourse about the present and future of the economic and political order. One of these, and a crucial one, I argue, is the amplified presence of these groups on the urban street and the virtual global street. As protesters and rioters occupied the urban street, from Cairo to London and from Kuala Lumpur to New York, they reached out to the centres of power and the urban dwellers in immediate proximity. But, as they appeared at the same time on global screens, the urban street was transformed into a node of the global street (Sassen 2010). From the urban street to the global street, groups which were usually marginal and invisible became hyper-visible. Does presence constitute a form of politics? Does politics constitute a form of presence? Or does presence represent only presence?

In this chapter, I discuss presence as the main – and often only – tool through which marginal and invisible social and political actors gain access to political process. I examine the ways in which presence becomes a kind of politics, or a possibility of politics, especially as the urban street and global virtual street merge. Inspired by Sassen's (2005, 2011) analysis, I discuss the many layers of politics that take shape in the city outside representational democracy and the established centres of political power. I locate presence within a politics which can be deliberative as well as chaotic, targeted as well as performative, as most notably but not exclusively observed on the streets of the global city.

With Sassen's analysis as a starting point, I move further to examine the constitutive role of the media in shaping the space and shape of revolt. When the urban riots in the United Kingdom started, a famous historian blamed urban music for making white people behave like blacks.[1] Numerous politicians and the popular press reproduced a narrative concerning the ills of rap, alongside widespread blaming of social media for allegedly enabling rioters to organize their criminal acts. And, while the state machine was struggling to obtain access to the locations of revolt, global audiences were closely observing on their screens live coverage and close-ups of action on the ground. Only weeks after these riots, the mediated city space moved yet again into the focus of global attention. The Occupy movement claimed urban public territories and the attention of global audiences, as within a few days it became a global, multi-nodal and trans-urban phenomenon. Mobile phones and laptops became recognizable as accessories to protest, as have popular cultural symbols, most strikingly captured in the 'Anonymous' mask. In the cases of the riots and of Occupy, the urban street became a site where urban and global divisions unfolded, where they were seen and marked on urban plateaus that began to look more like global mediascapes.

This chapter looks at the urban street in its continuum with the global street sustained through mediated communication. This continuum is the site where presence emerges as the predominant way in which marginalized groups seek visibility and recognition. Socially and politically marginalized groups, which lack economic capital and political power, demonstrate on the urban street the only capital that they have an abundance of: presence.

The two cases this chapter focuses on – Occupy and urban riots – could not be more different in so many ways, some of them discussed below. Yet there are three key commonalities that they share and that invite us to rethink the possibilities and limitations of progressive action and of a liberating cosmopolitanism (Harvey 2009: 280). The first relates to the hyper-visibility that protesters and rioters gained through the synergetic overexposure offered by the city and the media. Protest and 'destruction' on the urban street became largely framed through this hyper-visibility and visual imagery. The second commonality relates to the ways in which it was the media and the mediated spectacle that partly made the actors in the revolt. In the intense mediation of the events, participants became partly constituted by the media – both the media representing them and the media they themselves used. The third and consequent point where the two events converge is where a politics becomes possible through presence in the city's public space. In both cases, presence represents the only certainty; its outcome is uncertain and unpredictable. Yet, presence on the urban and the global street, either through progressive action or through mere revolt, becomes almost a prerequisite for visibility and for recognition (Fraser 2008). Protesters' and rioters' presence across the media and across the city reflects some possibilities for challenging hegemonic ideologies associated with the single, hierarchical and unquestioned political and social order of liberal representational democracy. It is this possibility that relocates social justice (or the lack of it) at the centre of a politics which makes urban riots and Occupy important. This politics not only recognizes difference – it can only exist through difference. Difference, recognition of difference and redistribution with the aim of sustaining difference become narratives and performances associated with protest and revolt as much as they constitute a vision for living with dignity in a mediated urban world.

The three elements of the discussion outlined above unfold in the following pages and reveal the ways in which urban politics, before anything else, become a matter of claims to the right to have a presence in spaces 'that matter' – the spaces where symbolic power is distributed and controlled. What is at stake is access – or the restriction of access – to public space, both mediated and physical. The tension is between the established order and the margins that are in revolt. On the one hand, a system of public order surrounds centres of power in the global city and becomes even more rigid and aggressive at times of crisis when established power is challenged. On the other hand, actors on the periphery of centres of power, increasingly excluded at times of crises, revolt against the dominant system of social and public order. In the case of Occupy, the revolt materializes as a visionary and globally oriented presence and, in the case of the riots, as angry demands for access to what others have. Engagement with communication technologies and the broader media culture demonstrates that the spaces that matter are largely symbolic, linking the urban street to other urban streets and symbolic power to claims to citizenship and identity. Media and communication technologies, as increasingly central elements of urban politics, are discussed here in relation to pre-existing but ever-changing cultures of marginality and political protest.

The city in the midst of global crises

The city at times of global crises becomes a location where change can be observed in all its physical and symbolic intensity. Anxieties and hopes associated with change and uncertainty unfold in political action and everyday practices. Unlike what many hoped for, the recession that started in 2008 was not a blip in a long and uninterrupted story of capitalism's advance. The global financial crisis of the early twenty-first century marks a point of change and a point of realization of western societies' economic vulnerabilities in a way unseen for generations. It comes after another key point in the realization of the vulnerabilities of the West: 9/11. A direct challenge to the 'taken-for-grantedness' of western power, the 9/11 attacks were followed by further violence and violations of human rights in the name of political and cultural righteousness, of an assumed *we*-ness against a named *other*-ness. As a result of both crises, cultural and religious difference has come to the fore yet again. New, or re-invented, narratives of the *other*-ness within became prominent in political and public mediated discourse: stories that tell of a pathological urban underclass, a dysfunctional European South, irresponsible unions resisting austerity, migrants taking locals' jobs. Alongside these powerful narratives, the boundaries between *we*-ness and *other*-ness have become extremely fragile. As the middle classes in the global North saw their financial security threatened or shattered, and political projects such as the EU perceived as on the verge of collapse, the positionalities of identity have shifted.

The vulnerable *we* has taken a hit that forced further reflection, as well as more violence directed against difference. New progressive and anti-capitalist movements, but also chaotic revolts, such as the urban riots seen in Athens in 2008 and in Britain in 2011, alongside the rise of xenophobia and racism spread from Australia to Sweden, reflect the explosive realization of the changes in global, national and urban sociocultural order. The new positionalities have challenged taken-for-granted categories and political narratives. Universalistic claims associated with the binary order of liberal democracy – citizens/non-citizens; Us/Others; underclass/middle class; Europeans/Others – have been under direct attack. In these messy, chaotic and dangerous times, hopes and possibilities for a new politics have (re-)emerged. This politics does not always represent a clear narrative, let alone a grand narrative. In many ways, it is through chaotic and destructive actions that the possibility of an alternative politics has emerged. This is not a new phenomenon in history. At other points of crisis and revolt in human history, chaos, resistance and deliberation have emerged alongside and in dialogue with one another.

It is in this context that both Occupy and the riots present interesting cases, not only of opposition but also of continuity in the politics of revolt. The possibilities on the one hand of a non-capitalist future and on the other of the marginalized poor occupying our streets have been entirely excluded from the mainstream media and from political narratives for a very long time. Their common starting point lies in this very exclusion of their political and social narrative and experience from the mainstream narrative of *our* society – at least until they came to the foreground at particular moments of hyper-visibility in the city. Yet both these became real and visible claims when streets and squares were occupied by protesters and rioters. Both moments of action emerged as a cry and a demand for the right to the city (Lefebvre 1996 [1968]), though primarily as a cry of alienation in the case of the riots and as a demand for struggle against alienation in the case of Occupy. Needless to say, the level of political intentionality behind the two events is very different. It is important to acknowledge this difference and to further examine it in analyses of the events, comparing participants' ideological and political backgrounds. This, however, is a topic beyond the focus of the present discussion. Intentionality only represents one element of the urban politics which, as history shows, can emerge in various and unpredictable ways. The realities of revolt, unsettling and diverse as they are in their expressions and consequences, reveal the complexities of the cosmopolitanization of urban action. The growing complexity of urban politics, emerging largely at the meeting of the city and the media, is the focus of the present discussion.

Mediating fear

The global city is increasingly recognized as a centre of intense concentration of power and risk, especially through its mediated representations, and particularly at times of crisis. The intensification of policing and surveillance as a result of the 'terrorist threat' from New York to Madrid and Mumbai has marked urban life, especially in certain neighbourhoods with a high concentration of the usual suspects. In western metropolises, migrant populations have been targeted as causes of demographic change and anomie, and popular media have long sustained public fears that conflate migration, the working class and the urban margins (Jones 2012). When the 2011 riots exploded across Britain, powerful media images of burning cities and urban chaos spread across the global media. A rioter standing in front of a burning car became a recognizable image across national and global media, not unlike the images of intercultural conflicts in Los Angeles after Rodney King's abuse by the police 20 years earlier. In both cases, the riots became symbols of the ultimate urban nightmare (Macek 2006). Such powerful images represent major spectacles of our times, marking and reproducing, alongside images of planes crashing into the Twin Towers (Chouliaraki 2006), recognizable televisual narratives of the city. Less so, but still powerful, are the images of the sacked Lehman Brothers' employees carrying their belongings out of the company's headquarters, and of Occupy banners with the message 'We are the 99 percent', which became a recognizable image, even a brand, associated with Occupy, as well as revealing the bridging that has taken place between global media representations and grounded action.

The legitimacy of the protesters' claim to represent 99 per cent of the people was achieved not when they set up their tents in Kuala Lumpur, New York, Oakland, London and São Paolo but when large audiences tuned in to television and other media to receive their message, to follow the protest and sometimes to communicate back, expressing their support. InterOccupy, a digital network calling activists across the United States and other parts of the world where the Occupy movement has a presence to 'connect, collaborate, organize' (interoccupy.org), represents this powerful link between the mediated and physical space of protest. Especially after the occupation of public spaces ended with the state machinery's expulsion of the protesters, the movement concentrated on occupying the mainstream and the hearts and minds of the wider public (Chomsky 2012).

Within the highly mediated and contested space of the city, the urban street and square have historically represented locations of conflict and of protest, as much as they have been travel routes or spaces for recreation and consumption. They have come to be recognized for their civic significance as the places where marginal and alternative political and social groups are most likely to be encountered. Socially and politically different from the hegemonic national imaginary, the poor, the homeless, the activists and the rioters can be seen in the street and its representations – from news and documentaries to films and television series. Signs of difference, such as the 'hoodie' and the dreadlocks encountered in the street and the mediated street, become powerful symbols of marginality, *other*-ness and threat (Dillabough and Kennelly 2010; Macek 2006), as much as they become performative and recognizable markers of the cosmopolitanization of the city. The presence of *other*-ness makes the city a dangerous place, an *other* to the nation, but also, if only momentarily, a space for these *others* to become part of the city's story, not unlike the moments of popular culture discussed in chapters 3 and 4. But presence can also become a powerful politics: shaped at the juncture of its physicality and its mediated representations, it can become equally visible to the next-door neighbour and to global audiences.

The politics of presence and the city

The politics of presence finds fertile ground in the city. In a way, it always has. The physicality of the urban space has historically been associated with protest and with claims to symbolic power. Proximity to centres of economic and political power – and more recently to centres of media power – has given the city an extra asset as the place where claims can be heard. In addition, the concentration of significant numbers of people who could be potential protesters and rioters has made the city a site of revolt. 'Places are not only the recipients of the effects of global forces, they are . . . the origin and propagator of them too,' argues Massey (2007: 15). Through its growing mediation, the city becomes even more fertile ground for the making of claims. Urban dwellers meet in the street and organize through digital networks (Cammaerts 2012). At the same time, they attract media attention to their actions and put their own representations of events 'out there' in alternative media, personal media and social networks.

Sassen (2002) argues that, within global modernity, urban politics has turned away from claims to property and towards claims to presence, with urban visibility providing the powerless with opportunities for presence, for making claims and for confronting the powerful. Agency is central to the realization of 'presence' and to claim making in the city (ibid.), especially when certain groups can only route their claims to cultural presence (identity) and political presence (citizenship) through the city. Sassen's analysis has a similar starting point to Phillips's influential thesis concerning the politics of presence, even though the two approaches have developed in parallel rather than by merging intellectual traditions. Phillips (1997) argues that, within modernity, mainstream politics has been overwhelmingly defined as the politics of ideas. Politics of ideas are 'blind' to difference, but as a consequence they reproduce the hegemony of the established political elite. Politics of ideas marginalize the significance of histories of exclusion and of the marginalization of ethnic and gender minorities in public political debates, and as a consequence they ignore and even reproduce such inequalities (ibid.). The marginalization of minorities in political life is an issue of concern to both scholars, although they adopt different analytical approaches to this realization. For Phillips, it is within parliamentary politics that inequalities need to be addressed. 'If political presence matters, it is because existing structures of power and representation have denied the pertinence of excluded perspectives and concerns,' she argues (1997: 182). 'Relatively autonomous voluntary groups', such as social movements, she continues, do not tackle the core of the problem. Political equality can be achieved 'in contexts which bring the differences together', and this is mainstream electoral politics (ibid.: 182). More than a decade after her influential thesis, concerns about the limited political representation and presence in mainstream politics of minorities remain as pertinent as ever. Synergies between political elites and the media are still powerful, if not more powerful than ever. As a consequence, groups that are marginal and oppositional to the status quo remain on the fringe or outside the mainstream political stage. It is in the light of the ongoing exclusion of minorities from mainstream politics and of the growing relevance of new political movements in setting alternative political agendas that the bridging of agency, non-representational politics and urban presence becomes important. The growing numbers of disadvantaged and marginal groups assume a distinctive presence when they take over the streets. The disadvantaged in global cities can gain 'presence' in their engagement with power, but also vis-à-vis one another:

> There is something to be captured here – a distinction between powerlessness and the condition of being an actor even though lacking power. I use the term presence to name this condition. In the context of a strategic space such as the global city, the types of disadvantaged people described here are not simply marginal; they acquire presence in a broader political process that escapes the boundaries of the formal polity. This presence signals the possibility of a politics. What this politics will be will depend on the specific projects and practices of various communities.(Sassen 2005: 91)

The politics of presence can become the strategic response of marginalized groups to the opportunities created in the city and a tool with which to access the symbolic power over-concentrated in the global city. In this discussion, presence is revisited for its potential to bring dispersed ideological positions together into common humanistic – or consumerist – values as well as for its inevitability as an outcome of inequality. In the intensely oppositional and unequal terrain of the city, presence becomes the main form of symbolic capital available to marginalized groups. Thus, there is an element of inevitability in the politics of presence, especially for socially rather than politically marginalized groups that enter the public domain without clear political goals. The combined physical and mediated visuality enables confrontation with established centres of power for a number of reasons. The global city holds sustained symbolic power. As marginalized groups enter the streets of the global city, they benefit from its concentrated and globally recognized symbolic power; as they become visible in the territory of the city, they also become visible across televisual and other mediated networks that continually connect the global city to trans-urban networks and to other centres of power. It is no coincidence that Occupy and the London riots became global news within hours of their emergence. While not on the same scale, other cities, especially capital cities, became sites of rebellion in the midst of the global recession. The cases of Madrid's Los Indignados[2] and Athens' rioters of 2008 and 2011–12 provided comparable and powerful material of local struggles linking to transnational mediated networks of protests and global audiences.

As presence spills into the urban street and the global digital highways, what takes place outside Parliament, Senate and other organized systems of political claim making matters. Lacking any other symbolic power, marginalized groups maximize their presence through the media. The media make political minorities and socially excluded groups momentarily visible, even heard. When no mainstream political platform is available to these groups, it is the media, effectively or ineffectively, that become an available platform of globalizing force. In media culture, presence – especially in its visuality – can itself become the message.

Hyper-visibility: seen, but also heard?

Two memorable pictures from the early hours of 28 February 2012, when police and bailiffs evicted the Occupy London protesters from St Paul's Cathedral, reached out to urban and global imagination in the different media. The first was that of a suited protester meditating as bailiffs dismantled his tent. The second picture was of a man standing silently with his laptop open, on the screen the message 'GET ORF MY LAND!' (*sic*). This was a digital response to the very old reality of urban conflict: the moment of the protester's resistance to the police. Now the protesters had a new tool through which to share their message. Did this new tool make a difference? The pictures went viral and circulated across global networks, as did protesters' mobile-phone pictures from Occupy Wall Street, Occupy Oakland and Occupy Tokyo. The images circulated across the world offered recognizable representations of protest alongside images of new forms of mediated action, familiar to global audiences. Protesters were doing what many of their audience did at home: using computers, phones, social networks. But they were out there doing it as a political act, as resistance.

Presence is a troubled reality of city life. The city is a place of surveillance and control, as well as a space of expression and liberation (Isin 2002). The growing presence of marginalized groups is partly a result of the saturation of cityscapes with cameras. The ever-present camera reaffirms, and sometimes even invents, what an urban street is for and what it represents. Being on camera – surveillance camera, television camera, mobile phone or iPad camera, to name but a few – has become a way of being an urban subject, an urban navigator who can do things while (inevitably) being watched. The culture of surveillance has become a regular constituent of city life and a practice that feeds into the logic of securitization and of a 'controlled' urban environment. CCTV is always there and is often used not only by the authorities but also by the mainstream media. The synergies between the media, the state and corporate surveillance are complex. When a crime is recorded on surveillance cameras, it can become powerful material reproduced in the media, as often happens in many television programmes on crime and policing. But the synergies become so complex that often it is not clear whether surveillance is initiated by the state and the media benefit from it, or the other way around. In the aftermath of the 2011 urban riots in British cities, the tabloid press reproduced photos of suspected rioters on their front pages, under titles such as 'The Most Wanted' (*Daily Mirror* 2011). Readers were invited to report anybody they recognized as a rioter. Protesters and rioters know that the cameras are there and they know they cannot avoid them. The 'hoodie' has become an icon of the urban street, at least in part as a response to the constant surveillance of street life since it can offer some visual protection from the cameras.

It is in big cities especially that surveillance has grown in response to increased securitization. Washington DC has used a network of traffic cameras to feed back information to a central police network (Associated Press 2003), while Chicago Mayor Richard M. Daley made a promise to have a surveillance camera on every street corner in his city's bid to host the 2016 Olympics (Britt 2009). In a 2006 CBS report on how Chicago's authorities 'keep an eye on the city' by expanding the systems of surveillance, reporter Daniel Schorn starts by pointing out: 'If we have learned anything in the last five years, it is this: one man's symbol of prosperity could be another man's target.' In arguments reflecting post-9/11 ideologies concerning *others* as a threat to western prosperity and the western 'way of life' (Schorn 2006), surveillance is referred to as a necessary tool for protecting the imagined *we* from a proximate *other*.

Surveillance cameras are as visible as the potential criminals recorded on them. The cameras do not need to be hidden. On the contrary, they need to be seen. The visibility of surveillance in the city, often celebrated by city authorities and the media, has helped to legitimate widespread personal communication surveillance. Cameras at the gates of privileged communities survey not only private property but also public spaces in the name of private interests, serving both economic interests and individuals' concerns for their own safety. State and media surveillance often merge, as demonstrated by the media campaigns to identify rioters caught on camera.

The state and the mainstream media make constant use of surveillance cameras, but not everyone can do this in the same way. Asymmetry of surveillance capacity reflects the asymmetries of power in the city. While we are never sure who is watching us, customers and visitors are usually banned from taking photos (Borden 2000b). It is not only the state that claims the exclusive privilege of surveillance but, increasingly, also corporations and the media. This asymmetry is also class-based. In 2010, the newly elected UK Conservative–Liberal coalition government, whose member parties had before the election emphasized in their manifestos the need to protect privacy, declared that it would use credit agencies to catch those involved in social benefits fraud. The celebration, on the one hand, of privacy and the incorporation, on the other, of a sophisticated system of surveillance of the urban poor merge in a paradoxical and selective application of privacy. This paradox was also observed when the political elites in many countries of the global North celebrated social media for their role in the 'Arab Spring', only to condemn the same social media a few months later for their role in the protests and riots that hit their own capital cities.

The omnipresence of cameras on the urban street represents a key element in the intensification of the city's mediation. As many debates and actions associated with urban riots and protests took place on media platforms, the media emerged as much more than mere tools for communication. They became protagonists in a politics that depends extensively on the media as platform, as managers of the discourse of protest and as technologies that record, testify and frame conflict through powerful images and narratives. The riots and the Occupy movement demonstrate some of the ways in which media representations of urban cultures as *other* to the nation and to hegemonic ideologies of social order both reinforce the pathologization of certain social and political groups and strengthen the presence of those groups. The narrative of difference thus becomes ubiquitous. The media play a key role in these processes, especially as they diversify their platforms, their reach and, most importantly, their role as technologies – being as much about the representation of *others*, as they are about the representation of the self. During the riots and the Occupy protests, participants became actors in media events. This happened when they could not escape the television cameras and surveillance cameras but also when they took the production of media narratives and images into their own hands, destabilizing the hegemonic balance of representational asymmetries. In personal and social media, by presenting themselves to cameras and television audiences, these actors were present on the street and in the media, performing simultaneously on a local and a global, mediated stage.

New politics in the city? Visible and virtual occupations

Occupy achieved great visibility and attracted sympathy across the spectrum of mainstream media, while reflecting the merging of urban protest and global movements (Cammaerts 2012). Through coordinated actions in cities across the world, Occupy showcased the effectiveness of mediation in organizing action and its global interconnectedness. At the same time, through the emphasis the movement placed on occupying physical spaces within financial centres, it confirmed the specificities of cities as centres of command and the symbolic value of occupying physical spaces. Cities not only hosted these movements, they also brought them to light. The heterogeneity of the participants reflected the sociocultural composition of the city and the ways in which cities can bring together difference in unforeseen constellations (Benjamin 1997 [1925]). Sassen calls these demonstrations, alongside the 'Arab Spring' and the urban protests in Chinese cities, the Global Street:

> In each of these cases, I would argue that the street, the urban street, as public space is to be differentiated from the classic European notion of more ritualized spaces of public activity, with the piazza and the boulevard the emblematic European instances. I think of the space of 'the street', which of course includes squares and any available open space, as a rawer and less ritualized space. The Street is a space where new forms of the social and the political can be *made*, rather than a space for enacting ritualized routines. (Sassen 2011: 2)

The openness of the global street leaves space for the diversity of voices within and for the circulation of shared ideas across space – the exposure to internal and global diversity becomes inescapable, forcing its actors to look at one another as elements in their own story of the city and of political action. The revival of the concept of social justice and anti-capitalist resistance in public political discourse reflects the advance of a political language that has emerged outside the dominant political centres of power but which spreads across multiple global streets, the digital and urban agora. The transnationality of such urban movements also demonstrates the difficulty of separating the urban from the global. But it also demonstrates that media technologies have become mechanisms that produce images and narratives: a movement's brand, its people, its urbanity and globality become visible largely through a system of media that starts with internal and local communication and expands to global media, both alternative and mainstream. These representations provide and feed into a strong symbolic system of the continuity and relevance of a movement across time and space.

The apparatus of representational power of new movements such as Occupy constantly feeds back into physical places of being and of being seen. Occupy has developed a series of platforms for enabling physical and virtual presence. 'An open space for global conversation: Occupy *Café*' (www.occupycafe.org) is only one of the fora where urban and trans-urban conversations between the movement's participants and supporters take place. As many of the urban occupations – with the two main camps in London and New York being the most influential – were evicted and dismantled, the virtual presence of the movement supported, and sometimes replaced, that interrupted and fragmented physical presence. The Occupy our Homes actions started simultaneously on the 6 December 2011 in 25 American cities (Gould-Wartofsky 2011). Global Teach-Ins, such as the one that took place online and in physical locations across 20 cities on 25 April 2012, represent both the movement's action and its sustained presence in and across spaces. And while it is the committed activists who are usually present in the physical place of action, supporters, voyeurs and even global audiences are also virtually co-present.

OccupyLive (www.livestream.com/occupylsx), an online news service that looks and acts like most mainstream online media (though of course taking a particular viewpoint in its news coverage), represents one of the most visible efforts of the Occupy movement to reach out to a diverse and dispersed public. Following the tradition of media-making by social movements (best captured by Indymedia in the anti-globalization and anti-capitalist movements of the 1990s and early 2000s), OccupyLive provides a radical viewpoint on the news. However, it does so within an aesthetic framework that locates it closer to CNN's and BBC's websites than to earlier forms of political online media. This interplay of the particular and the universal, of the alternative and the mainstream, is reflected both in the visual imagery associated with Occupy and in the ideological interplay between the 'majoritarian' discourse of the movement – best captured in its branded 'We are the 99 percent' – and its minority radical and anti-establishment actions. This interplay does not represent a paradox associated with new political trans-urban movements. Rather, it captures the continuities between political discourses and social realities that have replaced the discourses of given binaries that were predominant before 2008. In Beck's (2006) words, this is where cosmopolitan competence can develop. Translation and bridge-building, according to Beck, take place when 'situating and relativizing one's own form of life within other horizons of possibility; . . . the capacity to see oneself from the perspective of cultural others and to give this practical effect in one's own experience of boundary transcending imagination' (ibid.: 89). Indeed, the exposure to the new possibilities and risks associated with globalization (Giddens 1991), and more particularly to the post-2008 risks and threats, has shaped spaces of political imagination in new ways. The narratives, imagery and action of Occupy reflect one response to new realities: as hundreds of thousands of middle-class Americans found themselves below the poverty line and as

Europe has faced the threat of a previously unimaginable economic melt-down, the '99 percent' became a very diverse and shifting group, not clearly defined around the old *us* and *others*.

Uneasiness in producing clear narratives about the state of socio-economic realities has been seen not only in Occupy's delicate interplay between the mainstream and the alternative, the particular and the universal. It has been vividly captured in the mainstream media's representation of Occupy and of the financial crisis. Importantly, in the media's attempt to make sense of confusing and uncertain realities, the global city has become a key element in an interpretative framework, perhaps because it brings the different players closer together in the most intense way in an uncertain political and economic future. At the end of 2011 and beginning of 2012, when it became evident that the financial crisis had not gone away as hoped, two of the most influential international magazines, *Time* and *The Economist*, found themselves in the position not only of trying to explain the crisis, but also of proposing powerful frames for the events unfolding around it. *Time* named 'the protester' as its 2011 Person of the Year. Prominent within this story in its end-of-year issue were the Occupy protesters.

The wide interest the movement attracted in the mainstream media relates to the kind of movement this has been. Kurt Andersen's (2011) long piece in *Time* includes three special columns inspired by the protest language and action surrounding him as he wrote the piece. One is titled 'How to Occupy a Square', another 'How to Tweet on a Crisis' and a third, focusing on the Occupy movement's street libraries, 'How to Stock a Protest Library'. In these stories, the protester ceases to be the traditional *other* of the mainstream media and becomes present and a participant in a dialogical relation with the reader. This is one of the moments when the possibility of influencing dominant spaces of political engagement through presence becomes a reality. The language of the story is not that of an observing public but of an engaged public – both the reader and the protester have a presence in their mediated exchange. This is how the author puts himself in the picture while writing about the beginning of the Occupy Wall Street movement:

> Until late September, 99% of New Yorkers had never heard of Zuccotti Park, a privately owned public plaza . . . It was through my Twitter feed that I started noticing that something was going on in my city. The following week-end, I watched the YouTube video of a New York police deputy inspector casually pepper-spraying some random female protesters. A few days later, my 24-year-old nephew, Daniel Thompson, emailed from his small town in western New York: he was coming down to occupy Wall Street, and could he stay with us in Brooklyn? (Andersen 2011: 61)

The story dedicated to the protests across the world in 2011 creates a narrative where Cairo protesters are spoken about alongside New York protesters and where social media are integrated into a discourse that moves outside the West and back in such a way that, as the author argues at least, the discourse of global communication is changed, at least momentarily. Andersen's proposal is not far from Beck's claim to dialogical imagination – that is to a growing awareness and reflexivity concerning clashes within one's cultural worlds and the coexistence of contradictory realities in the world one occupies (Beck 2006). The embracing of Occupy – like that of the 'Arab Spring' – by the mainstream media reflects, if nothing else, the particular imaginary of a shared humanity addressing the injustice that sparked these movements. These messages embraced universalizing values of social justice and redistribution of power. The widespread use of personal and social media had its part in the way in which these protests became popular protests: the protesters were everyone and anyone, their diverse identities reflecting those of the public, especially the urban public. In their press release following their eviction from the grounds of St Paul's Cathedral on 28 February 2012, the organizers of Occupy London Stock Exchange shared a message many members of the public could identify with:

> We would like to thank all those who got the word out on social and traditional media overnight ... We'll miss Occupy London Stock Exchange but not because of the tents. Or even the kitchen shelves: it was a makeshift, loosely cooperative, occasionally quarrelling and fiercely idealistic group of people who came together to achieve something extraordinary. The relationships forged during these strange and beautiful four and a half months still have much further to run. This is only the beginning. (Occupy London 2012)

The mark that the protesters made is a mark on the city as much as on popular imagination. Their 'goodbye for now' statement reveals agency as much as it reveals a political vision. The presence achieved through the life of the protest was one that, as the organizers said, was sustained in 'social and traditional media', in face-to-face relationships and in a shared global vision of justice.

While this message could easily be interpreted as a discourse that mainstream media could share, and even disseminate, not all mainstream media embraced Occupy. It was in the first issue of 2012 that *The Economist* fought back, with an oversized cover headline sending a clear message: 'Save the City: the threats to the world's most global financial centre' (*The Economist* 2012). The picture behind the headline showed typical employees of the financial sector under attack in a grim London portrayed as a war zone. The editorial reads:

> Attacks on bankers by protesters from Occupy Wall Street, Occupy London and Occupy any city where a financier might have the temerity to turn a quick buck have spiced up the dreary economic news of the past year. Yet hostility is not confined to the Left. Even the bankers' supposed allies are putting the boot in – and nowhere more so than in Britain. (*The Economist* 2012: 7)

The discourse behind this editorial in *The Economist* portrays the financial sector as a scapegoat in the current crisis. Occupy is turned again into an *other*, a threat to *our* prosperity and *our* capitalism. The piece alerts its readers to the dangers of London losing its financial leadership to the likes of New York and other global cities in Asia. It is obvious, especially if one compares this to *Time's* big story on 'the protester', that the public debate has become polarized and that the media have taken a leading role in setting the rules of the game. The story in *The Economist* is a celebration both of global capitalism and of the global city. In this story, the city is the City, i.e. London's financial district. While the narrative emphasizes the globality of financial markets, it is interesting to see that the desired end in this case is for the British state – the nation-state – to intervene to limit regulation. As discussed in chapter 2, synergies between national governments, global cities and the media have advanced the hegemony of the financial industries in the city. Positive and negative publicity for Occupy in the mainstream media has perhaps advanced the movement's presence in mediated domains, but the mainstream media have not brought about the movement's presence single-handedly.

Taking the media into their own hands is now an established practice for social movements. Occupy embraced media and communication technologies in sustained and diverse ways. The urban and trans-urban Occupy movements appropriated the media in ways that helped the movement not only to organize itself, but also to 'speak' a language that global audiences share. The audience that the movement reaches out to directly or indirectly through the mainstream media is no different from its own participants or from the small audience reached through alternative media. The participants in this movement no longer need to be in the occupied public square – they can be spread across the city, the country and the world.

Between revolt and media culture

Media culture and its artefacts – from urban music to mobile phones – have became powerful identifiers of riots and protests, both in the mainstream media and in participants' self-presentation of the events. Selective, misinformed and moralistic, the identification in mainstream media and mainstream politics of rioters with particular media and cultural practices played a key role in the way the riots were framed during the 2011 events in national media and beyond. To some extent at least, the rioters adopted these mediated identifications. They did so when they targeted shops selling electronic goods for looting, when they made strategic use of personal media to organize actions or to communicate among themselves and when, in the aftermath of the riots, some used music and film to respond to mainstream representations of the riots. In the case of Occupy, the merging of popular culture and revolt was expressed in numerous ways, many of which were no different from those observed in the representations of the riots. Protesters and rioters were repeatedly represented in the media as technologically savvy users of personal and social media. Occupy protesters and rioters sustained the representation of revolt as mediated in actual practices that range from organizing actions to bringing media technologies to the centre of street life.

Parading the latest laptop was almost taken for granted among the diverse and multi-class Occupy protesters. This was less the case with urban rioters who were identified throughout the event as 'the urban underclass'. The London riots, which expanded to cities across the country, started in Tottenham, north London, on 6 August 2011, after the killing of a local man, Mark Duggan, during a chase by the police. A demonstration against police brutality and lack of respect for Mark Duggan's family was the initial public reaction. This was a protest which looked like many similar demonstrations following the many deaths of black men in custody in the UK. Media interest was almost non-existent. When, within a few hours, northeast London was burning and numerous locations in cities across the UK ended up burning for four days, the events ceased to be on the periphery of the city and of the media world. They became a major media event, not only in terms of coverage but also in the way the media themselves became incorporated into the story.

One of the most prominent ways in which the media became part of the story concerned the narrative that developed around the rioters' use of communication technologies and the looting of commodities associated with media culture. Communication and consumer culture represent core elements of mainstream urban culture – and are celebrated as such, as shown in earlier discussions in this book of fashion, shopping and technology. But in this case they became demonized. For the first time, the British government spoke publicly about the possibility of censoring personal media, after claims that Blackberry phones and social media had played a key role in the organization of the riots. Even the managing director of

Blackberry, Stephen Bates, was summoned to the Commons to explain the use of Blackberry phones during the riots (BBC Online 2011). The chair of a Parliamentary Committee asked him if he took responsibility for the 'Blackberry gangsters" use of mobile phones produced by his company to organize violent actions during the riots. Bates's response was to emphasize that the Blackberry is usually a 'force for good' (ibid.). He assured Members of Parliament that during the riots Blackberrys had mostly been used for people to communicate with their loved ones and let them know they were safe. What made this war of words interesting was the taken-for-granted role of digital media in driving certain behaviours. Old popular and populist arguments about violence on television leading to violent behaviours have increasingly been replaced by similar arguments concerning digital media (Cohen 1972; Livingstone 2003).

While moral panics about the media are familiar and go back to the early days of mass communication, there is something important in the way these have been adapted to digital media. Social media are discussed in terms of their becoming dangerous 'in the wrong hands'. Assumptions about 'worthy' and 'unworthy' users are reminiscent of classist arguments and moral judgements about the 'undeserving poor'. Perhaps not by coincidence, the notion of a divide between users of media technologies became powerful at the same time as the concept of the undeserving poor made a comeback. The liberal commentator Will Hutton spoke in 2010 about 're-moralizing' the welfare debate, 'not around the universal principle, but around the principle of deservingness' (BBC Online 2010), while the Conservative-led government aggressively pushed a similar agenda for welfare state reforms. I argue here, however, that this divide between the deserving and undeserving poor, or the 'right' and 'wrong' kind of Blackberry user, or even the right and wrong kind of diversity, comes with an underlying assumption of agency. The rioters' agency is dismissed in the hegemonic discourses of a 'harmonious' society reflected in the words of many politicians and public commentators. Yet it is unavoidably recognized as a property of the 'underclass' or the 'undeserving', of the 'criminal classes' or 'feral classes', as numerous leading politicians described the rioters. The criminalization of the rioters and the pathologization of the classes and sections of the society they presumably came from did not produce the kind of visibility that marginalized social groups can benefit from. But if presence on the street, and consequently in the media, advances their visibility in the public domain, does this not – effectively or ineffectively, rightly or wrongly – constitute a politics of presence in a highly mediated urban world? Could presence on the burning streets in itself be an attempt to counterbalance the invisible marginality that many people live with day in and day out on the fringes of the global city?

The enormous anxiety caused by the rioters' looting of commodities associated with media and popular culture – certain brands and types of clothing, television sets and mobile phones – confirmed the centrality of this culture to many urban dwellers' lives. One of the most widely circulated images during the riots was that of a woman calmly trying on a pair of trainers in a shop that was being looted. This image, alongside other visual representations of rioters carrying clothes, televisions and computers out of looted shops, gave rise to a powerful discourse about the alienation of the urban 'underclass' – a word that made a dynamic comeback during the riots. Britain's prime minister, David Cameron, said at the time: 'There are pockets of our society that are not only broken, but frankly sick. It is a complete lack of responsibility in parts of our society, people allowed to feel that the world owes them something' (*The Telegraph* 2011). Many Conservative public commentators followed this line, with little deviation from its narrative by the Labour Party, explaining the looting of goods as a reaffirmation of the culture of dependence, where the urban poor 'just take' from 'society' (Hastings 2011).

The pathologies associated with the 'urban underclass' prominently appearing in mainstream media and political discourse almost became a project of reaffirming the position of the urban poor as the social *other*. The different reception that the urban working class received in the public domain compared with the Occupy protesters demonstrates the limitations of cosmopolitan competence as described by Beck. These become most visible when the social *other* is reaffirmed as distant – even when physically proximate – and when class is marked as the most persistently defining category for social ordering. The case of the riots and the looting and violence associated with them presents the challenge of the shifting spatialities of the city and the (self-)representational world. What if these 'pathologies' become the tools for claiming a presence? And what if the adaptation of consumerist and mediated practices associated with the mainstream become the only way to engage with that mainstream? Presence is something that the rioters achieved, if only momentarily, through visibility. For the rioters, presence was achieved when the state lost control of the streets and the 'urban underclass' realized its momentary power to set the rules on the street and in the media, at least through the visuality of its presence. The aftermath of the riots is where the possibilities (or rather the limited possibility and sometimes impossibility) of destabilizing the social divides lie. In this case, there was very limited evidence of any policy change. But perhaps some change has occurred since it has become obvious to the popular imagination that the boundary for claims to the city and its streets is never quite set.

Anonymous: individuality in a mask

While trainers and mobile phones became the markers of the rioters' 'pathological consumption' (Bauman 1998), another popular culture symbol was appropriated and reclaimed as a vivid symbol of resistance in the case of Occupy. 'Anonymous', the mask now widely recognized as a symbol of Occupy and of the Hactivist movements, demonstrates the merging of individuality, mediation and protest. The mask was originally supposed to represent Guy Fawkes in the novel *V for Vendetta* written in 1982 by Alan Moore in the midst of the anti-Thatcher riots of the 1980s (Moore 2012). The figure of Guy Fawkes appeared in the novel as a symbol of resistance to totalitarian and conservative regimes. In 2005, the comic novel was adapted for the big screen in a successful Hollywood production with the same name. It was at this point that the mask became widely popular and began to be seen occasionally on protests, before recently becoming a widely used and recognized symbol associated with new online and offline social movements.

In relation to the adoption of the mask by Occupy, the author of *V for Vendetta*, Alan Moore, argues: 'It also seems that our character's charismatic grin has provided a ready-made identity for these highly motivated protesters, one embodying resonances of anarchy, romance, and theatre that are clearly well-suited to contemporary activism, from Madrid's Indignados to the Occupy Wall Street movement' (Moore 2012). The mask, which became known as 'the Anonymous', partly due to its representation of all protesters (or terrorists) in its fictional version, is as much about anonymity as it is about individuality. As Moore argues, it provides a sense of identity because it captures a number of symbols associated with current protest: from irony to anarchy and romance, as he argues, bringing agency and political action closer together. 'The Anonymous' is not faceless; the individual is represented in the mask of Guy Fawkes as sharing at least some of those elements of identity by his or her presence on the urban street. Part of this identity is the constant and complex interplay between individuals participating in a new movement and in media culture. This mask, which became popular through a Hollywood film and its appropriation of a historical political figure, reveals the familiarity that Occupy maintains with media culture. The cosy relationship of the movement with media culture is central to its rise and its existence. But it is the appropriation of this culture for the sustaining of presence that has made it politically significant. The similarity here with the riots is striking, yet usually unobserved. The appropriation of symbols and commodities associated with popular culture – trainers, television sets and mobile phones, and perhaps the 'Anonymous' mask – provided material for recognition, and partial interpretation, of a moment of conflict and of revolt in the city. It is through their use of certain commodities and communication technologies that rioters and protesters were partly 'made' in their representation of self and in the representation of them as the *others*.

New politics or old desperation?

The 2011 urban riots demonstrate the complexity of the politics of presence in the city. This is a politics that cannot be contained within systems of organized politics, and that can take the form of social unrest and destruction. The predominance of destruction and the lack of a clear political message is not the same as a lack of politics in the actions that came to be known as the urban riots. Not unlike Occupy, the riots demonstrated that parliamentary politics had become almost a distant observer of what was happening on the street and on the fringes of the city. Not unlike Occupy, the riots demonstrated that occupying public space, especially in unorthodox ways, attracts enormous attention. This kind of attention is not to be underestimated, especially when the groups primarily engaged in the riots have been largely invisible and unheard in mainstream politics for a long time. Unlike Occupy, though, the 2011 urban riots revealed a politics primarily expressed through acts of destruction and desperation, as did the violent riots of Athens in 2008 that followed mass protests at the killing of a 15-year-old boy by the police. The most marginal elements of the Athens protests-turned-riots, as much as of the London riots, demonstrated the limitations of the mere and momentary presence in the urban street when solidarity and political vision are absent. Unlike Occupy, the intentions of many of the Athens and London rioters were mixed and could in no way be identified as intentionally (or even effectively) political. Were these riots at all political? Was burning cars apolitical and looting mobile-phone shops a mere act of greed, as politicians and most media claimed at the time? Was there anything about these acts that related to recognition of the city's diversity and to claims to social justice?

As incidents of racism and social unrest have vividly shown in recent years (e.g. the Los Angeles riots, the Brixton riots, the Athens riots, the Paris riots), social segregation, racism and experiences of exclusion still stigmatize the life of many inhabitants of the city. Beyond the many differences between cities, inequality, poverty and segregation represent some of the biggest challenges for the urban world. The 2005 riots in the suburbs of Paris and of other French cities revealed in a violent manner the extent of a problem of geographical segregation, with disenchanted and disillusioned youth and a sense of political marginalization among many French Muslims. When a rioter was asked by a documentary-maker if he knew who the burned car that he was climbing on belonged to, the rioter replied, laughing: 'To Mr Everyone . . . It could be yours . . . I don't care' (Exandas 2005). The chilling discourse of indifference towards 'everyone' was followed by the same rioter saying: 'It was a message of despair . . . the only way to be heard.' The struggle for a presence, achieved only when marginalized urban dwellers become actors in a media event, is critical here. In front of a burning car, another rioter says:

> France has two faces. The one they show you, with the chic quarters, the Champs Elysées, the Eiffel Tower and the nice monuments. This is not France. France is what you see behind me. It's the tough suburbs, the misery. Two months ago you thought France was like that. You thought everything's fine. This is not France. You have no idea. (Exandas 2005)

Awareness of the asymmetries, not only in the distribution of wealth but also in the unevenness of the symbolic power that reproduces the representation of different social groups as 'unworthy' or as non-existent, can sustain both alienation and resistance to it. In the aftermath of the London riots of 2011, many opinions similar to those of the two young French rioters were recorded. Professor Green, a grime musician who grew up on an estate close to the areas where the London riots started, gave a very similar interpretation of the London events:

> People come to central London and think 'Oh, this is a lovely place', and the world can see that now. Robbery. Arson. Theft. Murder: it's been going on for years, but the government's been looking the other way. I see the riots and looting as young people thinking 'we've got an opportunity to answer back to the government', even though it's the wrong way to do it – because it's not harming them, it's harming innocent people. But I think they're just frustrated, trying to be heard. (In Hancox 2011)

A number of convicted rioters interviewed for an LSE and *Guardian* research project, *Reading the Riots,* in the aftermath of the 2011 riots spoke of their very different intentions. While these intentions varied greatly, two main reasons were given by many of the interviewees: taking 'revenge' for police brutality and expressing their sense of disengagement from the mainstream of society, which ignores or stereotypes them. In Professor Green's words, as with many rioters interviewed for the *Reading the Riots* project, the lack of visibility and recognition that accompanies marginalized communities in the city represents a painful reality with real consequences for their lives. A brief and violent explosion in the midst of heightened alienation associated with class and race politics in Britain, the riots became an opportunistic moment for people like the interviewee quoted below to respond to the institutionalized violence of the state apparatus:

> I was angry. Obviously I've been stopped a lot of times. I moved to London because I was getting stopped two or three days, two or three times a week. I moved to Brixton because I knew it was all full of black kids and they'd be getting stopped before me. I moved to Brixton and I enjoyed my life. I didn't get stopped once. I moved back to Liverpool and I get stopped, like, within the first week. (Carter 2011)

While the Occupy movement was a direct response to the recent crisis of capitalism, the links between the riots and the current economic crisis were not named so clearly by the rioters or the media. It is important to locate the current crisis and the moment of the riots within the broader context of urban and global inequalities. A Fiscal Policy Institute report on the recent recession's effect on New York City and its diverse inhabitants noted that the city's population experienced the highest unemployment on record in 2009 (Fiscal Policy Institute 2009a). The recession, notes the report, is characterized by disparities of effect along lines of race, ethnicity and neighbourhood. The same report (2009) notes black unemployment was above 15 per cent, with the black male population suffering the most, and reached 46 per cent in West Brooklyn. A story about the changing demographics of Harlem in *The Observer* quotes a jobless black financial adviser who was laid off during the recession and now plays his saxophone for cash in the street. He is quoted as applauding the fact that non-blacks are moving to his neighbourhood: 'If a new class of people is coming in, then I think the cultural life here will pick up. They can bring something to Harlem' (Harris 2010). At the same time, other locals expressed their fear of gentrification of their neighbourhood, which would marginalize the original inhabitants (ibid.). Stories of the same city are recorded in another Fiscal Policy Institute report, *A Tale of Two Recessions* (2009b). One story is about the financial recovery celebrated in sleek skyscrapers while the other is about an ongoing struggle in neighbourhoods of the city away from the centres of power and from the major media stories. Yet the second story is there, even if not on the first page. Even when it receives much less attention than the major headlines about number-crunching and decision making on the top floors of skyscrapers, it is a reflection of what happens many levels down.

Possibilities of a politics of difference

The line between politics and desperation is blurred in the case of the riots and, while it might be clearer in the case of Occupy, the grand shared narrative associated with older forms of political action is missing from that movement as well.

Rights, Iris Marion Young argues, are refined in opposition to the five faces of oppression (1990). The five faces referred to are: the marginalization of groups as a result of their identities; the lack of resources for participation in political life; the exploitation of labour at work and at home; cultural imperialism within and across societies; and violence at home and in society at large. She links this discussion to urban social movements, which is partly what the present discussion is about. While claims that the riots represented a social movement are inaccurate, if not totally confusing, the practices, performativity and presence that the riots, as much as the social movement of Occupy, represent reveal the faces of oppression observed in urban spaces. In part, the riots, as much as new social movements such as Occupy, represent a response to oppression, expanding across cities, across a nation and across the globe. The response, the claims to the right to respond, the struggles to establish recognizable rights are less clear in the two cases. Occupy highlights the shift of balance in the political discourse of protest, which redirects its attention from addressing particularistic progressive publics towards 'talking with' wider and diverse audiences that become attracted to the movement's humanistic and universalistic sets of values and ideas, such as social justice.

The riots became a less subtle reminder of the conflictual element in the close proximity of difference in the city. When leafy parts of London like Ealing and Dulwich felt the threatening presence of the rioters and looters, middle-class residents were terrified by the aggression of their neighbours. The riots that hit these parts of the city revealed the class warfare between the 'have-nots' and the 'haves' (who have more than the former, at least), living in close proximity, reaffirming the parallel described by Peter Hall (1999) between the polarization of rich and poor in the contemporary city and the Victorian divides recorded by Engels in Victorian England.

Harvey (2009) makes a call for understanding the broader terrain of 'conditions of possibility'. These conditions of possibility are what we observe in the cases of revolt discussed above – as the meanings of city space shift in times of crisis and as the mediated city space becomes a space for reflection and demand for change. Both the riots and Occupy show, in different ways, how moments of crisis come with anxieties (Giddens 1991), but are also moments of opportunity for political protest, as well as for reflexivity. The language of social justice, the images of injustice, the experiences of police brutality and the cynicism of the state towards the poor are most vivid and visible in the city – and, more and more, in the representations of the city.

Citizenship has always constituted itself through alterity, as citizens have defined themselves through non-citizens, those lacking rights, Isin argues (2002). The urban street is where exposure to difference and of those who have, or do not have, rights, has always taken place. With the advance of media and communication technologies, the momentary exposure to difference on the street has acquired some continuity and a frame for interpretation. As media diversify, so do frames; as protesters make their own media, the exposure to *other*-ness is not just mediated, but mediated as a production of the self, as self-presence. This is one of the most significant ways in which agency makes an advance in political life – as protesters and rioters are not only spoken about, but speak, and as they have a presence in the public arena. The mediated representations of city protests become a mirror image and a disturbed image of the protest, which the protesters see into and see through. The protest and the riot can become narcissistic, as the protesters see themselves on screen. They become communitarian, as comradeship develops not only with the person in physical proximity, but also with the audience-cum-participants beyond the locality who embrace the image of the protest (or who protest against the image of the protest when there is a sense of obstruction of its 'reality').

Strategically, or inevitably, as a result of media's ubiquity, a politics of presence in the city is enabled and enacted on the mediated local and global stage. Facebook or Blackberry messaging become constitutive elements of a social world which is increasingly mediated. This is an ecology associated with a sustained interaction of technologies and humans, of humans with other humans, with the exposure and production of vast numbers of messages that inform social action and ideology. The logic of mediation involves not only the act of engagement with technologies, either to make 'friends' or to protest in the street. It also relates to systems of filtering information, images and relationships. It involves the organization of systems of knowledge (Livingstone 2008) and of understandings of the world. It involves some of the most significant systems of organizing information for societies in the western world. Most of our knowledge of the world, both in proximity and at a distance, is filtered by information we receive through the media and managed through systems of communication and discourse that we share with our friends, peers and co-protesters in mediated environments. When Blackberry momentarily became the protagonist of the urban riots, this was a result of the ability of personal media to maintain an autonomous space of communication that supported action on the street. When the

Occupy movement's catchphrase, 'We are the 99 per cent', was repeated in the media, the global circulation of a movement's 'brand' was reaffirmed and legitimated.

As the global city becomes a stage where globally important questions – about inequality, poverty, access to commodities, information and decision making – are addressed, the visibility offered by the physical space of the city is no longer enough. The urban street is revived and extended to the global mediated street. It is in the continuity of the physical and mediated urban street that presence, as a strategy, as a tactic and as the inevitable politics of the *other* in the city, makes sense. The politics of presence depends on the merging of the grounded physicality of protest and conflict as much as on the sustainability of protest through its mediated representations. Increasingly, political movements, protesters and rioters use presence and visibility as their message, not just as their tool. Presence becomes part of the message, as the Occupy movements have demonstrated in the actual occupation of locations associated with global financial command. Yet it is not in the mere physicality of conflict and protest that this politics takes place. A movement, a protester, a rioter acts on the street, but the dissemination of the message takes place through the media. For groups that have no access to and receive no attention from dominant systems of representation (such as the urban poor) or for others who feel they represent 'silent majorities', as implied by the Occupy movement's 'We are the 99 per cent' message, visibility becomes an achievement in itself. The heterogeneity of both groups – the Occupy protesters and the rioters – demonstrates that there is only one message that is clear: that of visibility, of presence. The fact that most Occupy protesters were not actually sleeping in the tent camps demonstrates vividly the exact point of a politics of presence: the tents were not put up to accommodate protesters. Less than meeting practical needs, they symbolized continuity, perseverance and the commitment to constructing a city of protest (and an imagined city of protest and fairness) against a city of greed (and its sleek yet exclusive architecture). The powerful message of the tent city reached out to passers-by, as well as to the global audience. 'The movement is the message,' said one of the protesters' banners. The playful adaptation of 'the medium is the message' in itself reflects the powerful adoption of a media logic. The media logic becomes more than a tool; it is also part of the revolt itself, which spills into its imagination of and possibilities for a politics in urban and virtual global streets.

In different ways, both moments of revolt represent the uneven realities of the cosmopolitanization of action, ranging from globally oriented solidarity to the cry and turmoil associated with the internal cosmopolitanization of the city. From the beginning, Occupy projected its humanistic trajectories of justice and equality and linked its vision to other protests, expanding from New York to Cairo. For this movement, the cosmopolitan vision of a liberatory politics is clearly tied to the fate and action of other people living with the consequences of global capitalism. It is thus no surprise that Occupy has found no difficulty in attracting celebratory academic analyses of the humanistic and global orientation of new progressive politics (Castells 2012; Chomsky 2012; Gitlin 2012; Harvey 2013). The 2011 urban rioters, like the French rioters of the banlieue in 2005 and the migrant rioters of 2008 in Athens, on the other hand and ironically, have been treated as the underclass of urban revolt, not only in the dominant political discourse but also in the dominant academic discourse. The riots, no doubt, lacked the visionary and global intentionality of Occupy. Looting doomed them to be characterized as emerging out of the alienation of the urban working class. Even for the most radical commentators, the riots reproduced the lack of morality and the practice of capitalist greed that surrounds the urban working class (Harvey 2013). But there are two elements of the events that have gone largely unnoticed in these approaches. The political and media elite expressed enormous anxiety about the ethnic formation and the incorporation of popular culture and the media in the riots. The participation of the white working class in the riots, considered in the past as ethnic minority territory, was most vividly captured in the anxiety of David Starkey, the popular historian about 'whites turning black'. The redefinition of the riot beyond the 'colour line' presented the possibility of an internal cosmopolitanization, of a redefinition of the riot itself in the public imagination. In their heterogeneous ethnic composition, the rioters challenged the dominant order of revolt and destabilized the question of *who* has a right to the city and *how* – not intentionally perhaps, but in the way that for many the city is lived through despair. At the same time, the ways in which popular culture became part of a narrative of the rioters' pathology – with everything from rap to mobile phones at the core of debates – demonstrated vividly how fragile is the celebration of the cultural life of marginalized groups. The anxieties of the political and media elite around popular culture, communication technologies and the destabilization of racial order in the rioted city reveal the anxieties that the underbelly of the cosmopolitan city presents to the dominant class. Momentarily, the mobile phone 'un-surveilled' communication; the riot, even the looting, became a response from the margins to invisibility in a city that 'has been killed by rampant capitalist development' (Harvey 2013: xv). These unsettling realities, which are most limited in their cosmopolitan trajectories, but most vivid in their urban cosmopolitan roots, reveal the conflictual realities of cosmopolitanization and the ways in which these are resisted by the dominant political and media class. In chapter 4, I discussed the widespread celebration of certain forms of graffiti and music as evidence of the ways in which such encounters present cosmopolitan moments of communication across difference. The case of the riots presents another, less open-ended, reality associated with cosmopolitanization: the struggle around the recognition of the right of marginal groups to the city, especially when they have no systematic language for naming their claims. Different marginal groups may come together in difference. They may demonstrate in their action their openness to difference. But their difference, their many and dialogical differences, are constructed negatively in the dominant discourses of urban societies; yet again, the 'urban underclass' is an *other* to the difference that can be incorporated into the dominant narrative of the contemporary city, one that leaves some space for the world-oriented Occupy. As will be discussed in the concluding chapter, the realities of cosmopolitanization may run across the global city but they do not automatically turn into cosmopolitan possibilities. At least not for all.

7   Epilogue: Cosmopolitan Contradictions

In the heart of the city lie possibilities for identity, community and action, for reflexive engagement with others, but also for the commodification of difference and its selective celebration. The discussion that has unfolded in the pages of this book has explored these possibilities as they emerge through the multi-layered synergies of media and the city. This synergetic relation reveals different and conflicting cosmopolitan practices and visions. It exposes the ways in which the media are used to navigate the city and make sense of it as a place to live, consume and protest. It also explains how media and the city sustain and expand their symbolic power, precisely by maximizing the symbolic and monetary value of creativity, excitement, unpredictability, to name but a few of the qualities of urban difference.

Cosmopolitanization can be observed in every quarter of the city and reveals both its bottom-up and its top-down articulations: in the way in which people of different origins live cheek by jowl; in the ways in which the global city constructs its brand around its histories of cultural diversity; in the integration of different cultural traditions in music, performance and film. While cosmopolitanization as a process is singular, cosmopolitanism's meanings are plural and divergent. In the city, we can observe at least three different and conflicting cosmopolitan visions which are also reflected in particular sets of practices. As discussed in this book, these include neoliberal cosmopolitanism, vernacular cosmopolitanism and liberatory cosmopolitanism. They all have the same starting point: all recognize the value of difference, cultural diversity, urban openness and the ways in which media and communication can maximize access to difference and its cultural products. However, the incorporation of these values by different cosmopolitanisms and their visions is in each case very different. Neoliberal cosmopolitanism in the global city is ubiquitous, hegemonic and normalized. It has been widely incorporated into governance and business strategies as a way of managing and benefiting from difference: by selectively accepting the diverse histories of urban dwellers and marginalizing their complexities and by commodifying difference and its ability to sustain the city's symbolic power and appeal to global audiences, consumers and capital. Vernacular cosmopolitanism is the response to neoliberal cosmopolitanism at street level – it has less of a clear vision and more of a practice and a set of orientations emerging out of practice. It reflects the different ways in which urban dwellers try to live with difference, and how their inevitable and usually not chosen encounters with many different *others* become a daily reminder of the diverse and divergent worldviews, practices and moralities that surround them. Unintentional but inescapable, these encounters often lead to reflexive sensibilities and a sense of responsibility towards both close and distant others. After all, the global city and its mediation represent the most ordinary way of experiencing globalization in all its intensity and immediacy. Liberatory cosmopolitanism shifts the balance from being primarily about experience to being about vision. Liberatory cosmopolitanism represents a progressive cosmopolitan politics (Harvey 2009) which starts from urban encounters, but which raises questions about the significance of difference in advancing equality, recognition and redistribution. Liberatory cosmopolitanism is rarely seen as practice. Perhaps it is the Occupy movement that in recent years has most vividly grounded this vision on action. Even if it rarely becomes action, as a vision it gives the study of cosmopolitanization more significance. In this context, the study of media and the city represents not just an empirical, and not only an analytical, but also a political challenge. Liberatory cosmopolitanism, proposed by Harvey (2009) and investigated in this study as something that becomes possible at the meeting of media and the city, challenges neoliberalism precisely by translating the experiential reflexivity of vernacular cosmopolitanism into political action and sustained vision.

The four interfaces of the media and city synergies – consumption, identity, community, action – at the heart of this book represent a conceptual and empirical proposition for exploring and understanding the different, often mundane, cosmopolitan practices and visions. Representing the locations of the most intense struggle around the symbolic, communicative and territorial control of the city, the four interfaces also reveal moments of resistance where vernacular, and sometimes liberatory, cosmopolitanism emerges as a response to and as opposition to the neoliberal project. The fragile and incomplete process of cosmopolitanization expressed in these four interfaces, I have argued, helps us to read the city and the cosmopolitanisms it gives rise to. The four interfaces represent significant moments of struggle for access to and control of symbolic resources and for negotiations between *we*-ness and *other*-ness, between conviviality and separation. They most vividly demonstrate that diversity is about struggles that take place in the context of neoliberal capitalism's aggressive grip on the global city. It is important to emphasize this because none of these struggles would take the specific forms they do were it not for the attempts of urban dwellers to make sense of their life in the city and of one another against the background of powerful forces that segregate the city according to values of profitability, securitization and individualistic aggression. These struggles would not take the specific forms they do were it not for the hegemony of neoliberal values reproduced in the media and city synergies. But they also would not take these specific forms if these same synergies did not unintentionally open up spaces for self-representation and for alternative sets of values to emerge and to be circulated and shared locally and globally. Thus, diversity is not just about contestation, as will be discussed below. Constant exposure to difference is about communication; it is about the possibilities presented to urban subjects of developing cosmopolitan skills of recognition, respect and commitment to democracy, inclusivity and mutual understanding; it is about the advance of a moral and political responsibility to defend one another's rights, especially in times and spaces of extreme social injustice.

This last chapter represents the epilogue to an exploration of the close and complex relationship between media and the city. This relationship is still work in progress; it remains open and unknown in its consequences. This last part of the book engages with some possible consequences, especially in terms of the politics that the media and city synergies can give rise to. Focusing on the different cosmopolitan orientations that emerge in the city, this chapter cannot be conclusive: the conclusion of this story cannot yet be written. This chapter is a point of reflection. It does not draw together relevant literature; a systematic attempt to do so has run through all previous chapters. Instead, this chapter reflects on the different articulations of cosmopolitan practice and vision observed in the four interfaces studied and then moves on to discuss the political implications and possibilities that these present.

Four interfaces, four sets of tensions

The four interfaces that are the focus of this book demonstrate a number of key elements that cut across urban realities when urban dwellers develop tactics for managing the challenges presented by difference in the city. But also presented in the context of each interface are distinct strategies for domination through the incorporation of cosmopolitanization and particular tactics of resistance to neoliberalism. What becomes evident in relation to each interface are the distinct ways in which cultural industries and government incorporate difference in their efforts to maximize their symbolic power. What also is revealed is the way in which urban dwellers, mostly through experience and occasionally in purposeful and political projects, not only reproduce but sometimes even challenge the neoliberal project.

Consumption reflects the most uneven of these domains of struggle. The aggressive advance of consumerism in the global city is revealed in every element of city life: in the ways in which advertising merges consumerist ideals and urban symbols; in the ways in which different elements of urban culture are incorporated into brands and commodities; in the ways in which the city is celebrated as a cosmopolitan playground for the enjoyment of global tourists and consumers. Driven by the values of neoliberalism, contemporary consumption is about domination but also about an interesting tension: through consumption, more than any of the other interfaces, the cosmopolitan discourse becomes celebrated, ever-present and incorporated from the top down and from the bottom up into practices and cultures. The advance of cosmopolitan discourses was observed in the different ways in which Shoreditch and Stratford in East London are made sense of as spaces through consumption. Cosmopolitanism thus becomes less of a 'niche' or elitist reference and rather is diffused through discourses produced by urban planners, corporations and sometimes by consumers themselves. The nuance of the cosmopolitan discourse meets the nuances of mediation: in the ever-presence of advertising, in the repeated celebration of difference, and in the actual act of consumption of different food, music, streets and cities, cosmopolitanism becomes ordinary. Because of their ubiquity and their taken-for-grantedness, neither cosmopolitan discourses nor the media are usually challenged – although there are always exceptional moments. Advertising imagery and the organization of practices of consumption in malls and on the urban street promote cosmopolitan openness and diversity, yet in very specific commodified, western-centric framings of cosmopolitanism. Consumption does not present a politics of resistance to neoliberalism. But it represents the uneven interface where cosmopolitanism as discourse and cosmopolitanization as a process become appropriated. It is the field where capitalist organization allows space for exposure to difference. Unintentionally, this exposure becomes a confrontation with the realities of diversity – at least for some consumers, in some settings and at particular moments, especially in the city.

Consumption may be the interface where the hegemony of neoliberalism becomes most visible, but *identity* is an uneven domain in a different way. Cultural industries reach out to the creativity emerging on the margins of urban societies in order to expand their profit and their symbolic power. But creativity from the margins is grounded in experience, history and everyday struggles for access to symbolic and material resources, i.e. in the processes that make creativity a project of identity. While neoliberal cosmopolitanism is at work here, selectively celebrating difference for profit, the vernacular cosmopolitanism of the migrant and socially deprived city is experiential, inevitable and has no clear orientation: it is the way in which the city is lived, as the discussion on music and graffiti in chapter 4 demonstrated. Thus, while the interface of identity is not usually one of political struggle, it is certainly a domain of struggle and occasionally of resistance. Projects of self-representation made possible in the domain of popular culture are projects that act against the invisibility of the social and cultural *other*. Visual and aural representations of identities excluded from the mainstream political systems of recognition reflect attempts from the margin at cultural representation – sometimes the only kind of representation that certain groups are allowed to have within (neo)liberal western democracy.

Identity is an individual project, even if it is always located in social contexts. In the interface of *community*, we can observe much more intensively some of the tensions discussed in relation to identity. This is the case precisely because the opposition forces involve groups from both sides: cultural industries and policy makers on the one side and communities – both new and established – on the other. Importantly, these oppositions are not set: community is not by definition a site of resistance. Community can be a location where vernacular cosmopolitanism coexists with neoliberal cosmopolitanism and where the values of neoliberalism can be both incorporated and resisted. Most importantly, community needs to be investigated in the context of this discussion because it reflects the new and established social formations in the city that carry its histories and its present synergies with the media. Histories of migration make the city a place for living and a place of intense diversity. Long traditions of diasporic mobility have sustained the city as an open and transient space, a destination for hundreds of years. And media and communications have expanded the city's openness through networks that are sustained, multi-directional and ordinary and which affirm the city as a node in transnational cultural networks. As shown in chapter 5, there are different ways in which community makes the city: when people who share similar origins cluster in its territories; when people of different origins construct new communities in their urban locale; and, in recent times, when elite migrants use the global city as a node of their multi-nodal trans-urban communities. Always a site of many communities, the city represents a social space where we can investigate whether solidarity and hospitality are values reserved for members of one's own community or extend beyond communitarian boundaries. The contradictory and sometimes surprising answer to this question is offered by the examination of different cases, with new local communities reflecting most visibly cosmopolitan solidarities and elite migrants often reproducing selective transnational communitarianism.

The tensions associated with community show that assumptions about cosmopolitanism and parochialism as representing the two opposing poles for the future of urban societies are superficial. What is at stake is what kind of cosmopolitan vision will predominate – one that reproduces the privileges of elites by incorporating difference or one that respects difference and struggles for equality. The interface of *action* forces us to address these questions. The city has always been a site of political struggle, a site where claims are made. As a location of alterity, the city has also been a site where claim making has always been mediated by difference: class difference, cultural difference, and more recently difference as incorporated in the actual practice of political action and revolt. The political action and vision of the Occupy movement emphasizes solidarity in difference and for difference. Its political appeal has benefited from inclusionary representations of diversity. 'We are the 99 per cent' is a powerful brand. It is a recognition of difference and a recognition of commonality: humanity against capital, or the vision of liberatory cosmopolitanism against neoliberalism. But the city is not only a site of organized politics. Occupy might be the closest the western urban world has come to a liberatory cosmopolitan vision in recent years, but it is a rare moment of action in the city. Counterposed to this, I discussed the 2011 urban riots in London. A moment of revolt but without political intentionality, the riots capture the messiness of action in the city. Contradicting liberal, disciplinary and moralistic discourses that condemned the rioters and their media use, the riots represent a moment of making a claim to presence – in the city, on its streets, on the screens that make the city a global city. The vision was missing, but the anarchic convergence of cultural difference – although not of social difference – on rioting streets revealed both despair and desire. This desire was for presence, for recognition as human agents of an urban, mediated world, if nothing else.

Street agency

At the beginning of this book, questions were raised about the possibilities presented by cosmopolitanization for agency and for democratic and liberatory politics. What the four interfaces discussed have shown is that cosmopolitanization in not per se liberatory. To put it simply, cosmopolitanization should not be celebrated as a shift in consciousness and in political life. It is not. Yet it still carries some significance. Not as an end point but as a starting point, a process, a context for the development of skills of conviviality, cosmopolitanization challenges the limits of imagination through the intensification of mediated and physical encounters with difference. But cosmopolitan agency, politics and communities carry ideological burdens and do not themselves replace established structures and relations of power. Neoliberal, individualistic and thin articulations of cosmopolitanism represent a vision exported by global corporations, city governments and elite cosmopolitans. This cosmopolitanism either reaffirms existing boundaries or gives rise to new ones that advance inequality by capitalizing on cultural diversity, global flows of communication and interconnectivity. Indeed, previous forms of pathologization of difference have been challenged – the urban world does not allow unquestioned reproductions of the undesirable national *other* (although this does not mean that nationalist *othering* ceases to exist). Global consumerism and the circulation of cultural forms across boundaries makes the simple boundedness of *we*-ness and *other*-ness difficult. These already powerful actors increase their symbolic power through the opportunities provided by urbanization and mediation, especially the diversification of markers, creativity and mobility associated with cosmopolitanization. In this way, certain actors' economic and symbolic power increases as these new realities produce new and re-invented *others*. The social *other*, or the *other* who does not fit within the urban and global order of standardized consumerism and organized inequality, becomes a reflection of new and revisited discourses of inequality, for which cosmopolitanization allows space (and which it sometimes enables).

If cosmopolitanization only in exceptional cases becomes liberatory, representing new forms of solidarity and social justice, what – a critical reader might ask – is its significance? What the global city presents us with are the elusive, contradictory yet real expressions of cosmopolitanism. Literature on cosmopolitanism has spent a significant amount of space and time on persuading critical readers that there is a possibility of a cosmopolitanism *besides* the realities of sociocultural oppositions: between insularity and openness; nationalism and worldliness; inequality and freedom. Yet this defensive response to the 'other side' of openness, worldliness and freedom reflects the actual limitations of liberal theories of cosmopolitanism. Conceptual trajectories of cosmopolitan vision that set conditions for (or look for evidence of) overcoming these oppositions make cosmopolitanism either utopian or only possible for privileged elites. The tensions, conflicts and hard negotiations around the ownership and control of symbols and spaces in the city demonstrate the messiness, but social groundedness, of a cosmopolitanism that becomes embodied, enacted and produced through the very oppositions that challenge it as a possibility. Cultures of consumption, urban creativity, revolt and the projects of identity and community discussed here show that cosmopolitanism becomes a reality not beyond but precisely through the processes and symbolic forms that guide urban life.

This insight was enabled by the empirical focus of this book. Through it, I have aimed to understand when urban-mediated life links back to moments of self-reflexivity, of resistance to inequality and to the diversification of discourses of citizenship that include urbanity, transnationalism and identity. I approached these moments of possibility primarily from street level, by exploring the ways in which urban dwellers, visitors and audiences engage with elite cosmopolitan discourses of global consumerism, global culture and city branding, but also the ways in which they construct and negotiate alternative and vernacular cosmopolitan discourses and practices. By looking from the bottom up, through the experiences of the lower layers of the urban hierarchies, and horizontally, through the practices of urban dwellers, we can observe not only different cosmopolitan visions, but also the ways in which these merge: these visions become yet another point of encounter in the city. Neoliberalism sustains a good grip on the city and the media, as its symbolic power is reproduced, day in, day out, in the advance of consumerism; in the commodification of the city as a tourist and consumer destination for those who can afford it and for the many who aspire to afford it; in the symbolic legitimation of social divides; and in the celebration of the market in media representations and urban governance policies. But in the city's neighbourhoods, neoliberalism is also constantly challenged. The advance of surveillance systems and policing across the city is faced with moments of revolt and rebellion that demonstrate neoliberalism's fragility. More than in these moments, it is in the ordinariness of everyday city life that its grip becomes most fragile and conditional. While ideological hegemony is regularly reproduced in media representations and the organization of urban economic and political life, urban dwellers develop tactics for managing intensive juxtapositions in the media and in their city of difference, social inequalities and marginalization of the self and of proximate and distant others.

Cosmopolitan skills

Moving about on the streets of East London, listening to urban music and its contradictory representations of inequality, becoming a protester or a rioter, or finding oneself in intensive proximity to protesters and rioters turn everyday life into a political terrain. Seeing a stranger who is not hostile or threatening and speaking with others who may have different origins, but not necessarily a different destination, from oneself are ordinary acts of urban life. The possibility, then, of widening the limits of perception and action in order to recognize, respect and defend particular and diverse trajectories is real. Cosmopolitanism becomes relevant precisely because people who regularly experience close encounters with difference develop skills of recognizing, respecting and defending such trajectories. Cosmopolitan skills rely on the capacity to make sense of diversity, to talk across difference, to participate in the public life of culturally diverse societies, which is what the people described in this book do every day. For most people living in global cities, these are ordinary capacities of everyday citizenship. But they cannot be taken for granted; they need to be developed. These skills used to be associated primarily with migration; migrants have long been developing them because of their travels and constant exposure to others. The intensification of mediation and urbanization have today made it possible for many who do not necessarily themselves move, but who are surrounded by difference, to acquire these same skills.

Cosmopolitan skills start with awareness and recognition and occasionally expand all the way to developing action for the rights of the immediate members of new and old communities and those who may be culturally and spatially distant but are still fellows and co-citizens in shared urban societies. They make possible the diffusion of a politics that depends on commitment to values of respect, recognition and defence of difference across heterogeneous urban communities. The new, culturally diverse local communities discussed in chapter 5 reflect such moments of commitment to understanding and protecting the rights of those who have different cultural origins but a shared urbanity. The taking of action to protect these rights is usually grounded in the neighbourhood, and on occasion expands across urban and trans-urban spaces where questions about citizenship and democracy are directly addressed. The moments when the big questions of democracy, solidarity and conviviality are tackled head on are scarce, but they demonstrate the value and potential of cosmopolitan skills.

But we need not focus only on these skills when we explore liberatory cosmopolitanism. Throughout the book, I have avoided a focus on alternative and radical systems of representation that clearly oppose the hegemonic systems dominating mainstream national and transnational media. Instead, I chose to explore primarily the space around the media, the participation of different players from either privileged or marginal positions in media culture and the intentional and unintentional publics formed around and through mediated communication. These media practices include production, use and consumption that often merge local media, social networks and mainstream national and transnational media. If we accept that mediascapes converge and that the city is partly lived and partly made sense of within them, we need to understand what particular kinds of possibility for cosmopolitan politics they give rise to.

We need to track their links to long-standing and nuanced processes associated with intensive juxtapositions of difference. Mediated urban proximity expands the terrains of negotiation, both in terms of meanings and in terms of space. Close proximity to difference is no longer something only experienced by urban dwellers or by neighbours. It is experienced in mediated local, national and transnational spaces. This means that the stakes are higher and involve a wide range of participants. The spatial expansion of negotiations also affects their meanings. The negotiations that matter most are about the technologies that allow access to urban and global resources, and about the ability to support identity, community and equality in a diverse and interconnected world. These negotiations are neither formalized nor controlled, but most often they involve oppositional intentions as well as changing positionalities (Harvey 2009). The changing positionalities of individuals are most evident in the rearticulated spaces of the city as spaces for belonging, being and playing through encounters and through contact and communication with others – old others, new others and those just passing through.

While refusing the individual, free-floating quality of liberal cosmopolitanism, this book has developed a particular empirical focus. I have been more interested in parts of the city and in urban subjects that have not been associated with given and privileged cosmopolitan positions. Acts associated with the ordinariness of everyday life and with managing and contesting marginality in the city demonstrate the role of urbanity and mediation in challenging the limits of the self and of engagement with others and with social and political forms of solidarity and hospitality. It is indeed the current condition most urban subjects live in, where commodities, information and money are constantly in flux, that provides a constant reminder of current risks, uncertainties and insecurities. It is the growing awareness of difference close by and at a distance and the associated risks to immediate subjectivity and to the world that creates moments of resistance, engagement and even subversive appropriations of neoliberal discourses. The negotiations and conflicts observed at urban meeting points are more often than not mediated.

Justice

In studying urban cultures of consumption, communication, community and action, questions of recognition, redistribution and representation (Fraser 2008) have emerged as the most urgent. What I have tried to show is that highly cultural and, in the first instance, non-political practices, such as many communication practices, are actually used when people seek – deliberately or as a practice of everyday life – representation and access to valuable symbolic resources in the city and in the world. Recognition of and respect for difference and for the cultural sphere represent specific skills associated with the mediated urban world and present a starting point for addressing the challenges of unequal distribution of valuable (symbolic) resources, a point to take serious account of in politics and policies that oppose social injustice.

Unlike what often happens in our engagement with national media – where it is journalism and the clearly defined sphere of media and information that organize representation and knowledge – personal, social and mass media, in their convergence and diversity, destabilize representations of self and other. In this mere destabilization, possibilities for different viewpoints, reflections and claims open up. Sometimes, there is more to say about cosmopolitan articulations of citizenship when studying urban pirate radio or mobile-phone use in the city than when studying national broadcasting and its reproduction of the rightfulness of present hegemonies (Fenton 2012). Behind the social divides of the city lie small-, medium- and large-scale actions that shape dynamics in the immediate locale, but also sometimes the discourses and diverse meanings of citizenship – and non-citizenship. Explorations of and demands for citizenship become an interplay between the very specific potentials and restrictions available in urban neighbourhoods and the possibilities given through mediation for 'ways out' and for access to knowledge and understanding of what happens 'outside' the very specific locale. It is in the creation of different representations that sometimes compensate for the lack of political representation, in the recognition of inequality and in collective struggles for access to different images, discourses and materialities that human agents can produce new spaces and new forms of relations. These are the moments discussed in this book: the moment when close proximity to people of different backgrounds in the city provides a valuable context for interpreting international news as issues of intimate relevance; the moment when music-making on the margins becomes a possibility of having an unheard voice podcast across the world; the moment when protesting or rioting on the urban street becomes a moment for claiming the long overdue representation that mainstream media and politics have denied and digital media will guarantee. These moments, of course, are forcing us to ask important questions that surpass the moment, questions about belonging and citizenship. Most importantly, they are forcing us to ask: what possibilities does the city present for a politics of difference which is not about *other*-ness, strangeness and suspicion, but about coexistence, communication and equality?

The preceding discussion aimed to reflect on the possibilities presented by the city for identity, representation and recognition outside, beyond or in addition to exclusive and national forms of citizenship. If it matters that the media expand spaces for the representation of marginality, if it matters that they challenge geographical boundaries by linking urban neighbourhoods with other urban neighbourhoods across the world, it is in this way: citizenship can no longer be organized or imagined merely around a national and vertical system of rights and responsibilities. Global-city literature has helped us to understand the ways in which communication technologies have decentralized and decoupled corporate activities from a vertical system of control and from the circulation of products and information through global networks. This book has presented an attempt to contribute to understanding some of the ways in which media and communication technologies have decentralized citizenship and decoupled its meanings from the complete control of the neoliberal nation-state. The city has always presented a major challenge to the power and control of the nation-state, sustaining throughout its history at least some cultural and political autonomy vis-à-vis the nation. The long-standing quality of the city as a counterpoint to the nation has intensified and become exemplified by the case of the global mediated city. Systems of (self-)representation produced and consumed in the city, but also and importantly shaped, circulated and shared across transnational networks, have advanced the legitimacy of claims that are not directed to or controlled by the nation-state.

Digital networks and the diversification of information and communication flows have not only expanded the connections of the city beyond the nation but also opened up spaces of imagination and reflection about a present and a future that are not only locally grounded, but also globally shared. Access to multiple images and narratives of identity, community and humanity on the internet, but also on television, has advanced urban subjects' capabilities of seeing the self and others on common platforms. The capabilities of linking the city to the rest of the world and personal experience to the experience of others close by and at a distance have been changing the meaning of belonging and of community: mediated by the city, but also by the media, community has become more fragile than ever but also more possible than ever. Living with difference is something that urban subjects have always done. But the realization that living with difference has become the only way in which life can be lived in present times has a great symbolic significance for the way in which the city and citizenship are imagined (and enacted).

The question of what urban subjects do with their new capabilities of engaging and understanding difference remains open. The possibility of switching off or even of aiming for more rigid boundaries against difference are realities of urban life, as much as cosmopolitan sensibilities. Closure and selective engagement with difference find expression in the behaviour of urban elites and in the ideologies and the practice of socially and politically marginal groups. The intensification of exposure to difference means not only shifts in the limits of community. It also means a retreat within narrower boundaries, be these elite or working-class, local or transnational. But there is something that runs across both realities: nobody can really and fully switch off difference. It is always in the media, as the case of the urban riots has shown, and can never be fully escaped from – with consequences for awareness and for fear. While awareness by no means comes with a ready-made commitment to solidarity, it provides a starting point for it. As discussed in the case of multi-ethnic, urban local communities, cosmopolitan sensibilities sometimes emerge as a result of urban encounters and of mediated exposure to suffering. The groundedness of such sensibilities in the urban experience and in mediated encounters represents a counterpoint to the current hegemonic political discourse. This by far dominant political discourse reinforces the ideological pathologization of the complexities of difference – especially in anti-migration politics, in the demonization of the urban poor and in international politics that reduce global inequalities to a charitable cause.

To conclude

The media can play a key role in reducing and commodifying differences. In their diverse production, consumption and use, they can also open up avenues for communication, allowing and even forcing encounters with difference. In both cases, they mediate communication, miscommunication and frame meanings of *we*-ness and *other*-ness. When in the latest Batman blockbuster the villains jail the superhero in a prison that looks and feels medieval, they still manage to install a television set so that Batman is forced to watch the destruction of his beloved city. On that screen, the city is opened up to be watched around the world. Unlike Batman's captivity, the city is open. This openness, which is almost inevitably mediated, comes with experience, risks and togetherness. But, in contrast to the blockbuster's neoliberal fantasy of a city's unconditional togetherness around an existing order and against the threat of the outsiders, the city of possibilities, imagination and consumption can never be just about order and togetherness. Even in its most superficial, commodified and neoliberal media representations, the global city is a site of meeting and mixing, thus inevitably also of tension and sometimes conflict. Those mixed realities of the city are never totally absent from media representations of the city. At the same time, what happens on the urban street can no longer ever be enacted outside or beyond mediation: the music, the graffiti, the advertisement, the telephone call that links friends who live close to one another and relatives who live on different continents. It is the street that allows us to understand these synergies in their ubiquity and in all their complexity. Here, the happy ending of the blockbuster meets many other (self-)representations – marginality, protest, graffiti and urban music – which are just as mediated as Gotham City's victory.

In the 'real' city, loud and contesting musical themes emerging from passing cars, multilingual signs on high streets, competing religious symbols in neighbouring places of worship and exchanges of products, including music, film and personal technologies, all reveal the multiplicity of possibilities for belonging *here* (and as a consequence also belonging *elsewhere*). As the representational and experiential material at the core of this book has shown, it is *within* cosmopolitanism that many of the most important struggles of our times take place, not between cosmopolitanism and parochialism or nationalism. Living with cosmopolitanization in urban societies of the global North is no longer a novelty or a choice. And it increasingly seems that this is not only a phenomenon concerning the global North alone. The erosion of boundaries and the intensive juxtapositions of difference are as much a reality in the lives of elites as they are in the lives of working-class people, as argued throughout this book. But the positions that these different groups take within the process of cosmopolitanization vary enormously and reflect the latent and explosive struggles associated with a mediated and largely unequal urban world. Many of these struggles will continue in the future, revealing the ideological repositioning of different actors, partly through addressing old problems – especially those associated with capitalism – and partly through managing new conditions, especially the intensification of proximity and awareness of one another's sociocultural realities and moral responsibilities. The three predominant kinds of cosmopolitanism discussed above – neoliberal, vernacular and liberatory – reflect the continuities and new challenges that inequality and local and global proximity entail.

The moments of liberatory cosmopolitanism are where we may seek, and hopefully occasionally find, a shared language of communication and of polity: in the specificity of the city for its dwellers, in their practices and their appropriation of its territory and representations, in its particular and particularistic histories, in its old and new communities and its ongoing struggles. It is these specificities which are grounded in the city but which are – now more than ever and inescapably – connected to other cities, other villages, other continents of the world. This is the point where universalism and particularisms meet, where humanistic values and commitment to equality and the redistribution of local and global resources take on global relevance and turn into local action.

Notes

Chapter 1 Introduction

1 I am referring to *others* as well as *the other*, choosing to emphasize the plurality of *other*-ness and of difference in the city.

Chapter 3 Consumption: The Hegemonic and the Vernacular

1 One need only think of the powerful representations of Paris as the fashion capital, appearing in tourist brochures of the city, films and advertisements for commodities, or of similar representations of New York as trendsetter, and most recently of London as the capital of street fashion and independent fashion design.

Chapter 4 Identity: Popular Culture and Self-Making

1 Convergence of production and consumption, in the case of urban cultures of communication, is very ordinary. It is often encountered in the digital environments where music and graffiti are produced, shared and manipulated, as well as on the street, where the limits of their production and consumption often become blurred.

2 I choose not to separate 'graffiti' from 'street art', which is a current trend, especially in urban policy. The reason is that such a division in the characterization and recognition of graffiti/street art is primarily ideological, tied to the estimated value of graffiti and the perceived graffitists' or street artists' identities. This is an important debate, especially as it reflects the commodification of street culture and the selective appropriation of graffiti into mainstream art systems. However, such debates go beyond the scope of the present discussion.

3 Urban music and graffiti represent different forms of urban creativity, with their distinct histories and artistic trajectories. However, as they are here discussed as examples of urban cultures linked to questions of identity, they are not extensively addressed in their differences, but mostly of their commonalities, i.e. as forms of creativity that become both forms of identity expression and forms of commodification of the city as a space of production and consumption.

4 In October 2006, Banksy's six prints of Kate Moss's face were sold for £50,400 and a Mona Lisa stencil for £57,600 at Sotheby's (http://news.bbc.co.uk/1/hi/entertainment/6069384.stm, accessed 16 May 2013). In February 2013, a transnational debate involving residents, local authorities, the FBI and an auction house in Miami exploded when a Banksy graffiti was detached from a wall in North London and was taken for an auction to Miami (Harper 2013).

5 Authenticity here refers to the popular meaning of the concept, not its articulations in philosophical or critical theory. More specifically, it refers to the perceived originality and truthfulness of urban creativity, seen to reflect the lives and cultural heritage of its agents. Fascinating debates on authenticity and urban music go back to the Frankfurt School's critique of jazz. However, these debates, precisely because of their complexity, would need significant attention and, since they fall outside the focus of the present discussion, are not dealt with here.

Chapter 5 Community: Transnational Solidarities

1 The focus groups discussed here were conducted during two periods between 2009 and 2011. They represent a major element of a cross-European research project that investigated the relation between transnational media consumption and Arabic speakers' experiences of citizenship across Europe. The cross-European project *Media & Citizenship: Transnational Television Cultures Reshaping Political Identities in the European Union* received funding from the European Community's Seventh Framework Programme FP7/2007-2013 under Grant Agreement No. 217480. The research team was a consortium of five European universities (consortium leader: C. Slade). The author led the team conducting research in London, Madrid and Nicosia.

2 A survey conducted for the *Media & Citizenship* project in six European capital cities (Amsterdam, Berlin, London, Madrid, Paris, Stockholm) with 2,470 self-identified Arabic speakers, showed that in all cities more than 90 per cent of respondents watched Arabic-language television. Focus groups in the six cities, and also in Nicosia, Cyprus, followed the survey.

Chapter 6 Action: Presence and Marginality

1 Historian David Starkey, participating in *Newsnight* on BBC television said that white people speak and act 'like blacks' and rap music is partly to blame for this. See www.huffingtonpost.co.uk/2011/08/13/white-have-become-blacks_n_926087.html (accessed 16 May 2013).

2 Los Indignados (The Outraged) became a popular movement against austerity with global appeal. It was initiated on 15 May 2011 when demonstrators set up a camp in Madrid's Puerta del Sol. This movement inspired many other similar movements across Europe, most influentially in Athens in the second half of 2011.

References

Adorno, T. (1991) *The Culture Industry: Selected Essays on Mass Culture*. London: Routledge.

Amin, A. and Thrift, N. (2002) *Cities: Reimagining the Urban*. Cambridge: Polity Press.

Andersen, K. (2011) 2011: Person of the Year. *Time*, 26 December, pp. 42–81.

Anisef, P. and Lanphier, M. (2003) *The World in a City*. Toronto: University of Toronto Press.

Appadurai, A. (1996) *Modernity at Large: Cultural Dimensions of Globalization*. Minneapolis, MN: University of Minnesota Press.

Appadurai, A. (2006) *Fear of Small Numbers*. Durham, NC: Duke University Press.

Associated Press (2003) Another tool for Big Brother? 2 July. Available at: www.wired.com/politics/law/news/2003/07/59471 (last accessed 23 April 2013).

Atta, Dean (2012) I am nobody's nigger. Available at: http://soundcloud.com/deanatta/i-am-nobodys-nigger (last accessed 10 May 2013).

Augé, M. (2008 [1995]) *Non-Places: An Introduction to Supermodernity*. London: Verso.

Banksy (2010) *Exit Through the Gift Shop*. A Banksy Film Production.

Barthes, R. (1997) Semiology and the urban. In N. Leach (ed.), *Re-thinking Architecture*. London: Routledge, pp. 166–71.

Baudrillard, J. (1994) *Simulacra and Simulation*. Ann Arbor, MI: Michigan University Press.

Bauman, Z. (1998) *Work, Consumerism and the New Poor*. Buckingham: Open University Press.

Bauman, Z. (2005) *Liquid Life*. Cambridge: Polity Press.

BBC Online (2008) Calls to rename East End station. 20 May. Available at: http://news.bbc.co.uk/1/hi/england/london/7411512.stm (last accessed 23 April 2013).

BBC Online (2010) The deserving or undeserving poor. 18 November. Available at: www.bbc.co.uk/news/magazine-11778284 (last accessed 23 April 2013).

BBC Online (2011) Blackberry boss defends messenger's role in riots. 15 September. Available at: www.bbc.co.uk/news/technology-14931348 (last accessed 22 April 2013).

BBC Online (2012a) Knifepoint robberies rise by 10%, crime figures show. 19 January. Available at: www.bbc.co.uk/news/uk-16626558 (last accessed 23 April 2013).

BBC Online (2012b) Census shows rise in foreign-born. Available at: www.bbc. co.uk/news/uk-20677515 (last accessed 23 April 2013).

Beck, U. (1999) *World Risk Society*. Cambridge: Polity.

Beck, U. (2006) *Cosmopolitan Vision*. Cambridge: Polity.

Beck, U. (2009) Foreword. In M. Nowicka and M. Rovisco (eds), *Cosmopolitanism in Practice*. Farnham and Burlington: Ashgate, pp. xi–xii.

Bell, D. A. and de-Shalit, A. (2011) *The Spirit of Cities: Why the Identity of a City Matters in a Global Age*. Princeton, NJ: Princeton University Press.

Bell, D., Holloway, S. L., Jayne, M. and Valentine, G. (2008). Pleasure and leisure. In T. Hall, P. Hubbard and J. R. Short (eds), *The Sage Companion to the City*. London: Sage.

Benhabib, S. (2008) *Another Cosmopolitanism*. Oxford and New York: Oxford University Press.

Benjamin, W. (1997 [1925]) *One-Way Street and Other Writings*. London: Verso.

Benjamin, W. (2004) *Selected Writings*. Edited by M. Bullock and M. W. Jennings. Cambridge, MA: Harvard University Press.

Bennett, M. (2011) Hackney soldiers: The birth of jungle. *Clash Music*, 11 April. Available at: www.clashmusic.com/hackney-soldiers (last accessed 23 April 2013).

Berker, T. (2005) The everyday of extreme flexibility – the case of migrant researchers' use of new information and communication technologies. In R. Silverstone (ed.), *Media, Technology and Everyday Life in Europe*. Burlington: Ashgate.

Bernal, V. (2006) Diaspora, cyberspace and political imagination: The Eritrean diaspora online. *Global Network* 6(2): 161–79.

Binnie, J. and Skeggs, B. (2006) Cosmopolitan knowledge and the production and consumption of sexualised space: Manchester's gay village. In J. Binnie, J. Holloway, S. Millington and C. Young (eds), *Cosmopolitan Urbanism*. London and New York: Routledge, pp. 220–45.

Binnie, J., Holloway, J., Millington, S. and Young, C. (2006) Introduction. In J. Binnie, J. Holloway, S. Millington and C. Young (eds), *Cosmopolitan Urbanism*. London and New York: Routledge, pp. 1–34.

Bodaar, A. (2006) Multicultural urban space and the cosmopolitan 'Other': The contested revitalization of Amsterdam's Bijmermeer. In J. Binnie, J. Holloway, S. Millington and C. Young (eds), *Cosmopolitan Urbanism*. London and New York: Routledge, pp. 171–86.

Borden, I. (2000a) Boundaries. In S. Pile and N. Thrift (eds), *City A–Z*. London and New York: Routledge, pp. 20–2.

Borden, I. (2000b) CCTV. In S. Pile and N. Thrift (eds), *City A–Z*. London and New York: Routledge, pp. 35–6.

Borough of Hackney (2010) *Children and Young People*. London: Borough of Hackney.

Bourdieu, P. (1985) The market of symbolic goods. *Poetics* 14: 13–44.

Bourdieu, P. (1993) *The Field of Cultural Production*. Cambridge: Polity.

Brenner, N., Marcuse, P. and Mayer, M. (2012) Introduction. In N. Brenner,

P. Marcuse and M. Mayer (eds), *Cities for People, Not for Profit*. New York: Routledge, pp. 1–10.

Bridge, G. (2004) *Reason in the City of Difference*. London and New York: Routledge.

Britt, P. (2009) Chicago mayor wants more surveillance cameras. *Heartlander*, 1 May. Available at: http://news.heartland.org/newspaper-article/2009/05/01/chicago-mayor-wants-more-surveillance-cameras (last accessed 23 April 2013).

Brown, G. (2006) Cosmopolitan camouflage: (Post-)gay space in Spitafields, East London. In J. Binnie, J. Holloway, S. Millington and C. Young (eds), *Cosmopolitan Urbanism*. London and New York: Routledge, pp. 130–45.

Bull, M. (2007) *Sound Moves: iPod Culture and Urban Experience*. London and New York: Routledge.

Burd, G (2008) The mediated metropolis as medium and message. *International Communication Gazette* 70(3–4): 209–22.

Burdett, R. and Rode, P. (2013) Our cities, our future. *LSE Research*. London: LSE.

Burdett, R. and Sudjic, D. (eds) (2007) *The Endless City: The Urban Age*. London: Phaidon.

Butler, T. and Lees, L. (2006) Super-gentrification in Barnsbury, London: Globalization and gentrifying global elites at the neighbourhood level. *Transactions of the Institute of British Geographers* 31: 467–87.

Butt, R. (2006) Is Hackney really the worst place to live? *Guardian News Blog*, 26 October. Available at: www.guardian.co.uk/news/blog/2006/oct/26/ishackney real (last accessed 22 April 2013).

Calhoun, C. (2002) The class consciousness of frequent travellers: Towards a critique of actually existing cosmopolitanism. In S. Vertovec and R. Cohen (eds), *Conceiving Cosmopolitanism: Theory, Context and Practice*. Oxford: Oxford University Press, pp. 86–109.

Cammaerts, B. (2012) Protest logics and the mediation opportunity structure. *European Journal of Communication* 27(2): 117–34.

Carter, H. (2011) Rioter profile: 'I knew the black kids would be stopped before me'. The *Guardian*, 8 December. Available at: www.guardian.co.uk/uk/2011/dec/08/rioter-profile-battle-against-police (last accessed 22 April 2013).

Castells, M. (1989) *The Informational City: Information Technology, Economic Restructuring and the Urban-Regional Process*. Oxford: Blackwell.

Castells, M. (1996) *The Rise of the Network Society. Vol. 1 of The Information Age: Economy, Society and Culture*. Cambridge, MA and Oxford: Blackwell.

Castells, M. (2009) *Communication Power*. Oxford: Oxford University Press.

Castells, M. (2012) *Networks of Outrage and Hope*. Cambridge: Polity.

Champion, M. (2013) Give us back our Banksy. 18 February. *Evening Standard*.

Chan, W. F. (2006) Planning Birmingham as a cosmopolitan city: Recovering the depths of its diversity. In J. Binnie, J. Holloway, S. Millington and C. Young (eds), *Cosmopolitan Urbanism*. London and New York: Routledge.

Cheah, P. (2007) *Inhuman Conditions: On Cosmopolitanism and Human Rights.* Cambridge, MA: Harvard University Press.

Chomsky, N. (2012) *Occupy.* New York: Penguin.

Chouliaraki, L. (2006) *The Spectatorship of Suffering.* London and New York: Sage.

Chouliaraki, L. (2012) Re-mediation, inter-mediation, trans-mediation: The cosmopolitan trajectories of convergent journalism. *Journalism Studies*, iFirst, pp. 1–17.

Chouliaraki, L. (2013) *The Ironic Spectator: Solidarity in the Age of Post-Humanitarianism.* Cambridge: Polity.

City of London (2012) *Key Facts.* Available at: http://217.154.230.196/NR/rdonlyres/77C91659-E1A3-421A-85C5-0607C1E093CC/0/MC_keyfactsJune 2011.pdf (accessed 16 May 2013).

Clifford, J. (1992) Travelling cultures. In L. Grossberg, C. Nelson and P. A. Treichler (eds), *Cultural Studies.* London: Routledge, pp. 96–116.

Cohen, S. (1972) *Folk Devils and Moral Panics: The Creation of Mods and Rockers.* London: Routledge.

Coomes, P. (2011) Don't call me urban! The time of grime. *BBC News*, 2 June. Available at: www.bbc.co.uk/news/in-pictures-13608668 (last accessed 23 April 2013).

Couldry, N. (2003) Media, symbolic power, and the limits of Bourdieu's Field Theory. Media@LSE Electronic Working Papers. Available at: www2.lse.ac.uk/media@lse/research/mediaWorkingPapers/pdf/EWP02.pdf (last accessed 22 April 2013).

Couldry, N. (2012) *Media, Society, World: Social Theory and Digital Media Practice.* Cambridge: Polity.

Couldry, N. and McCarthy, A. (2004) Introduction. In N. Couldry and A. McCarthy (eds), *MediaSpace: Place, Scale and Culture in a Media Age.* London: Routledge, pp. 1–18.

Creative Activism (2012) Culture jamming, hoaxes and other 'radical' acts of aesthetic resistance. 22 January. Available at: http://gapierre.wordpress.com/2012/01/27/creativact-week-3/ (accessed 16 May 2013).

Curtin, M. (2003) Media capital: Towards the study of spatial flows. *International Journal of Cultural Studies* 6(2): 202–28.

Daily Mirror (2011) London riots 'most wanted' suspects pictured. 15 December, p. 1.

Davis, M. (2000) *Magical Urbanism: Latinos Reinvent the US City.* London and New York: Verso.

De Certeau, M. (1984) *The Practice of Everyday Life.* Berkeley: University of California Press.

Demant, F., Maussen, M. and Rath, J. (2007) *Muslims in the EU (The Netherlands): Cities Report; Preliminary Research Report and Literature Survey.* London: Open Society Institute and EU Monitoring and Advocacy Program.

Department for Culture, Media and Sport (UK) (2011) Olympics boost East

London's regeneration. Available at: www.culture.gov.uk/news/news_stories/8461.aspx (last accessed 22 April 2013).

Derrida, J. (2001a [1972]) *Derrida: Writing and Difference*. London and New York: Routledge.

Derrida, J. (2001b) *On Cosmopolitanism and Forgiveness*. London and New York: Routledge.

Dillabough, J.-A. and Kennelly, J. (2010) *Lost Youth in the Global City: Class, Culture and the Urban Imaginary*. London and New York: Routledge.

Diminescu, D. (2008) The connected migrant: An epistemological manifesto. *Social Science Information* 47(4): 565–79.

Du Gay, P. (ed.) (1997) *Doing Cultural Studies: The Story of the Sony Walkman*. London: Sage.

Eade, J. (ed.) (1997) *Living the Global City: Globalization as Local Process*. London and New York: Routledge.

Eade, J. (2000) *Placing London: From Imperial Capital to Global City*. New York and Oxford: Berghahn Books.

Economist, The (2008) Nomads at last, 10 April. Available at: www.economist.com/node/10950394 (last accessed 22 April 2013).

Economist, The (2012) Save the city. 402(8766): 7.

Elliott, A. and Urry, J. (2010) *Mobile Lives*. London and New York: Routledge.

Ellsworth-Jones, W. (2012) *Banksy: The Man Behind the Wall*. London: Aurum Press.

Exandas Documentary Series (2005) Paris 2005. Available at: www.smallplanet.gr/en/documentaries/chronologically/2005-2006 (accessed 17 May 2013).

Fenton, N. (2012) Cosmopolitanism as conformity and contestation. *Journalism Studies,* iFirst: 1–15.

Ferjani, R. (2007) Les télévisions arabophones en France: une transnationalité postcoloniale. In T. Mattelart (ed.), *Médias, migrations et cultures transnationales*. Paris: De Boeck & Larcier, pp. 103–20.

Fine, R. (2007) *Cosmopolitanism*. London and New York: Routledge.

Firmstone, J., Georgiou, M., Husband, C., Marinkova, M. and Stiebel, F. (2009) *Representation of Minorities in the British Press*. Vienna: EU Fundamental Rights Agency.

Fiscal Policy Institute (2009a) New York city in the Great Recession: Divergent fates by neighbourhood and race and ethnicity, December. Available at: www.fiscalpolicy.org/FPI_NeighborhoodUnemployment_NYC.pdf (last accessed 23 April 2013).

Fiscal Policy Institute report (2009b) New York city: A tale of two recessions. Available at: www.fiscalpolicy.org/FPI_NewYorkCitysTwoRecessions_20091119.pdf (last accessed 22 April 2013).

Florida, R. (2002) *The Rise of the Creative Class*. New York: Basic Books.

Fraser, N. (2003) Social justice in the age of identity politics: Redistribution, recognition and participation. In N. Fraser and A. Honneth (eds), *Redistribution or Recognition? A Political–Philosophical Exchange*. London: Verso.

Fraser, N. (2008) *Scales of Justice: Reimagining Political Space in a Globalizing World*. New York: Columbia University Press.

Garnham, N. (2011) The political economy of communication revisited. In J. Wasko et al. (eds), *The Handbook of Political Economy of Communications*. London: Wiley-Blackwell, pp. 41–61.

GaWC (1998) *Inventory of World Cities*. Available at: www.lboro.ac.uk/gawc/citylist.html (last accessed 22 April 2013).

Georgiou, M. (2006) *Diaspora, Identity and the Media*. Cresskill, NJ: Hampton Press.

Georgiou, M. (2008) Urban encounters: Juxtapositions of difference and the communicative interface of global cities. *International Communication Gazette* 70(3–4): 223–35.

Georgiou, M. (2010) Media representations of diversity: The power of mediated images. In A. Block and J. Solomos (eds), *Race and Ethnicity in the 21st Century*. Basingstoke: Palgrave.

Georgiou, M. (2012) Watching soap opera in the diaspora: Cultural proximity or critical proximity? *Ethnic and Racial Studies* 35(5): 868–87.

Georgiou, M. and Coleman, S. (2008) *New Media and Development: Young Audiences' Engagement with the Media and the World*. London: IBT.

Giddens, A. (1987) *Social Theory and Modern Sociology*. Cambridge: Polity Press

Giddens, A. (1991) *Modernity and Self-Identity: Self and Society in the Late Modern Age*. Cambridge: Polity.

Gilroy, P. (1997) *The Black Atlantic: Modernity and Double Consciousness*. London: Routledge.

Gilroy, P. (2004) *After Empire: Melancholia or Convivial Culture?* Abingdon: Routledge.

Gitlin, T. (2012) Written for the late, lamented occupied London. *Open Democracy*, 5 March. Available at: www.opendemocracy.net/ourkingdom/todd-gitlin/written-for-late-lamented-occupied-london (last accessed 22 April 2013).

Global Street Art (2013) Global street art. Available at: http://globalstreetart.com/ (last accessed 22 April 2013).

Golding, P. and Murdock, G. (2005) Culture, communications and political economy. In J. Curran and M. Gurevitch (eds), *Mass Media and Society*, 4th edn. London: Arnold, pp. 60–83.

Gordon, E. (2010) *The Urban Spectator: American Concept-Cities from Kodak to Google*. Lebanon, NH: Dartmouth College Press.

Gordon, I. (2003) Capital needs, capital growth and global city rhetoric in Mayor Livingstone's London Plan. Paper presented at Association of American Geographers Annual Meeting. Available at: www2.lse.ac.uk/geographyAndEnvironment/pdf/Capital_Needs.pdf (last accessed 22 April 2013).

Gould-Wartofsky, M. (2011) Occupy Wall Street goes home. *Possible Futures: A Project of the Social Science Research Council*. Available at: www.possible-futures.org/2011/12/13/occupy-wall-street-home-postcards-east-york (last accessed 22 April 2013).

Guardian, The (2012) Reading the riots: Investigating England's summer of disorder. Available at: www.guardian.co.uk/uk/series/reading-the-riots (last accessed: 16 May 2013).

Gumpert, G. and Drucker, S. (2008) Communicative cities. *The International Communication Gazette* (70)3–4: 195–208.

Hackney Solidarity Network (2008) 'Hackney's not crap' gentrification tour, 28 September. Available at: www.hackneysolidarity.info/latest-news/hackneys-not-crap-gentrification-tour-28-september-2008 (last accessed 22 April 2013).

Hackworth, J. (2007) *The Neoliberal City: Governance, Ideology, and Development in American Urbanism.* Ithaca, NY: Cornell University Press.

Hall, S. (1990) Cultural identity and diaspora, in J. Rutherford (ed.), *Identity: Community, Culture, Difference.* London: Lawrence and Wishart.

Hall, P. (1999) *Cities in Civilization.* London: Phoenix Giant.

Hall, S. (2001) *The Multicultural Question.* Milton Keynes: The Pavis Centre.

Hall, S. (2003) Calypso kings. In M. Bull and L. Back (eds), *The Auditory Culture Reader.* Oxford and New York: Berg.

Hall, S. (2008) Cosmopolitanism, globalisation and diaspora: Stuart Hall in conversation with Pnina Werbner. In P. Werbner (ed.), *Anthropology and the New Cosmopolitanism: Rooted, Feminist and Vernacular Perspectives.* ASA Monograph No. 45. Oxford: Berg, pp. 345–60.

Hancox, D. (2011) Rap responds to the riots: 'They have to take us seriously.' The *Guardian*, 12 August. Available at: www.guardian.co.uk/music/2011/aug/12/rap-riots-professor-green-lethal-bizzle-wiley (last accessed 22 April 2013).

Hannerz, U. (1990) Cosmopolitans and locals in world culture. *Theory, Culture and Society* (7)2–3: 237–51.

Hannerz, U. (1996) *Transnational Connections: Culture, People, Places.* London: Routledge.

Harris, J. (2006) A cloistered metropolitan elite is in denial about Britain. *Guardian*, 24 October. Available at: www.guardian.co.uk/commentisfree/2006/oct/24/britishidentity (last accessed 22 April 2013).

Harris, P. (2010) There goes the neighbourhood: Change sweeps Black America's cultural home. In *The Observer.* Available at www.guardian.co.uk/world/2010/mar/28/harlem-african-american-barack-obama (last accessed 17 May 2013).

Harris, P. (2012) Portland, the US capital of alternative cool, takes TV parody in good humour. In the *Guardian.* Available at: www.guardian.co.uk/world/2012/feb/12/portland-portlandia-tv-alternative-culture (last accessed 16 May 2013).

Hartley, J. (2010) Connected communities and creative economy; clash, cluster, complexity, creativity. Paper presented at *Research Development Workshop – Connected Communities*, 6–8 December, 2010, Birmingham, UK.

Harvey, D. (1989) *The Condition of Postmodernity.* Oxford: Wiley-Blackwell.

Harvey, D. (2001) *Spaces of Capital: Towards a Critical Geography.* Edinburgh: Edinburgh University Press.

Harvey, D. (2007) Neoliberalism and the city. *Studies in Social Justice* 1(1).

Available at: http://phaenex.uwindsor.ca/ojs/leddy/index.php/SSJ/article/view-File/191/183 (last accessed 16 May 2013).

Harvey, D. (2009) *Cosmopolitanism and the Geographies of Freedom*. New York: Columbia University Press.

Harvey, D. (2013) *Rebel Cities: From the Right to the City to the Urban Revolution*. London: Verso

Hastings, M. (2011) Years of liberal dogma have spawned a generation of amoral, uneducated, welfare dependent, brutalised youngsters. *Daily Mail*, 5 August. Available at: www.dailymail.co.uk/debate/article-2024284/UK-riots-2011-Liberal-dogma-spawned-generation-brutalised-youths.html (last accessed 23 April 2013).

Hayward, K. and Yar, M. (2006) The 'chav' phenomenon: Consumption, media and the construction of a new underclass. *Crime, Media, Culture* 2(1): 9–28.

Held, D. (2010) *Cosmopolitanism: Ideals, Realities and Deficits*. Cambridge: Polity.

Herman, E. S. and McChesney, R. W. (1997) *The Global Media*. London: Cassell.

Hesmondhalgh, D. (2007) *The Cultural Industries*, 2nd edn. London: Sage.

Highmore, B (2005). *Cityscapes: Cultural Readings in the Material and Symbolic City*. New York: Palgrave.

Hitchens, C. (2008) Last call, Bohemia. *Vanity Fair*, July. Available at: www.vanityfair.com/culture/features/2008/07/hitchens200807 (last accessed 23 April 2013).

hooks, b. (1994) *Teaching to Transgress: Education as the Practice of Freedom*. New York: Routledge.

Hoxton FM (2011) About us. Available at: www.hoxtonfm.co.uk/?p=193 (last accessed 23 April 2013).

Hoyler, M. and Watson, A. (2012) Global media cities in transnational media networks. *GaWC Research Bulletin 358*. Available at: www.lboro.ac.uk/gawc/rb/rb358.html (last accessed 15 May 2013).

Hussein, M. (2007) *Muslims in the EU (Denmark): Cities Report; Preliminary Research Report and Literature Survey*. London: Open Society Institute and EU Monitoring and Advocacy Program.

IOM (2010) *World Migration Report 2010*. Geneva: International Organization for Migration.

IPPR (2011) New poll shows Londoners are proud of their city but don't want stronger London government. Press release, 6 December. Available at: www.ippr.org/press-releases/111/8350/new-polling-shows-londoners-are-proud-of-their-city-but-dont-want-stronger-london-government- (last accessed 22 April 2013).

Isin, E. (2002) *Being Political: Geneologies of Citizenship*. London and Minneapolis: Minnesota University Press.

Jacobs, J. M. (1996) *Edge of Empire: Postcolonialism and the City*. London: Routledge

Jansson, A. (2002). Spatial phantasmagoria: The mediatisation of tourism experience. *European Journal of Communication* 17(4): 429–43.

Jones, O. (2012) *Chavs: The Demonization of the Working Class*. London: Verso.

Karanfil, G. (2009) Pseudo-exiles and reluctant transnationals: Disrupted nostalgia on Turkish satellite broadcasts. *Media, Culture & Society* 31(6): 887–99.

Keith, M. (2005) *After Cosmopolitanism? Multicultural Cities and the Future of Racisms*. London: Routledge.

King Adz (2010) *Street Knowledge*. London: Harper Collins.

Klein, N. (1999) *No Logo*. New York: Picador.

Kosnick, K. (2009) Conflicting mobilities: Cultural diversity and city branding in Berlin. In S. Hemelryk Donald, E. Kofman and C. Kevin (eds), *Branding Cities: Cosmopolitanism, Parochialism, and Social Change*. New York and London: Routledge.

Koutroumpa, M. (2012) Graffiti: Art versus vandalism. *Streets of London*, 7 February. Available at: http://streetslondon.co.uk/articlepage/graffitinew.html (last accessed 23 April 2013).

Krätke, S. (2003) Global media cities in a worldwide urban network. *European Planning Studies* 11: 605–28.

Krätke, S. (2011) How manufacturing industries connect cities across the world: Extending research on 'multiple globalizations'. *GaWC Research Bulletin* 391. Available at: www.lboro.ac.uk/gawc/rb/rb391.html (last accessed 15 May 2013).

Krätke, S. and Taylor, P. J. (2004) A world geography of global media cities. *European Planning Studies* 12(4): 459–77.

Krims, A. (2007) *Music and Urban Geography*. London and New York: Routledge.

Lefebvre, H. (1996 [1968]) The right to the city. In H. Lefebvre, E. Kofman and E. Lebas (eds), *Writings on Cities*. Cambridge, MA: Blackwell, pp. 63–184.

Lemke, T. (2001) 'The birth of bio-politics': Michel Foucault's lecture at the Collège de France on neo-liberal governmentality. *Economy and Society* 30(2): 190–207.

Lentin, A. and Titley, G. (2011) *The Crises of Multiculturalism*. London: Zed Books.

Lethal Bizzle (2006) David Cameron is a donut. The *Guardian*, 8 June. Available at: www.guardian.co.uk/commentisfree/2006/jun/08/davidcameronisadonut (last accessed 22 April 2013).

Lin, W.-Y., Song, H. and Ball-Rokeach, S. J. (2010) Localizing the global: Exploring the transnational ties that bind in new immigrant communities. *Journal of Communication* 60(2): 205–29.

Lindsay, I. (2012) *Olympicisation: Life in the Shadow of the Olympic Torch*. Presentation at Global Studies Association 11th International Conference, Manchester: Manchester Metropolitan University, 6 July.

Livingstone, S. (2003) Children's use of the internet: Reflections on the emerging research agenda. *New Media and Society* 5(2): 147–66.

Livingstone, S. (2008) Engaging with media – a matter of literacy? *Communication, Culture & Critique* 1(1): 51–62.

London First (2008) East London regeneration. Available at: www.londonfirst.

co.uk/planning--development2/east-london-regeneration (last accessed 23 April 2013).

Lott, T. L. (1999) *The Invention of Race: Black Culture and the Politics of Representation*. Oxford: Blackwell.

Lury, C. (2011) *Consumer Culture*, 2nd edn. Cambridge: Polity.

Macek, S. (2006) *Urban Nightmares: The Media, the Right, and the Moral Panic over the City*. Minneapolis, MN: Minnesota University Press.

Malpas, J. (2009) Cosmopolitanism, branding, and the public realm. In S. Hemelryk Donald, E. Kofman and C. Kevin (eds), *Branding Cities: Cosmopolitanism, Parochialism and Social Change*. London and New York: Routledge, pp. 189–97.

Martín-Barbero, J. (1993) *Communication, Culture and Hegemony: From the Media to Mediations*. London: Sage.

Massey, D. (1991) A global sense of place. *Marxism Today* (June): 24–9.

Massey, D. (2005) *For Space*. London and Thousand Oaks, CA: Sage.

Massey, D. (2007) *World City*. Cambridge: Polity.

Matsaganis, M., Katz, V. S. and Ball-Rokeach, S. J. (2011) *Understanding Ethnic Media: Producers, Consumers, and Societies*. Thousand Oaks, CA: Sage.

Mayor of London (2012) *Cultural Metropolis: The Mayor's Cultural Strategy – 2012 and Beyond*. London: Greater London Authority.

McClary, S. (2003) Bessie Smith: 'Thinking Blues'. In M. Bull and L. Back (eds), *The Auditory Culture Reader*. Oxford and New York: Berg, pp. 27–34.

McQuire, S. (2008) *The Media City: Media, Architecture and Urban Space*. London and Thousand Oaks, CA: Sage.

McQuire, S. and Papastergiadis, N. (eds) (2005) *Empires, Ruins + Networks: The Transcultural Agenda in Art*. London and Chicago: Rivers Oram Press.

Meyrowitz, J. (1985) *No Sense of Place: The Impact of Electronic Media on Social Behavior*. Oxford: Oxford University Press.

Miles, S. (2012) The neoliberal city and the pro-active complicity of the citizen consumer. *Journal of Consumer Culture* 12(2): 216–30.

Miles, S. and Miles, M. (2004) *Consuming Cities*. London: Palgrave.

Miller, D. (2010) *Stuff*. Cambridge: Polity.

Moore, A. (2012) Viewpoint: *V for Vendetta* and the rise of Anonymous. *BBC News*, 10 February. Available at: www.bbc.co.uk/news/technology-16968689 (last accessed 23 April 2013).

Muhe, N. (2007) *Muslims in the EU (Germany): Cities Report; Preliminary Research Report and Literature Survey*. London: Open Society Institute and EU Monitoring and Advocacy Program.

Nightingale, C. (1993) *On the Edge*. New York: Basic Books.

Norwood, G. (2013) Global prime: The real costs. *Financial Times*, 16/17 February 2013.

Occupy London (2012) A promise from Occupy London: This is only the beginning. *Open Democracy*, 28 February. Available at: www.opendemocracy.net/ourkingdom/occupy-london/promise-from-occupy-london-this-is-only-beginning (last accessed 23 April 2013).

O'Connor, J. (2007) The cultural and creative industries: A review of the literature. University of Leeds. Available at: http://kulturekonomi.se/uploads/cp_litrev4. pdf (last accessed 16 May 2013).

Ofcom (2010) The Communications Market 2010. Available at: http://stakehold ers.ofcom.org.uk/market-data-research/market-data/communications-market-re ports/cmr10/ (last accessed 15 May 2013).

Papastergiadis, N. (2012) *Cosmopolitanism and Culture*. Cambridge: Polity.

Park, R. E., Burgess, E. W. and McKenzie, R. (1925) *The City*. Chicago: University of Chicago Press.

Phillips, A. (1997) *The Politics of Presence: The Political Representation of Gender, Ethnicity and Race*. Oxford: Oxford University Press.

Philo, C and Kearns, G. (1993) Culture, history, capital: a critical introduction to the selling of places. In G. Kearns and C. Philo (eds), *Selling Places: The City as Cultural Capital, Past and Present*. Oxford: Pergamon.

Pine, B. J. and Gilmore, J. H. (2011) *The Experience Economy*. Cambridge, MA: Harvard Business School Press.

Portes, A. (2001) Introduction: The debates and significance of immigrant transna-tionalism. *Global Networks* 1(3): 181–93.

Powell, A. (2004) Space, place, reality and virtuality in urban internet cafés. In *Proceedings of the Second Annual Canadian Association of Cultural Studies Conference*.

Pratt, A. C. (2008) Creative cities: The cultural industries and the creative class. *Geografiska Annaler: Series B, Human Geography* 90, pp. 107–17.

Pratt A. C. (2012) The cultural economy and the global city. In B. Derudder, M. Hoyler, P. J. Taylor and F. Witlox (eds), *International Handbook of Globalization and World Cities*. Cheltenham: Edward Elgar, pp. 265–74.

Recording Industry Association of America, The (2007) Consumer profile. Available at: http://76.74.24.142/44510E63-7B5E-5F42-DA74-349B51ED-CE0F.pdf (last accessed 22 April 2013).

Reuters (2011a) Gap between US rich, poor is widest in Atlanta. Available at: www.reuters.com/article/2011/10/26/usa-states-incomes-idUSN1E79P1O 120111026 (last accessed 22 April 2013).

Reuters (2011b) Number of 'majority minority' US cities grows-Brookings. Available at: www.reuters.com/article/2011/08/31/usa-states-cities-populations-idUSN1E77U0WQ20110831 (last accessed 22 April 2013).

Robertson, R. (1992) *Globalization: Social Theory and Global Culture*. London: Sage

Robbins, B. (1998) Introduction Part I: Actually existing cosmopolitanism. In P. Cheah and B. Robbins (eds), *Cosmopolitics: Thinking and Feeling Beyond the Nation*. Minneapolis, MN: University of Minnesota Press, pp. 1–19.

Robins, K. (2001) Becoming anybody: Thinking against the nation and through the city. *City* 5(1): 77–90.

Rofe, M. W. (2003) 'I want to be global': Theorising the gentrifying class as an emergent elite global community. *Urban Studies* 40(12): 2511–26.

Rose, N. (2000) Governing cities, governing citizens. In E. Isin (ed.), *Democracy, Citizenship and the Global City*. London: Routledge.

Said, E. (1994) *Culture and Imperialism*. London: Vintage.

Sandercock, L. (2003) *Towards Cosmopolis: Planning for Multicultural Cities*. New York: Wiley.

Sassen, S. (2001) *The Global City*. Princeton, NJ: Princeton University Press.

Sassen, S. (2002) *Global Networks, Linked Cities*. London and New York: Routledge.

Sassen, S. (2003) *Guests and Aliens*. New York: The New Press,

Sassen, S. (2004) Local actors in global politics. *Current Sociology* 54(4): 649–70.

Sassen, S. (2005) The repositioning of citizenship and alienage: Emergent subjects and spaces for politics. *Globalizations* 2(1): 79–94.

Sassen, S. (2010) When the city itself becomes a technology of war. *Theory, Culture & Society* 27(6): 33–50

Sassen, S. (2011) The global street comes to Wall Street. In *Possible Futures: A Project of the Social Science Research Council*. Available at: http://www.possible-futures.org/2011/11/22/the-global-street-comes-to-wall-street/ (last accessed 23 April 2013).

Schorn, D. (2006) 'We're watching'. CBSNews. Available at: www.cbsnews.com/stories/2006/09/05/five_years/main1968121.shtml (last accessed 16 May 2013).

Sennett, R. (1990) *The Conscience of the Eye: The Design and Social Life of Cities*. New York: Norton & Company.

Sennett, R. (2002) Cosmopolitanism and the social experience of cities. In S. Vertovec and R. Cohen (eds), *Conceiving Cosmopolitanism: Theory, Context and Practice*. Oxford: Oxford University Press, pp. 42–7.

Shaw, S., Bagwell, S. and Karmowska, J. (2004) Ethnoscapes as spectacle: Reimaging multicultural districts as new destinations for leisure and tourism consumption. *Urban Studies* 41(10): 1983–2000.

Sheller, M. and Urry, J. (2003) Mobile transformations of 'public' and 'private' life. *Theory, Culture and Society* 20(3): 107–25.

Short, J. R. (2004) *Global Metropolitan: Globalizing Cities in a Capitalist World*. London: Routledge.

Silverstone, R. (1999) *Why Study the Media?* London, Thousand Oaks, CA and New Delhi: Sage.

Silverstone, R. (2005) Mediation and communication. In C. Calhoun, C. Rojek and B. Turner (eds), *The Sage Handbook of Sociology*. London: Sage.

Silverstone, R. (2007) *Media and Morality: On the Rise of the Mediapolis*. Cambridge: Polity Press.

Silverstone, R. and Georgiou, M. (eds) (2005) Introduction to special issue on media and minorities in multicultural Europe. *Journal of Ethnic and Migration Studies* 31(3): 433–41.

Simmel, G. (1997) The metropolis and mental life. In D. Frisby and M. Featherstone (eds), *Simmel on Culture: Selected Writings*. London and Thousand Oaks, CA: Sage, pp. 174–85.

Skórska, M. J. and Kloosterman, R. (2012) Performing on the global stage: exploring the relationship between finance and arts in global cities. GaWC Research Bulletin 412. Available at: www.lboro.ac.uk/gawc/rb/rb412.html (last accessed 2 May 2013).

Smith, M. P. (2001) *Transnational Urbanism: Locating Globalization*. Malden, MA and Oxford: Blackwell.

Stevenson, N. (2003) *Cultural Citizenship: Cosmopolitan Questions*. Maidenhead: Open University Press.

Taylor, P., Walker, D., Catalano, G., and Hoyler, M. (2002) Diversity and power in the world city network. *Cities* 19(4): 231–41.

Tebbakh, S. (2007) *Muslims in the EU (France): Cities Report; Preliminary Research Report and Literature Survey*. London: Open Society Institute and EU Monitoring and Advocacy Program.

Telegraph, The (2011) London riots: water cannons to be used on 'sick society'. 10 August. Available at: www.telegraph.co.uk/news/uknews/crime/8694401/London-riots-water-cannons-to-be-used-on-sick-society.html (last accessed 22 April 2013).

Thompson, J. B. (1995) *The Media and Modernity*. Cambridge: Polity Press.

Thrift, N. (2004) Driving in the city. *Theory, Culture and Society* 21(4/5): 41–59.

Thussu, D. (2006) *International Communication: Continuity and Change*. London: Arnold.

Time Out (2012) Why fashion matters. *Time Out* 2165: 13–20.

Topping, A. (2011) Farewell youth clubs – hello street life and gang warfare. The *Guardian*, 29 July. Available at: www.guardian.co.uk/uk/2011/jul/29/young-people-gangs-youth-clubs-close (last accessed 22 April 2013).

Tower Hamlets Borough (2010) *The Borough*. Available at: www.towerhamletsschoolsport.org/?_id=490 (last accessed 22 April 2013).

Turgis, C. (2011) Vancouver named best city to live in. Available at: http://uk.travel.yahoo.com/ideas/vancouver-named-best-city-live-080000725.html (last accessed 22 April 2013).

United Nations (2010 [2009]) Revision of world urbanization prospects. Press release. Available at: http://esa.un.org/unpd/wup/Documents/WUP2009_Press-Release_Final_Rev1.pdf (last accessed 22 April 2013).

Urry, J. (2007) *Mobilities*. Cambridge: Polity.

Vertovec, S. (2009) *Transnationalism*. London and New York: Routledge

Vogel, C. (2011) Guggenheim outpost as a pop-up urban lab. In *The New York Times*. Available at: www.nytimes.com/2011/08/03/arts/design/bmw-guggenheim-lab-to-open-as-pop-up-in-east-village.html?_r=0 (last accessed 22 April 2013).

Werbner, P. (1999) Global pathways: working class cosmopolitans and the creation of transnational ethnic worlds. *Social Anthropology* 7(1): 17–35.

Werbner, P. (2006) Understanding vernacular cosmopolitanism. *Anthropology News* 47(5): 7–11.

Werbner, P. (ed.) (2008) *Anthropology and the New Cosmopolitanism: Rooted, Feminist and Vernacular Perspectives*. ASA Monograph No. 45. Oxford: Berg.

Westfield Stratford City (2011) Community. Available at: http://uk.westfield. com/stratfordcity/community (last accessed 22 April 2013).

Williams, R. (1961) *The Long Revolution*. London: Chatto & Windus.

Williams, R. (1997) *Culture and Society 1780–1950*. New York: Columbia University Press

Wilson, D. (2008) Segregation and division. In T. Hall, P. Hubbard and J. R. Short (eds), *The Sage Companion to the City*. London and Thousand Oaks, CA: Sage.

Young, I. M. (1990) *Justice and the Politics of Difference*. Princeton, NJ: Princeton University Press.

Žižek, S. (2011) Shoplifters of the world unite. *London Review of Books*. Available at: www.lrb.co.uk/2011/08/19/slavoj-zizek/shoplifters-of-the-world-unite (last accessed 22 April 2013).

Zukin, S. (1995) *The Cultures of Cities*. Oxford and Malden, MA: Blackwell.

Zukin, S. (2011) *Naked City: The Death and Life of Authentic Urban Places*. Oxford: Oxford University Press.

Index